I0803270

IMAGES
of America

PITTSBURGH'S MANSIONS

On the Cover: Lyndhurst was built by William Thaw Sr. in 1888. The home stood on a nine-acre plot of land at Fifth Avenue and Beechwood Boulevard in Point Breeze. It was demolished in the 1940s. (Pittsburgh History & Landmarks Foundation.)

IMAGES
of America

PITTSBURGH'S MANSIONS

Melanie Linn Gutowski

ARCADIA
PUBLISHING

ISBN 978-1-4671-2015-9

Published by Arcadia Publishing
Charleston, South Carolina

Printed in the United States of America

Library of Congress Control Number: 2013931868

For all general information, please contact Arcadia Publishing:
Telephone 843-853-2070
Fax 843-853-0044
E-mail sales@arcadiapublishing.com
For customer service and orders:
Toll-Free 1-888-313-2665

Visit us on the Internet at www.arcadiapublishing.com

To Mom, for sparking my lifelong interest in old houses and in reading about them; and to Dad, for all that early writing practice.

Contents

ACKNOWLEDGMENTS

As a lifelong devotee of old houses, I consider this book very much a labor of love, though not one I could have completed alone. I am deeply indebted to an excellent group of archivists and librarians, including Martin Aurand, Carnegie Mellon University Libraries; Art Louderback, Heinz History Center Archives; Julie Ludwig, Frick Art Reference Library; Miriam Meislik, University of Pittsburgh Archives Service Center; Rachel Grove Rohrbaugh, Chatham University Archives; and Albert Tannler, Pittsburgh History & Landmarks Foundation.

Thanks also go to Frank and Maura Brown, Jack Carpenter, Charlotte Cohen, Mary Del Brady and Richard Pearson, Al Mann, and the East Liberty Valley Historical Society for sharing stories and images.

I would not have had the wherewithal to complete this project without the unending support (and patience) of my husband, Marc; my parents; and other friends and family members, especially my aunts. An honorable mention goes to Mommy's little research assistant, who, though not much actual help, did chime in frequently with kicks of encouragement.

The bulk of the images in this volume appear courtesy of Carnegie Mellon University Libraries (CMU), Chatham University Archives (Chatham), and Senator John Heinz History Center, Library & Archives Division (HHC). Images from other institutions and/or individuals are credited as such. All uncredited images appear courtesy of the author's collection.

INTRODUCTION

A man's home is his castle.

—English aphorism

It is said, though difficult to verify, that during Pittsburgh's peak years—roughly 1830 to 1930—the city had more millionaires than New York City. Western Pennsylvania had long been a manufacturing center, first of glass, then iron, and then coal, oil, and steel. At that time, local industry was enabling the building of the world, which in turn enabled many men who profited from this fact to build their own world, largely cosseted away from the very evidence of their business success. Wealthy neighborhoods—at the time considered suburbs—began to emerge in the city's East End and in neighboring Allegheny City. The sprawl of affluence continued into areas that today are considered the city's suburbs and into the countryside. Immense homes with scores of rooms, sometimes nearly 100, soon lined the streets of the city and its surrounding region.

The ready availability of inexpensive household help and low heating costs enabled owners to build larger and ever more extravagant mansions. At the same time, the popular idea of making one's home a sanctuary led to an increasing effort to place more space between oneself and one's neighbors, and especially between the family home and the threats—real or perceived—of pollution, poverty, and crime.

George Gall, author of *Homes and Country Estates of Pittsburgh Men*, published in 1905, noted that Pittsburgh did not enjoy the "fame for beauty" that other cities, such as Cleveland, Buffalo, Boston, New York, and St. Paul, did at the time. "Yet in order to demonstrate that Pittsburgh men have been successful in building up as beautiful a city as it is prosperous, one has only to show what has been accomplished in residence building here," Gall wrote. "Pittsburgh's best residence section is not confined to any one locality or street. This has been brought about by the beautiful and varied topography as seen in the many high elevations and numerous valleys, stretching out in all directions. Her representative people have taken advantage of these natural building localities and erected thereon their homes, in most cases away from the manufacturing districts, where they may obtain rest and quiet after spending many hours amid the noise and din of this great manufacturing and commercial center. As they have selected these naturally beautiful and quiet retreats, so have they in most cases tried to build, selecting mostly, as represented in later work, a style of architecture adapted to the site selected."

While individual prosperity made these homes financially possible, it was a small army of architects that brought the whims and fantasies of the city's industrialists to life. Alden & Harlow, Janssen & Abbott, MacClure & Spahr, and Rutan & Russell are just a few of the partnerships that were active in the area at this period. Individuals such as Louis Stevens, Frederick J. Osterling, Paul W. Irwin, George Orth, and Olaf M. Topp were in high demand among Pittsburgh's millionaires, who no doubt traded architect recommendations over Scotch at their private clubs. Gall noted that many of the architects and landscape designers who created these homes had made their own homes in Pittsburgh, a further recommendation of the area's architectural pedigree.

It must be noted that the people represented in this book are overwhelmingly white, male, Anglo-Saxon Protestants. The few women represented herein are generally wealthy widows of these men. Pittsburgh society—indeed, upper-class society as a whole at the time—was not welcoming of Eastern and Southern European immigrants, to say nothing of African Americans, Roman Catholics, Jews, or women.

Many of the homes within these pages no longer exist. While specific reasons vary from family to family, in general, the destruction followed a pattern. Often, the home's original owner would decide to relocate, either to a country home or to another major metropolitan area, such as Boston, New York City, or Washington, DC. The home left behind in Pittsburgh would be sold or left to heirs, who eventually either decided to relocate themselves or could no longer afford to keep the home.

Sometimes, these homes would be donated to the city of Pittsburgh in the hopes that officials would make good public use of the building and its surrounding land. But, the city was in no better position to afford the upkeep of these massive homes than were their former owners, and the houses were often demolished and the land put to other use. It was in this manner that several of the city's public parks came into being. Some owners did look ahead with an eye toward preservation, usually donating their properties to educational or other civic institutions that could not afford to construct their own buildings. If these magnificent homes survived the 1940s to 1960s, when Victorian and Edwardian designs were decidedly out of fashion, the chances were good that they would catch the wave of historic preservation activism brought on by nostalgia, and so remain intact.

Though the people named in these pages are deceased and many of their homes gone, their legacies live on in the names of neighborhoods, streets, schools, parks, and other community institutions. While this book is by no means a definitive catalog of western Pennsylvania's stately homes, the history of Pittsburgh's mansions is also a history of the building of the city itself.

One

Around the East End

Pittsburgh's East End was host to an explosion of construction between 1830 and 1925 as the rapidly expanding iron and steel industries created freshly-minted millionaires. As the newly wealthy sought an escape from the pervasive pollution of the city's industrial areas, fashionable suburbs emerged in Squirrel Hill and Point Breeze. Highland Park was another popular location for stately homes, though other parts of the East End were not without their impressive residences. The growth of the Pennsylvania Railroad enabled these neighborhoods to flourish, offering a convenient commute for the businessmen who built their mansions there. All of these areas are now part of the city proper, but, at the time, they were referred to by residents as "the country," due to the spacious lawns and wide boulevards that saw a fraction of the traffic they currently convey.

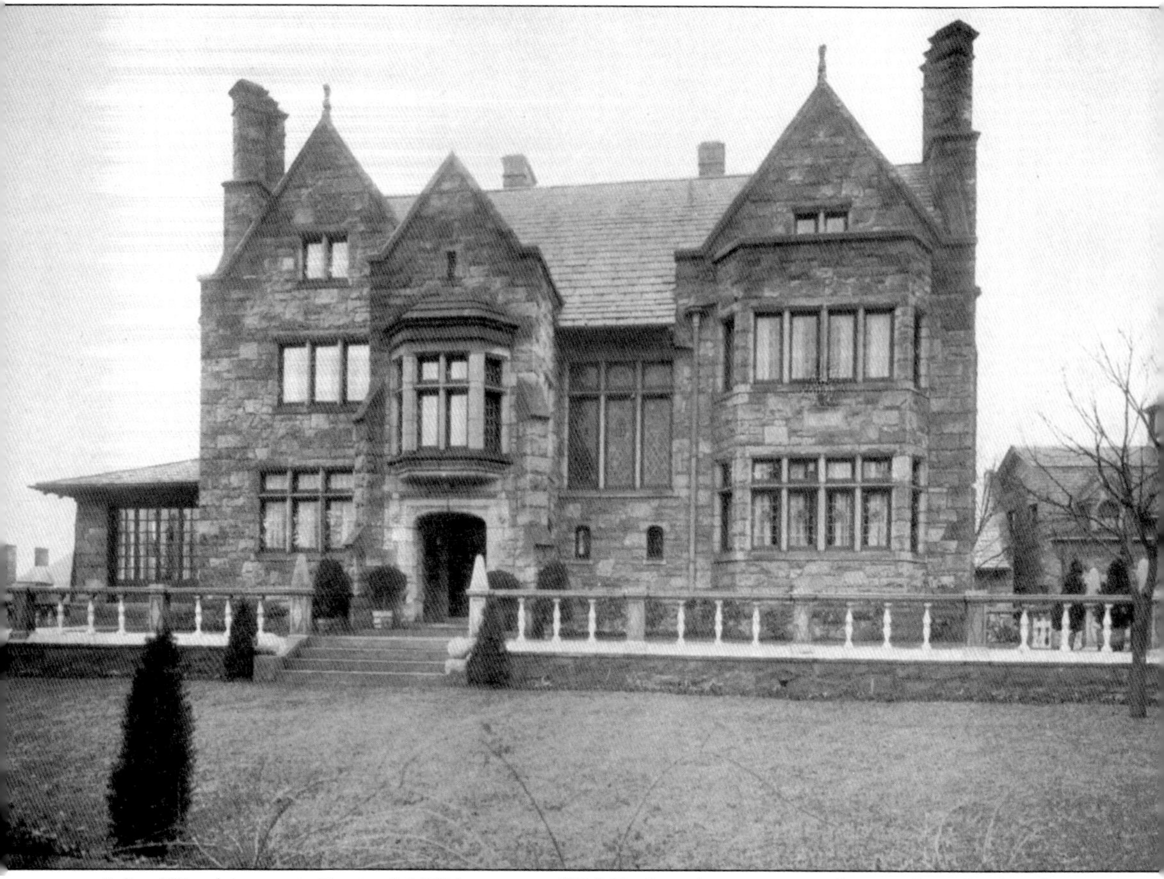

John Worthington's Squirrel Hill home, at 5505 Forbes Avenue, was designed in the Jacobean Revival style by Louis Stevens around 1909. Worthington, a Welsh immigrant, was a superintendent of South Penn Oil Company, charged with developing oil and natural gas resources in West Virginia. (CMU.)

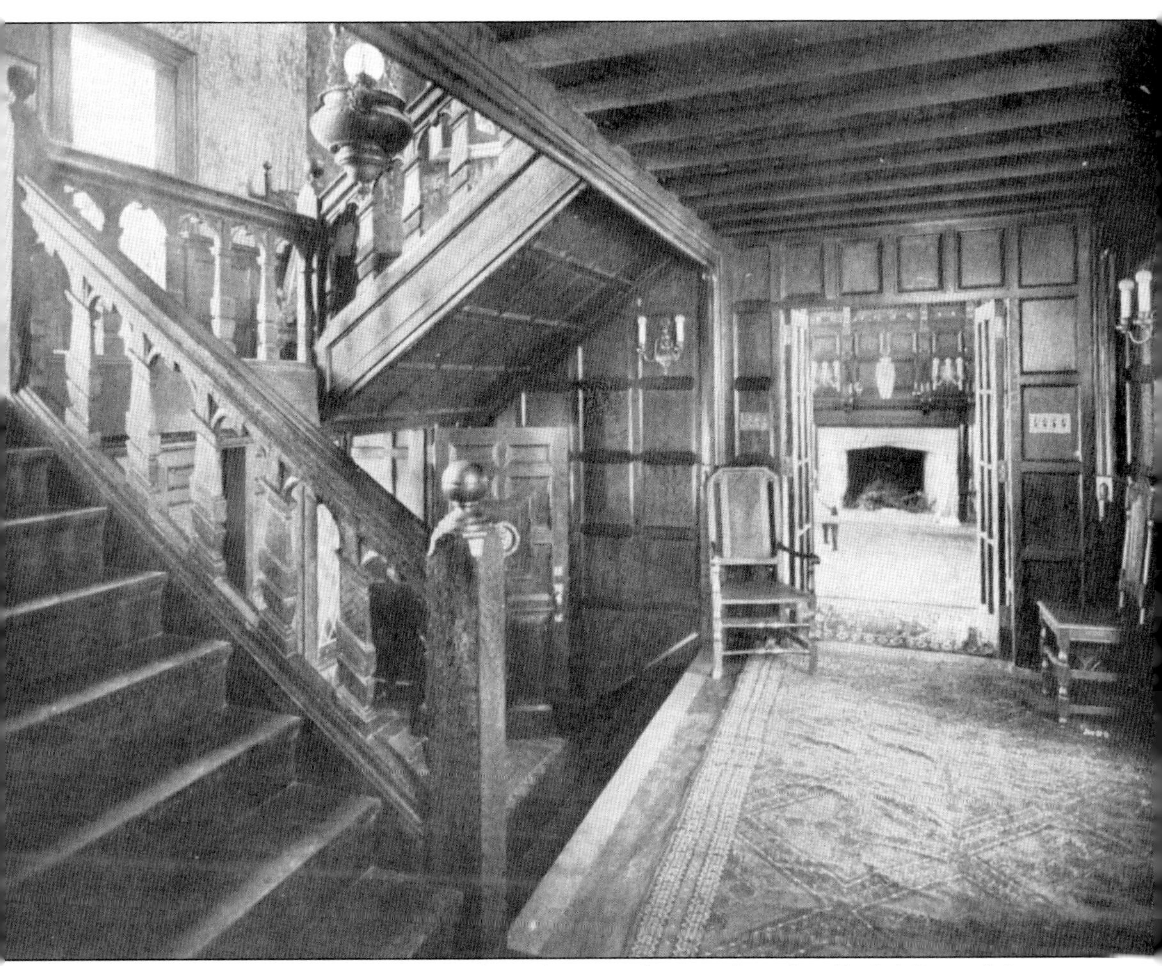

In keeping with its façade, the interior of Worthington's home reflected an English Revival decor. From the front door, guests ascended several steps into the hall, then were likely led into the sitting room, seen through the doorway at right. (CMU.)

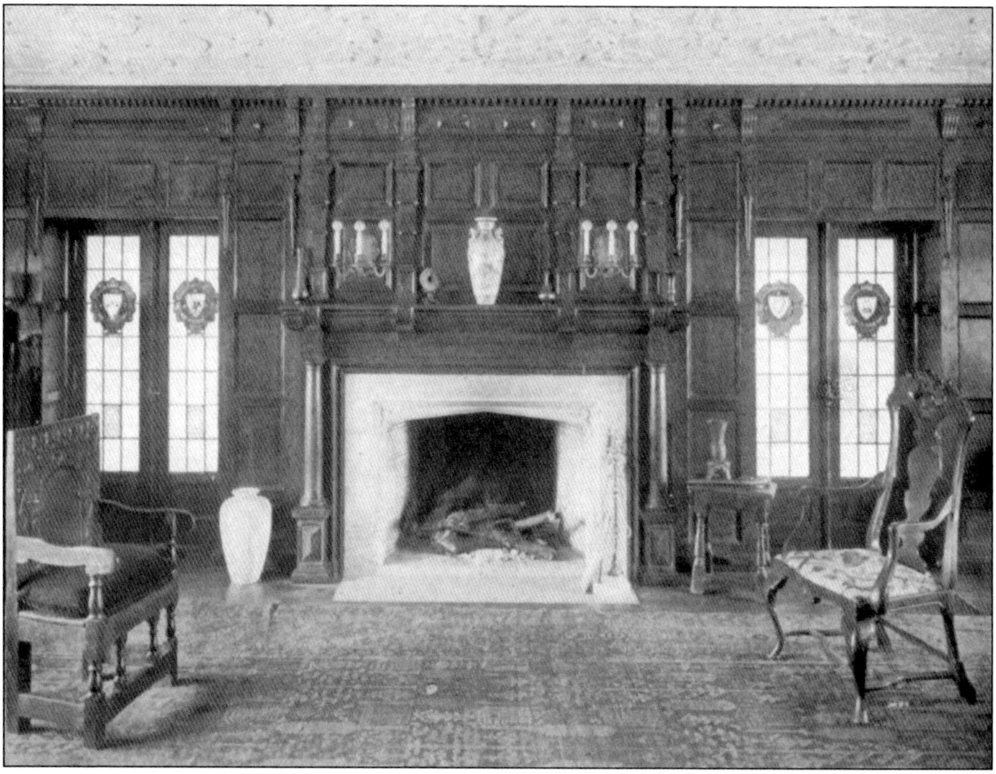

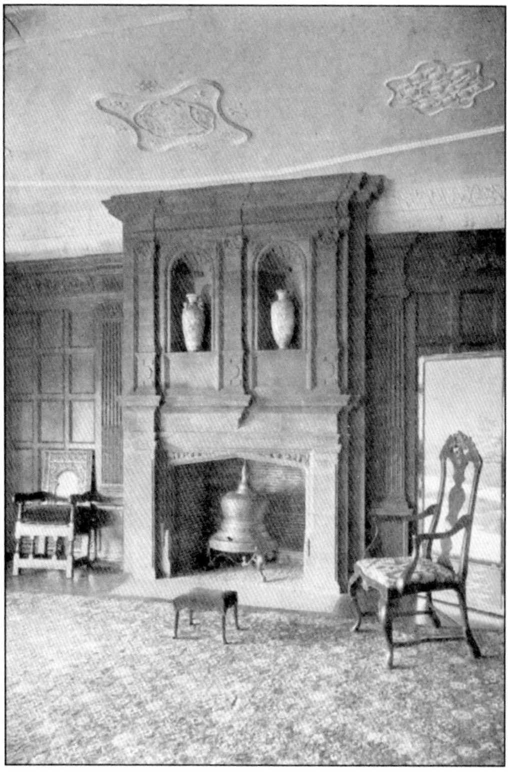

The features of John Worthington's sitting room—heavy, throne-like furniture, stone fireplace insert, heraldic motifs in the stained-glass windows, and decorative strapwork on the ceiling—continue the home's English manor character. (CMU.)

With its carved mantel niches, the Worthington dining room takes on an almost Colonial feel. The great expanse of what appears to be machine-loomed carpeting further displays the family's wealth; at the time, machine-loomed floor coverings were more expensive than those that were hand-loomed. The decorative screen on the right likely hid an entrance for the home's servants. (CMU.)

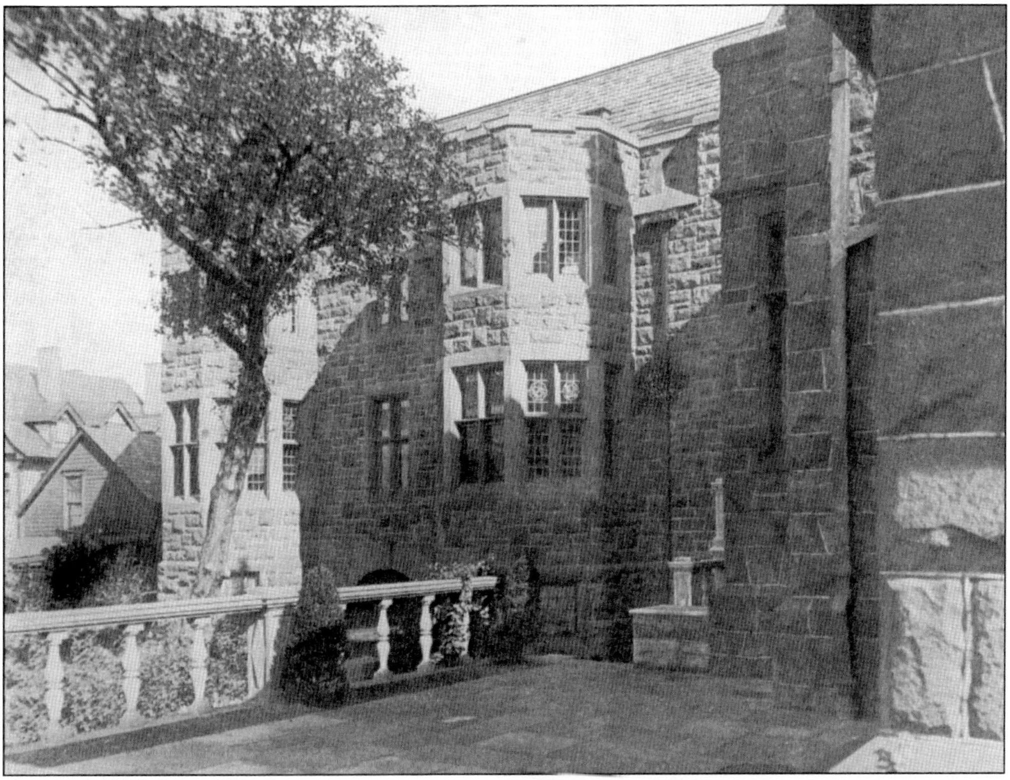

Around 1915, John Worthington commissioned Louis Stevens to add a new wing to his home. This image offers a closer look at the home's crenellated parapets, one of the hallmarks of Jacobean Revival design. Today, the structure serves as a house of worship for the Temple Sinai congregation. (CMU.)

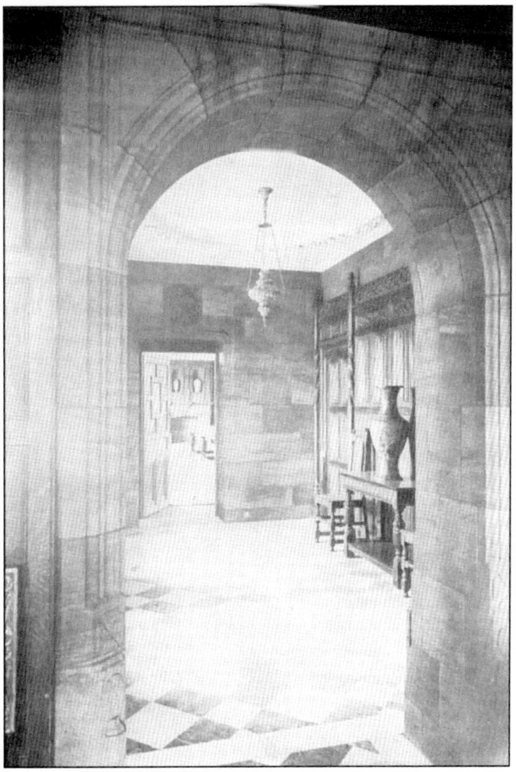

The new wing of the Worthington home led off of the dining room, seen here through the archway. The wing was connected to the main house by a garden hall, which was flooded with natural light. The garden hall door led onto a stone terrace. (CMU.)

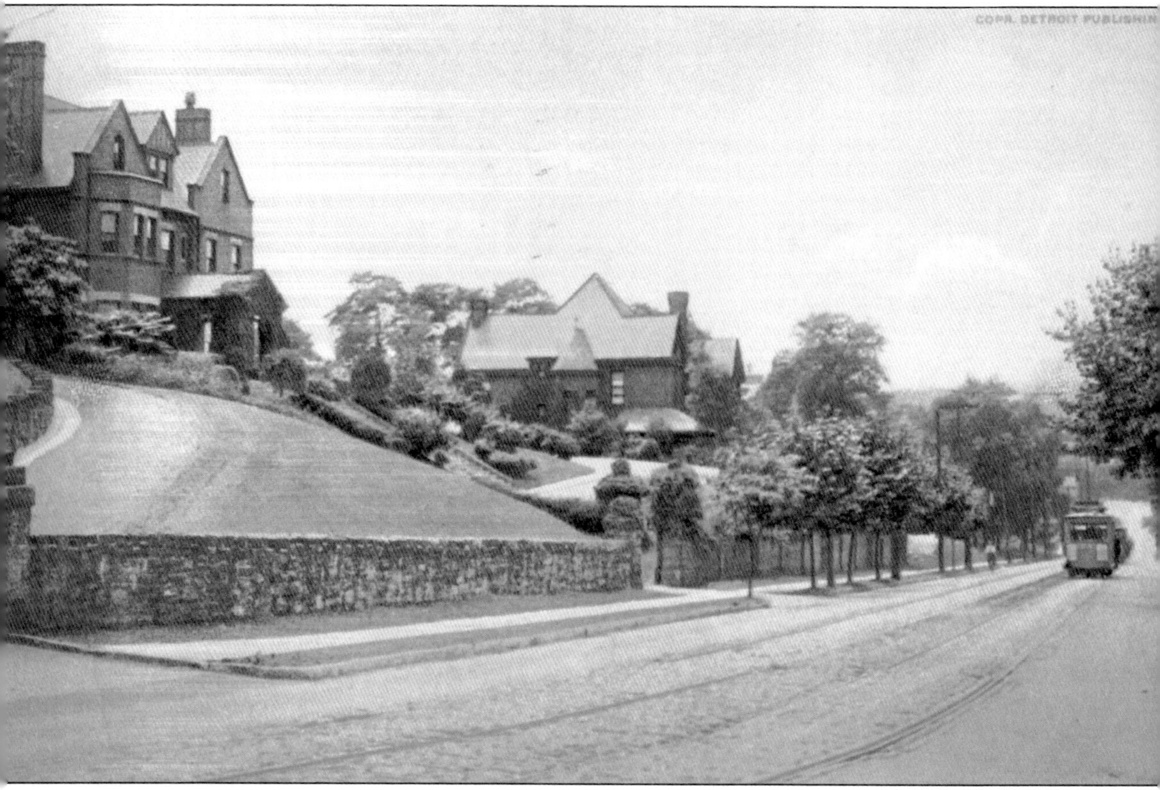

The home of James S. Kuhn can be seen at left in this postcard depicting Forbes Avenue, then called Forbes Street. Kuhn was president of both the Pittsburgh Bank for Savings and the First National Bank of McKeesport. The home's design appears to be what is called Jacobethan Revival, combining the shaped parapets of Jacobean Revival with a half-timbered dormer, borrowed from the Elizabethan Revival style.

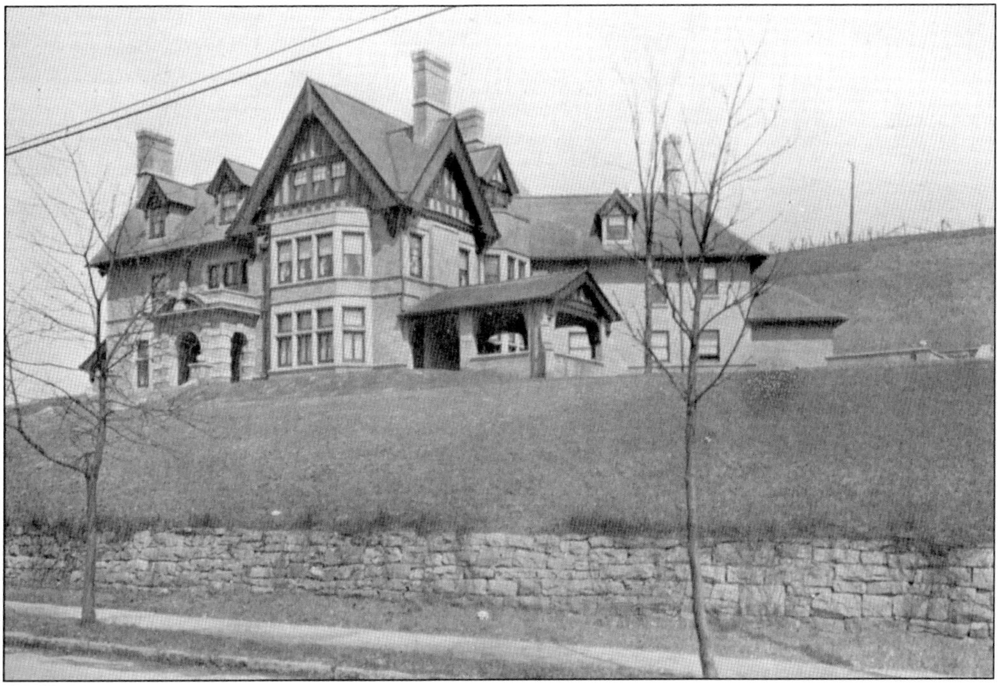

William Bacon Schiller's Elizabethan Revival home, at 5075 Forbes Avenue, was designed by MacClure & Spahr around 1905. Schiller, president of the National Tube Company, was charged with managing all of the company's works at McKeesport. (CMU.)

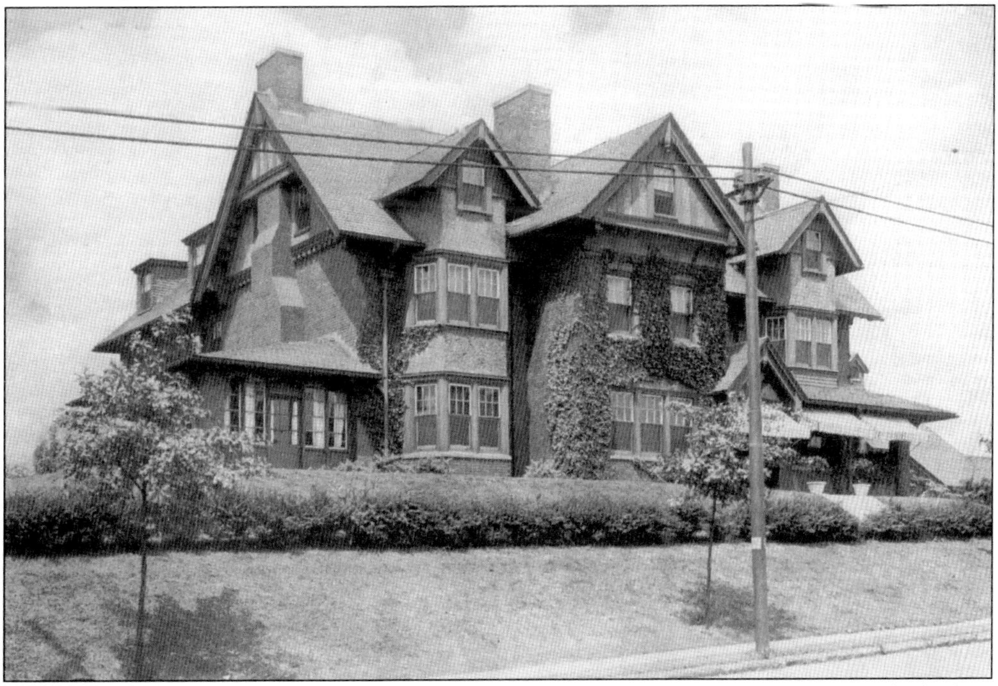

Eugene L. Messler's home, at 5423 Forbes Avenue, displays another good example of the Elizabethan Revival style, this time executed by Alden & Harlow. Messler, an engineer, was at one time general superintendent of Jones & Laughlin's Eliza Furnaces & Coke Ovens. (CMU.)

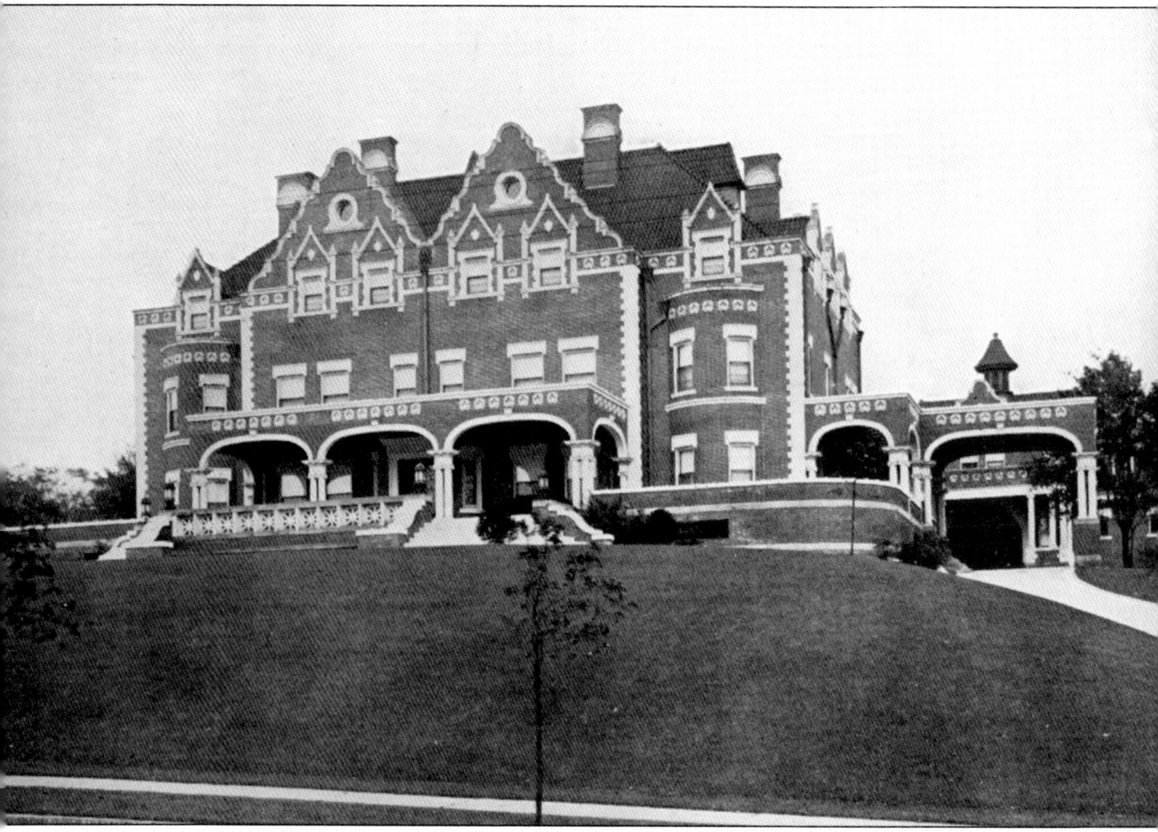

August A. Frauenheim was the proprietor of this gargantuan home at Beacon and Murdoch Streets in Squirrel Hill. While predominantly Flemish-style Tudor Revival, the house also seems to have had a châteauesque flair about it. Frauenheim held interests in pumps and hydraulic machinery.

As in the present day, property situated in or near a park was a desirable commodity. Ben Elm, the estate of William Larimer Mellon, sat close to the Forbes and Darlington entrance to Schenley Park. The home was designed by Alden & Harlow around 1903, and the landscape was done by Olmsted Brothers. The name of the home derives partially from Irish Gaelic and means "Mount Elm."

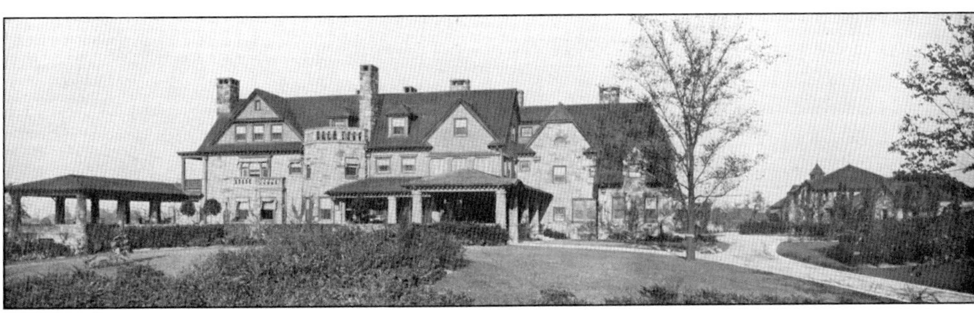

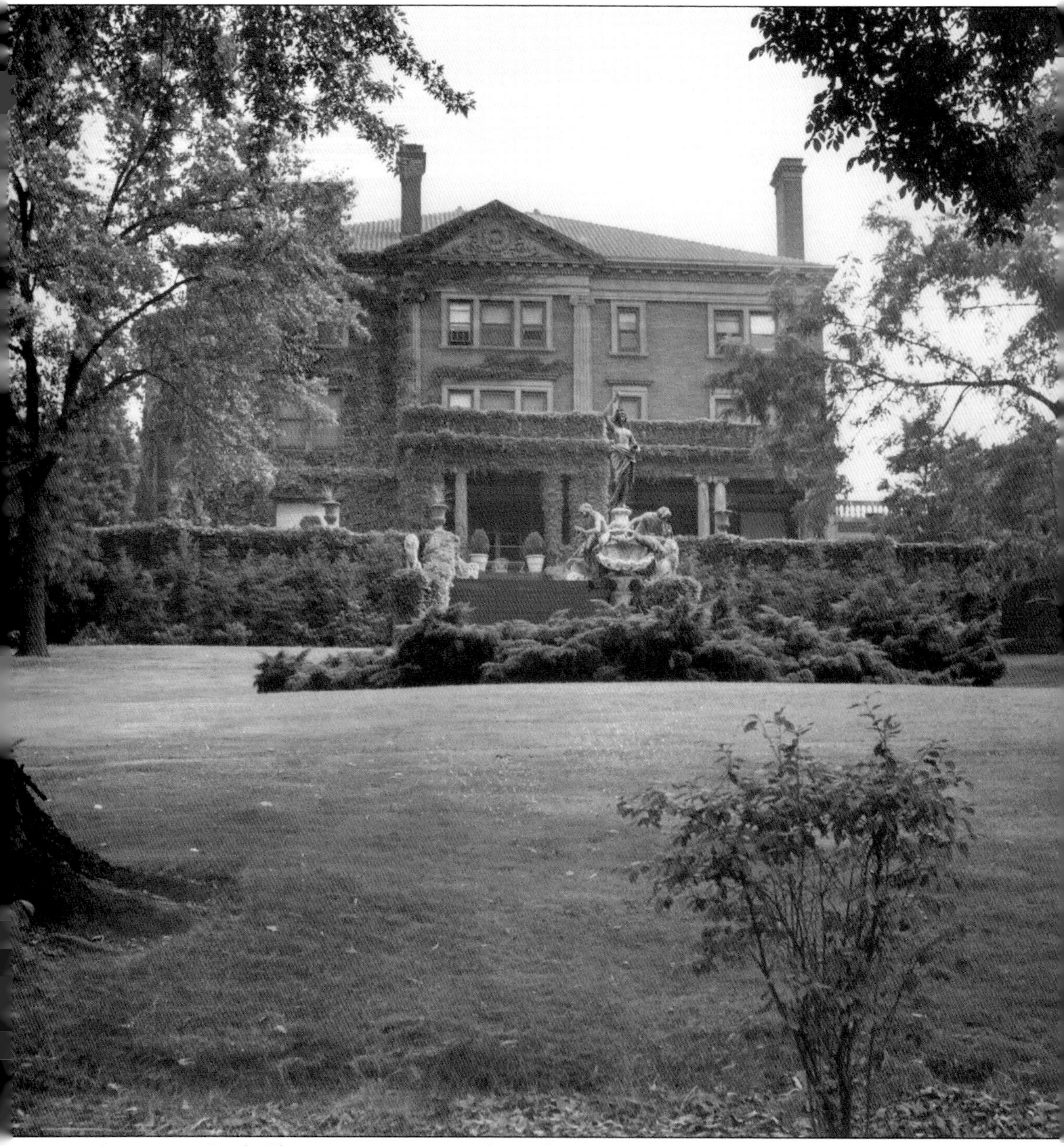

Lawrence Cowle Phipps was a vice president of Carnegie Steel and served two terms in the US Senate (1918–1929). Grandview, his Neoclassical Revival mansion on Warwick Terrace, was one of the city of Pittsburgh's greatest losses when it was torn down in the late 1970s. (Pittsburgh History & Landmarks Foundation.)

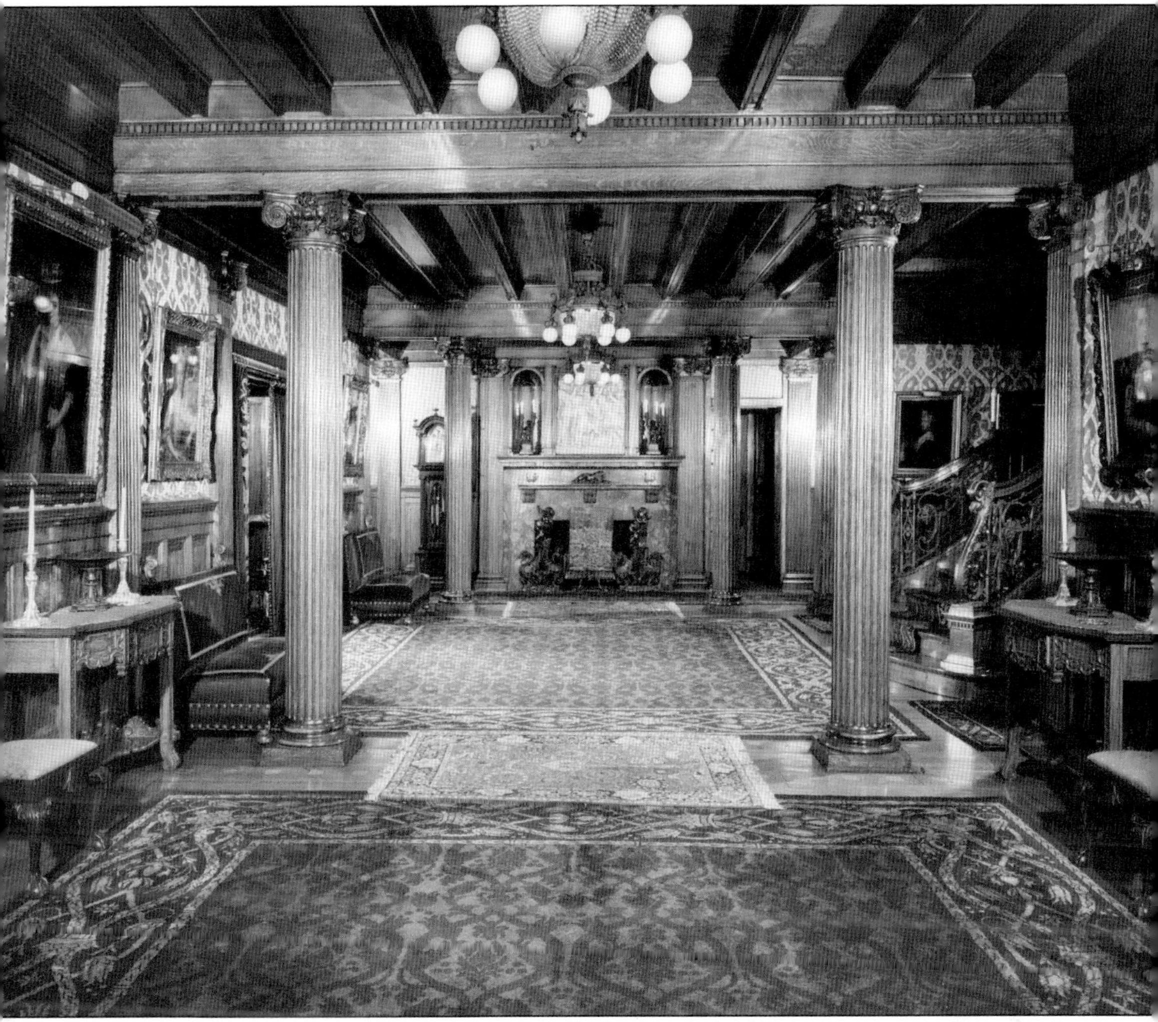

The long entrance hall at Grandview partially bisected the home. James Van Trump of Pittsburgh History & Landmarks Foundation once called the house a "spacious Edwardian symphony," with all of its key notes struck here at a visitor's first glance. (Pittsburgh History & Landmarks Foundation.)

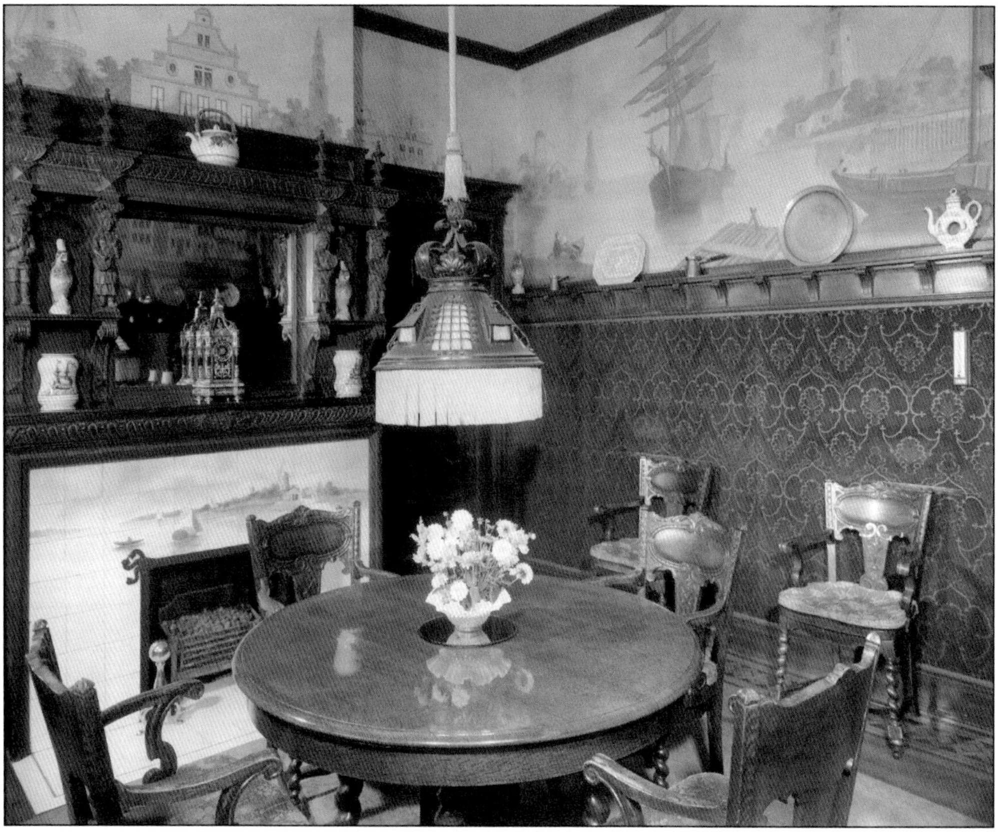

Grandview's breakfast room offers a peek into the Phipps family's private space. Though formal-looking to modern eyes, this room has a more relaxed feel than its adjoining areas. The room's decor incorporates the family's exotic travel interests. (Pittsburgh History & Landmarks Foundation.)

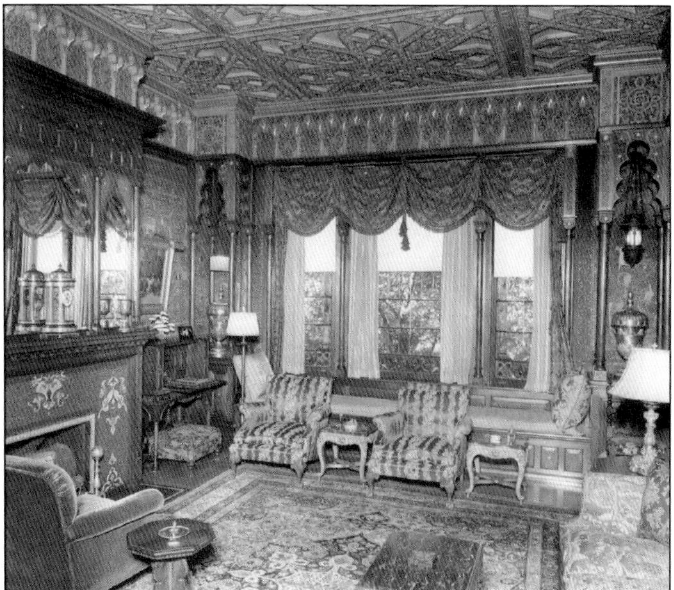

The smoking room at Grandview offers further evidence of the family's exotic tastes. The woodwork around the mantel and cornices reflects a Middle Eastern influence. The wall covering appears to depict peacock motifs. (Pittsburgh History & Landmarks Foundation.)

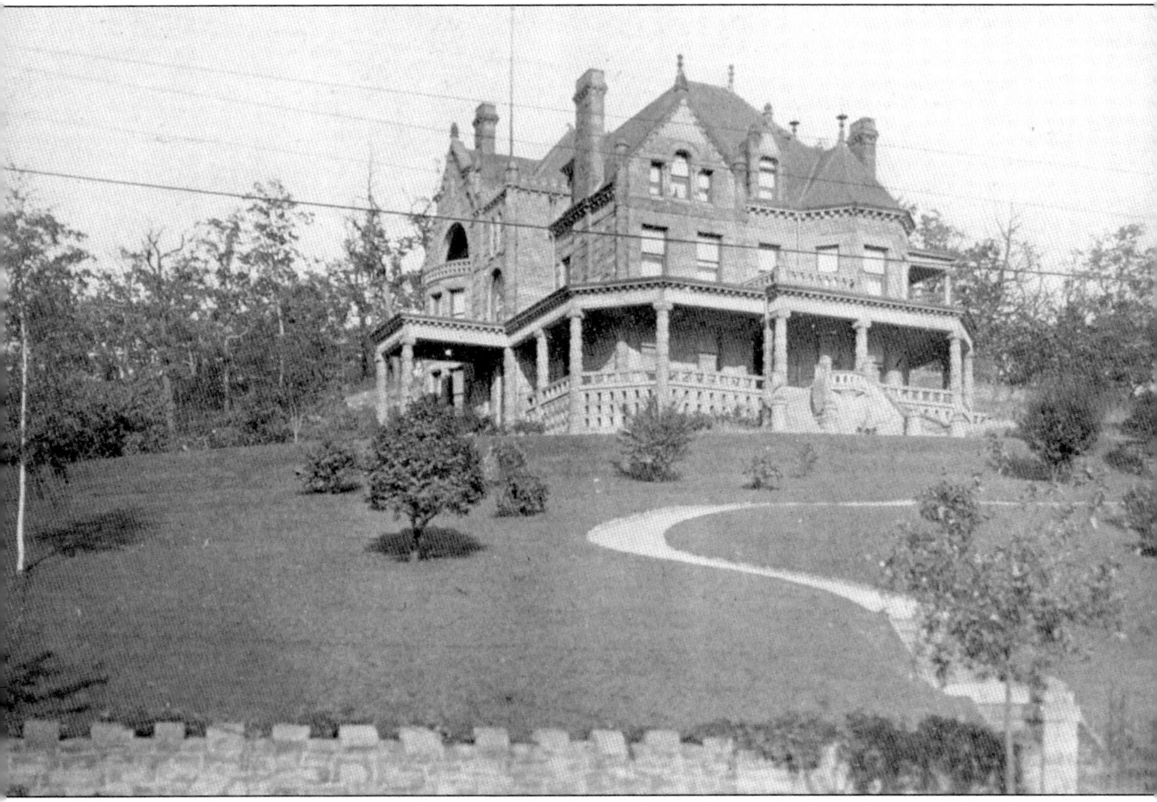

Thomas R. Loughrey's home at Forbes Avenue and Woodlawn Street displays elements of Jacobean Revival and Romanesque styles. Loughrey held interests in Western Pennsylvania mining and smelting operations.

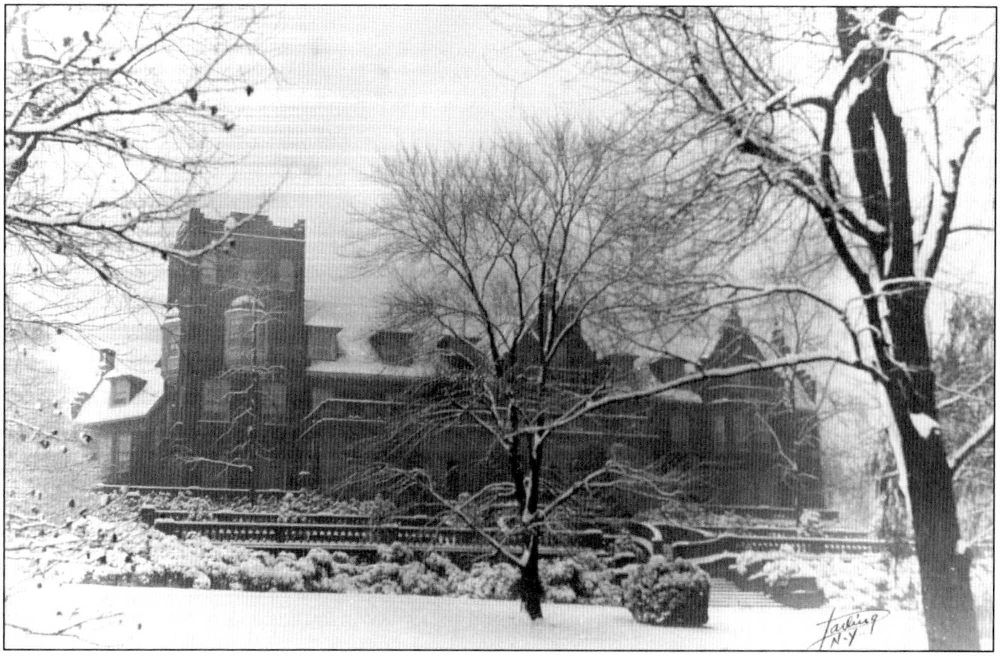

Located at Fifth Avenue and Beechwood Boulevard in Point Breeze, Lyndhurst, designed by Theophilus Parsons Chandler Jr., was the expansive estate of the William Thaw Sr. family. Thaw was a financier, steamboat operator, and a director of the Pennsylvania Railroad. He lived here with his second wife, Mary Copley Thaw, and their five children. A daughter, Alice Cornelia Thaw, was married in the house in 1903 in a lavish wedding to the Seventh Marquess of Hertford and was eventually styled Countess of Yarmouth. The home, dubbed by the *Pittsburgh Press* as "Pittsburgh's last castle," was demolished in 1944. (Above, Pittsburgh History & Landmarks Foundation.)

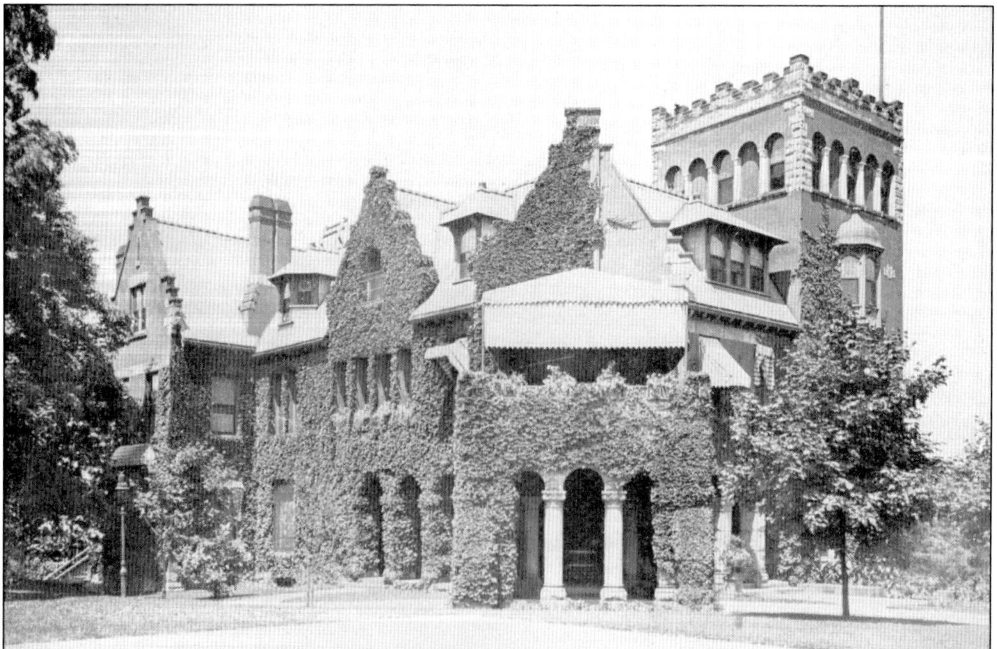

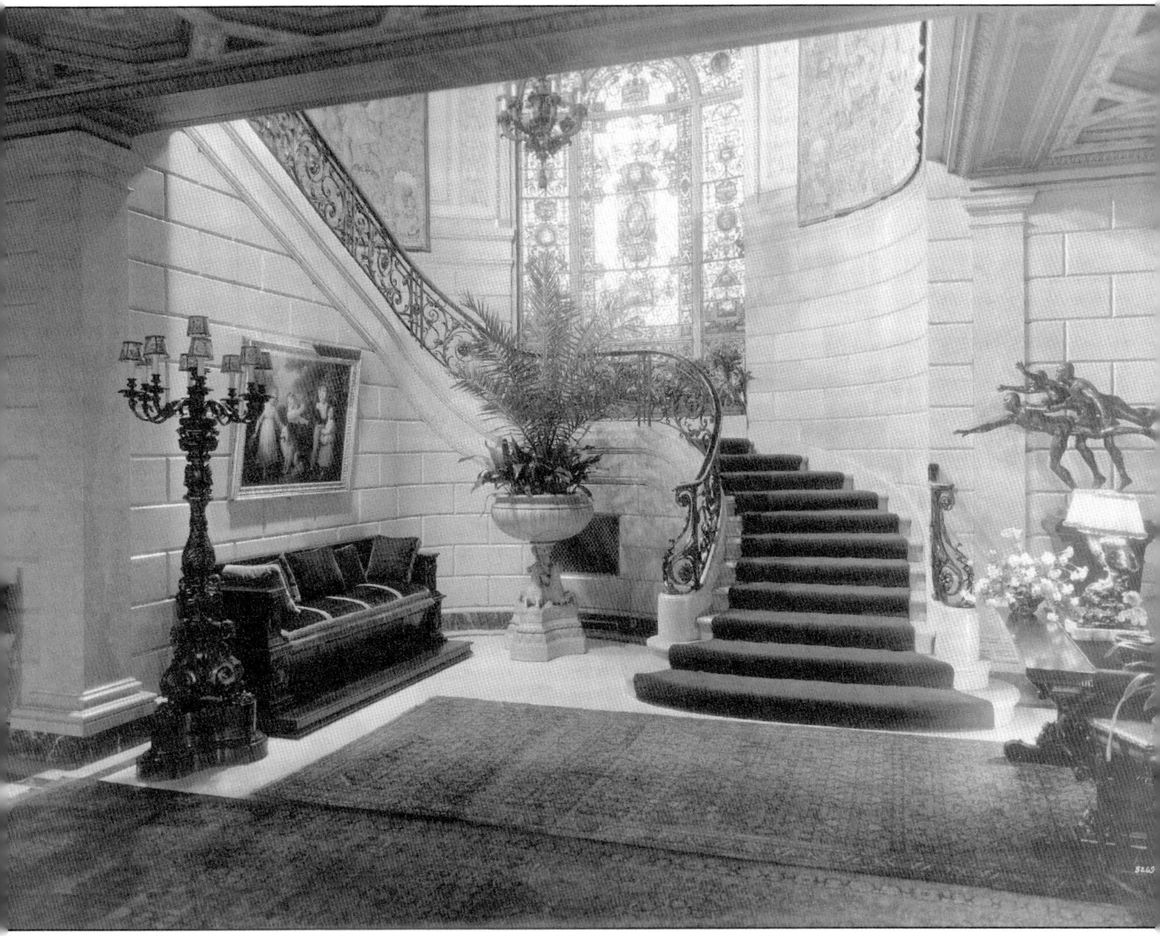

Lyndhurst's entrance hall set the stage for the lavish interiors that visitors were to encounter throughout the house. Elaborate ironwork, stained-glass panels, and tapestries greeted guests arriving at the Thaw home. (Pittsburgh History & Landmarks Foundation.)

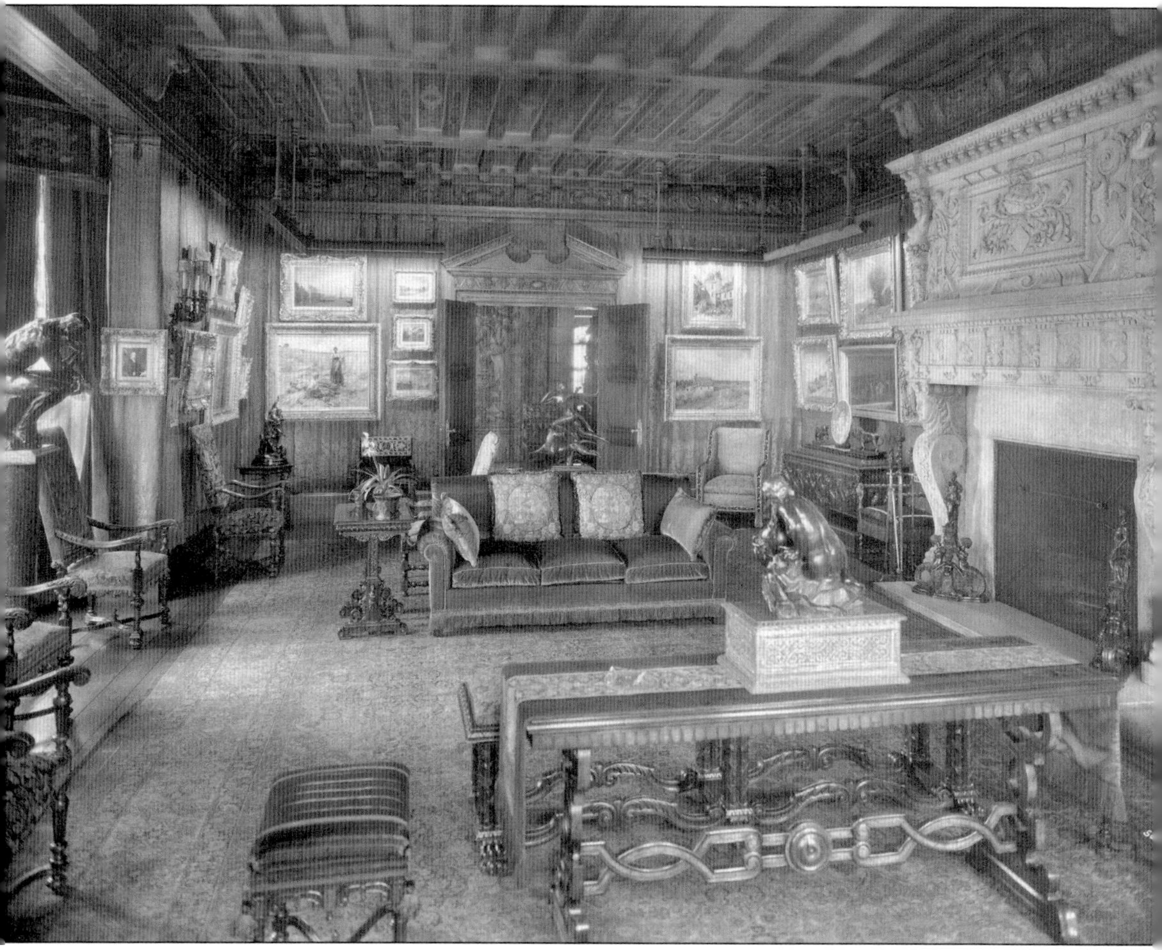

The living hall at Lyndhurst echoes the home's Jacobean Revival façade. With its enormous fireplace, coffered ceiling, and dark wood, the room had a cluttered feel that was typical for the period. A small portion of the Thaw family's art collection can be seen at the far end of the room. (Pittsburgh History & Landmarks Foundation.)

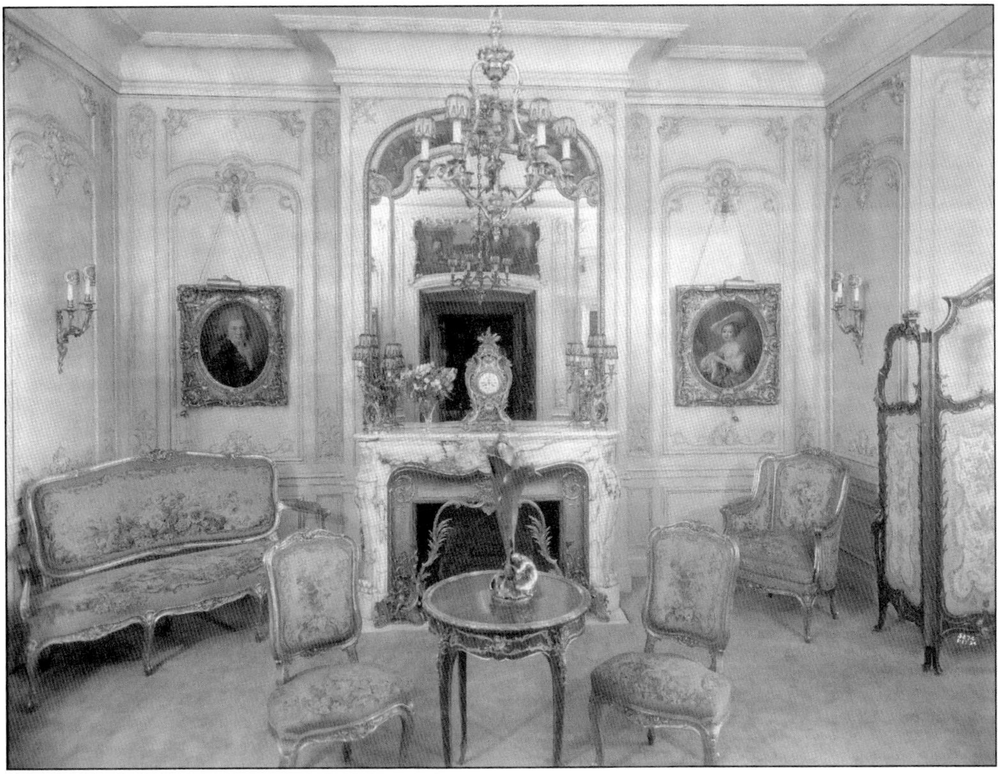

Lyndhurst's sitting and dining rooms reflected a Louis XV decor that was highly popular at the time. Gold-edged portières, hand-painted murals, and elaborate oil paintings completed the furnishings for these extravagant spaces. (Pittsburgh History & Landmarks Foundation.)

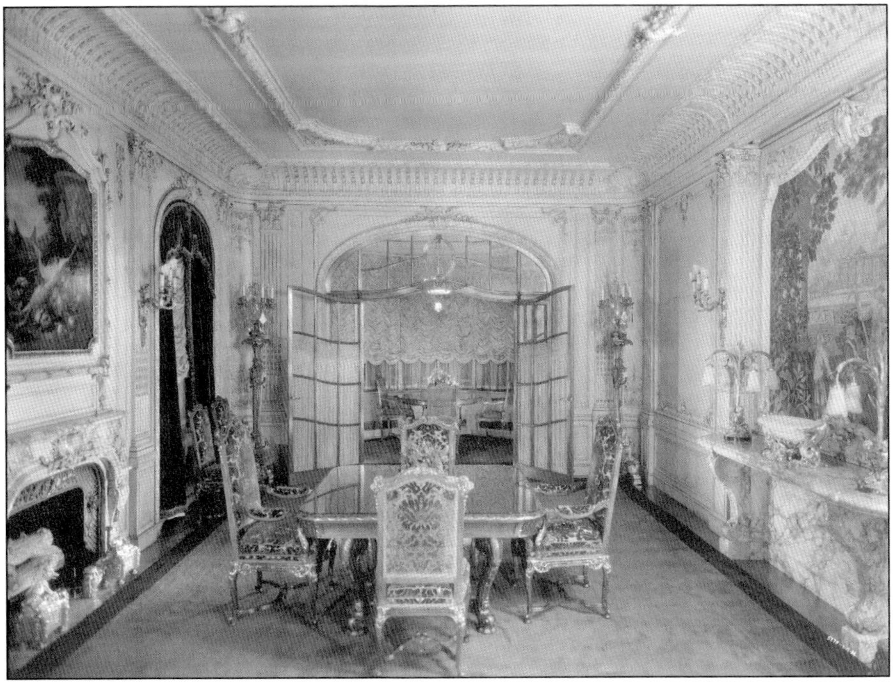

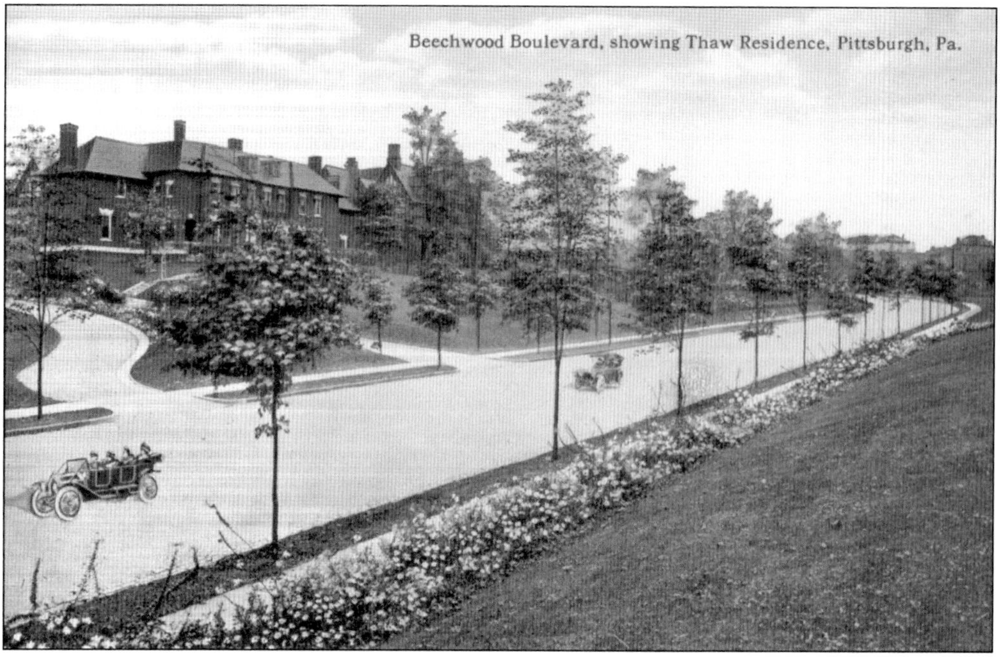

The postcard above shows Beechwood Boulevard and the home of Mary Copley Thaw. The Elizabethan Revival gable of the house can be seen at center, peeking out from the tree line. Oaklawn, as the house was known, was Mrs. Thaw's second and much smaller house; she lived here from about 1906 until her death in 1929. It is said that she abandoned the family's larger home, Lyndhurst, shortly after her son Harry K. Thaw murdered the architect Stanford White to end a love triangle involving Evelyn Nesbit, a society model. She never returned to Lyndhurst during her lifetime.

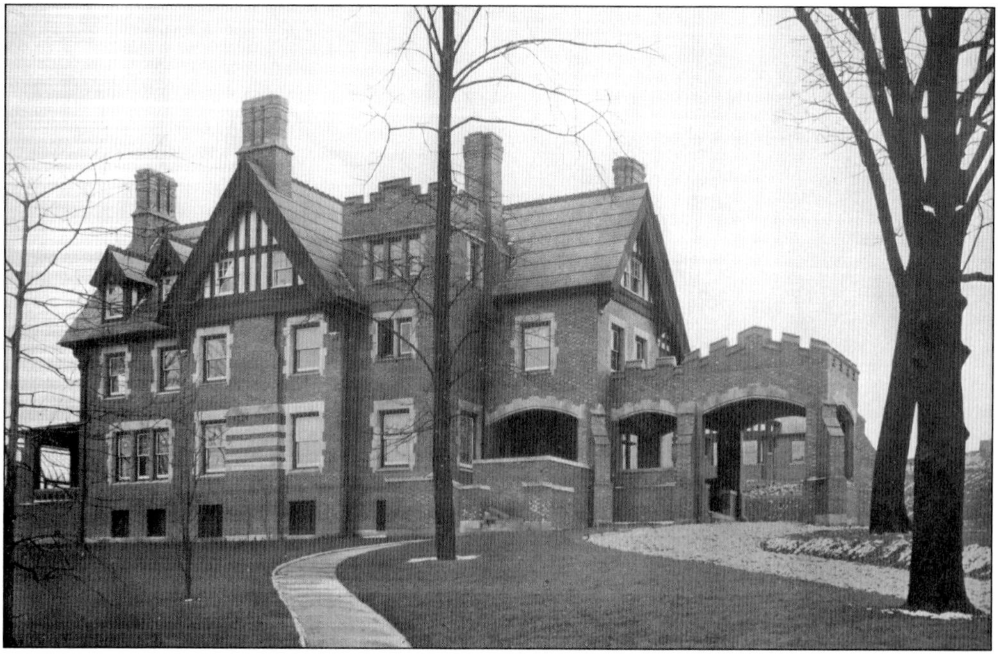

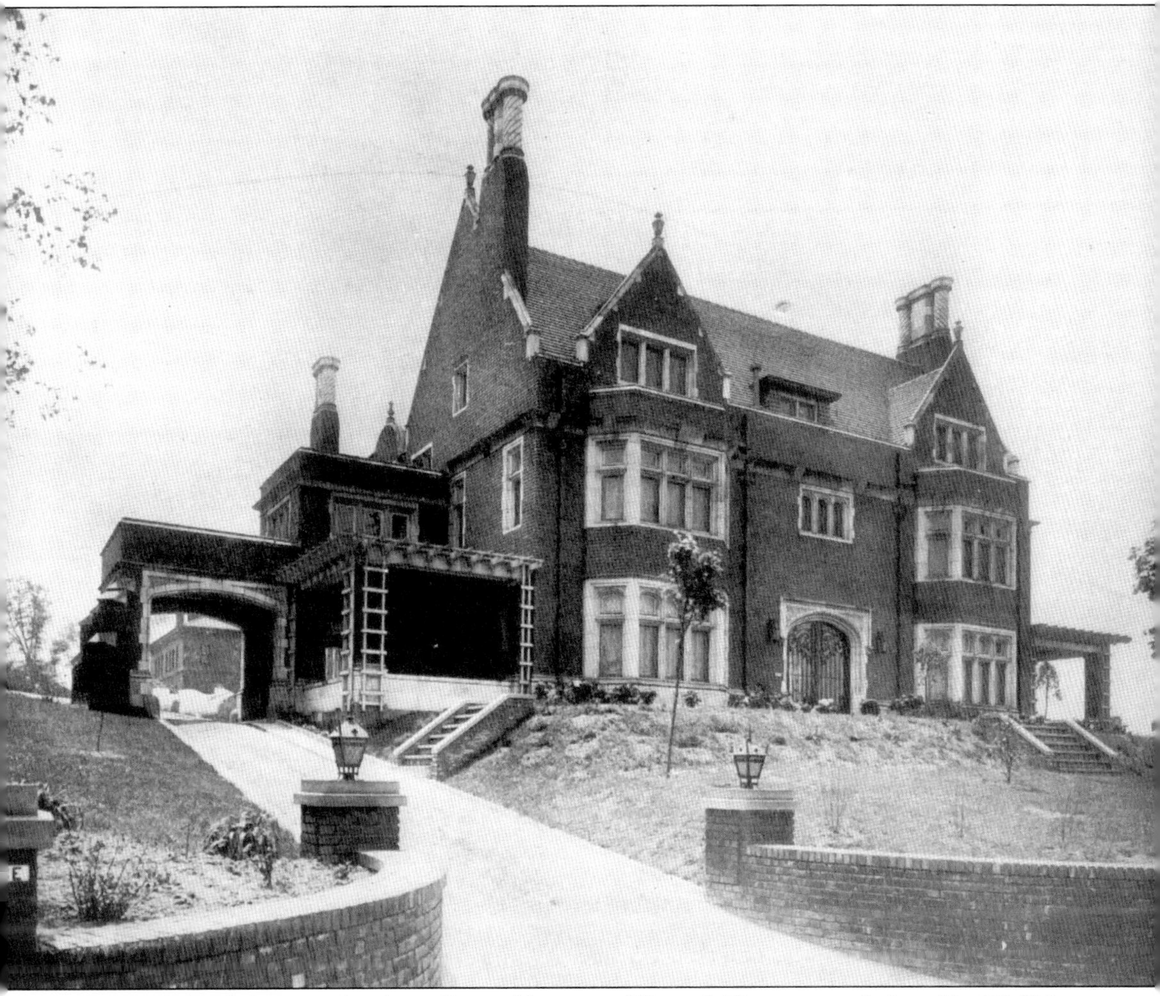

Herbert DuPuy's 24-room Jacobean Revival home on Warwick Terrace was designed by Olaf M. Topp around 1913. DuPuy was an owner of the Pennsylvania Rubber Company and, in later years, developed a series of rental row houses in neighboring Allegheny City. More recently, until its sale in 2009, the home was owned by the Roman Catholic Diocese of Pittsburgh, serving as the home of five different bishops.

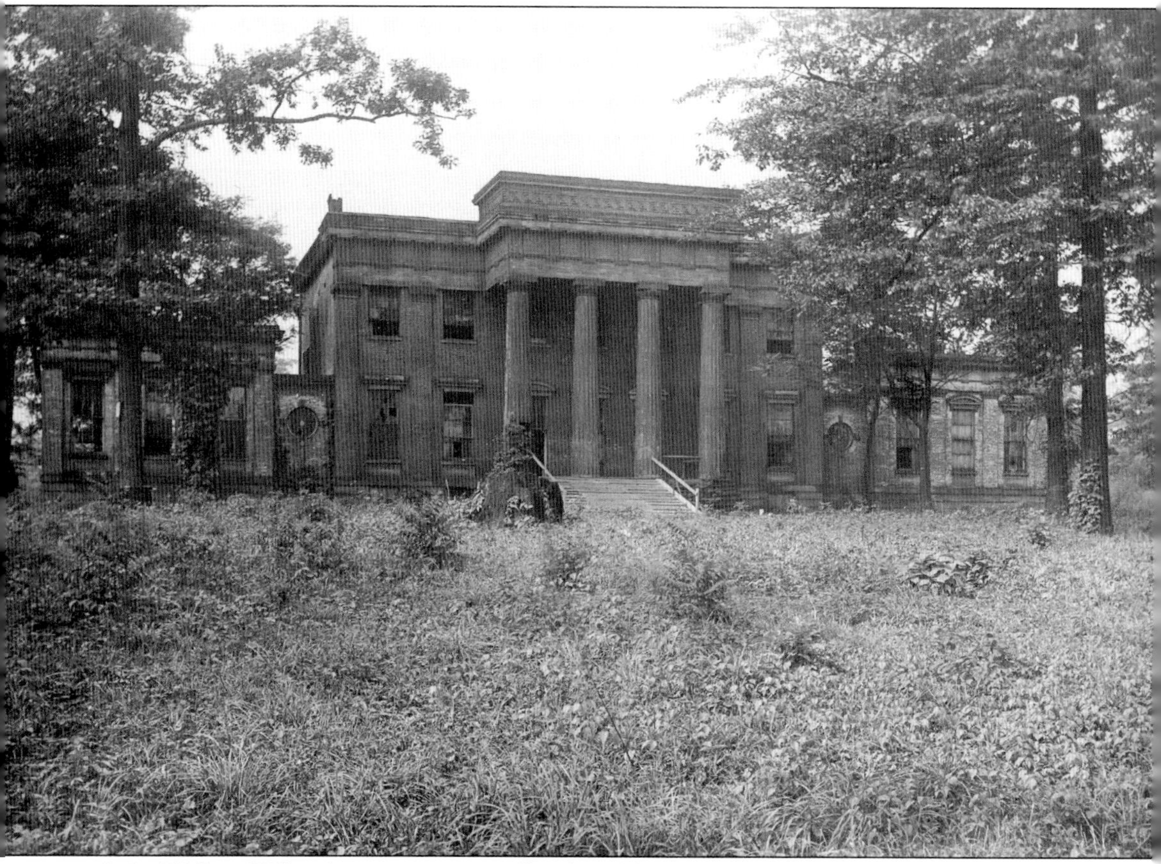

Judge William Wilkins's expansive tract of land straddled parts of present-day Point Breeze, Squirrel Hill, and Wilkinsburg. It is said that Wilkins designed his mansion, Homewood, himself around 1835. Many illustrious Americans visited Homewood, including presidents Andrew Jackson and Zachary Taylor. The residence stood until 1922, at which time the building was demolished and the remaining land sold. (HHC.)

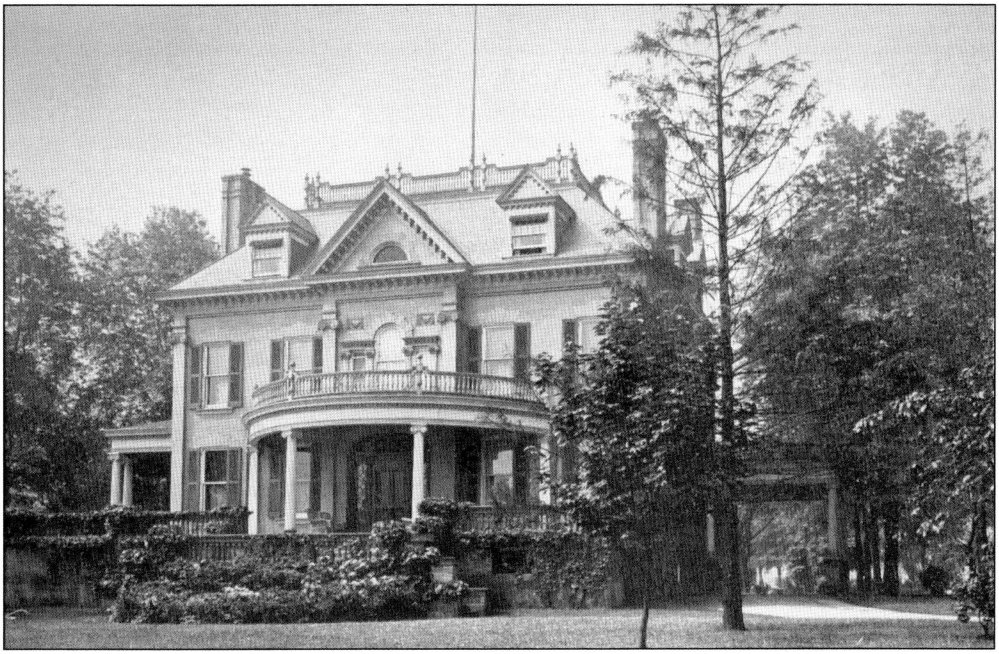

Pennham, home of John B. Jackson, stood at 6842 Penn Avenue. Jackson was the president of Fidelity Trust Co. and held positions on the board of directors for many local banking institutions. He was also active with organizations serving the deaf, blind, and insane. It is said that Jackson was the first Pittsburgher to present an oil painting to the permanent collection at the Carnegie Institute. A lifelong bachelor until his death in 1908 in a horse-riding accident, Jackson resided at Pennham with his sisters.

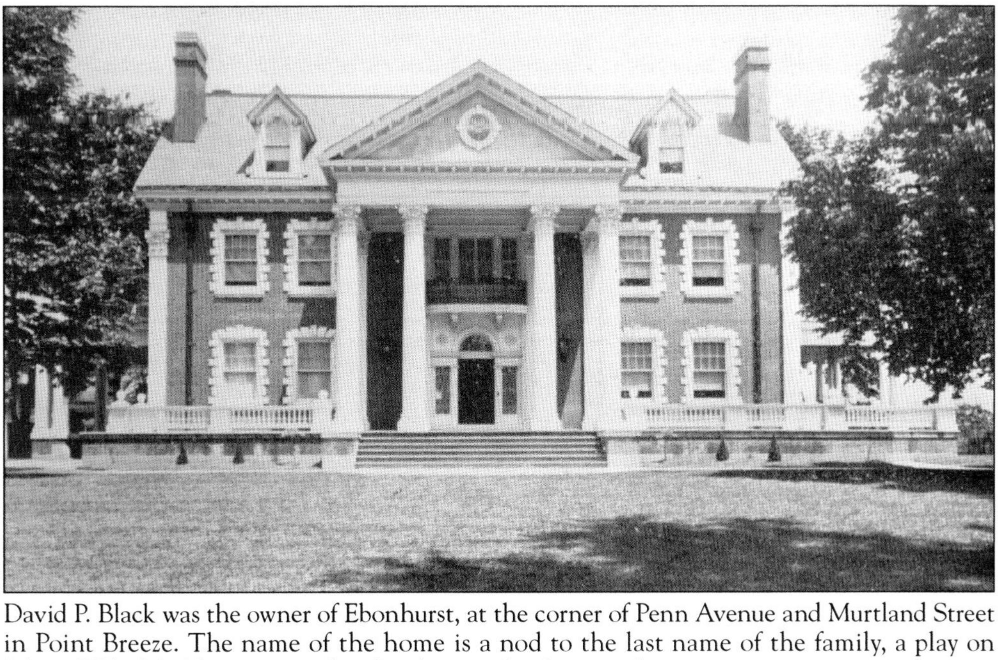

David P. Black was the owner of Ebonhurst, at the corner of Penn Avenue and Murtland Street in Point Breeze. The name of the home is a nod to the last name of the family, a play on "ebony." Black held interests in local real estate, banking, and insurance institutions and was an avid motorist.

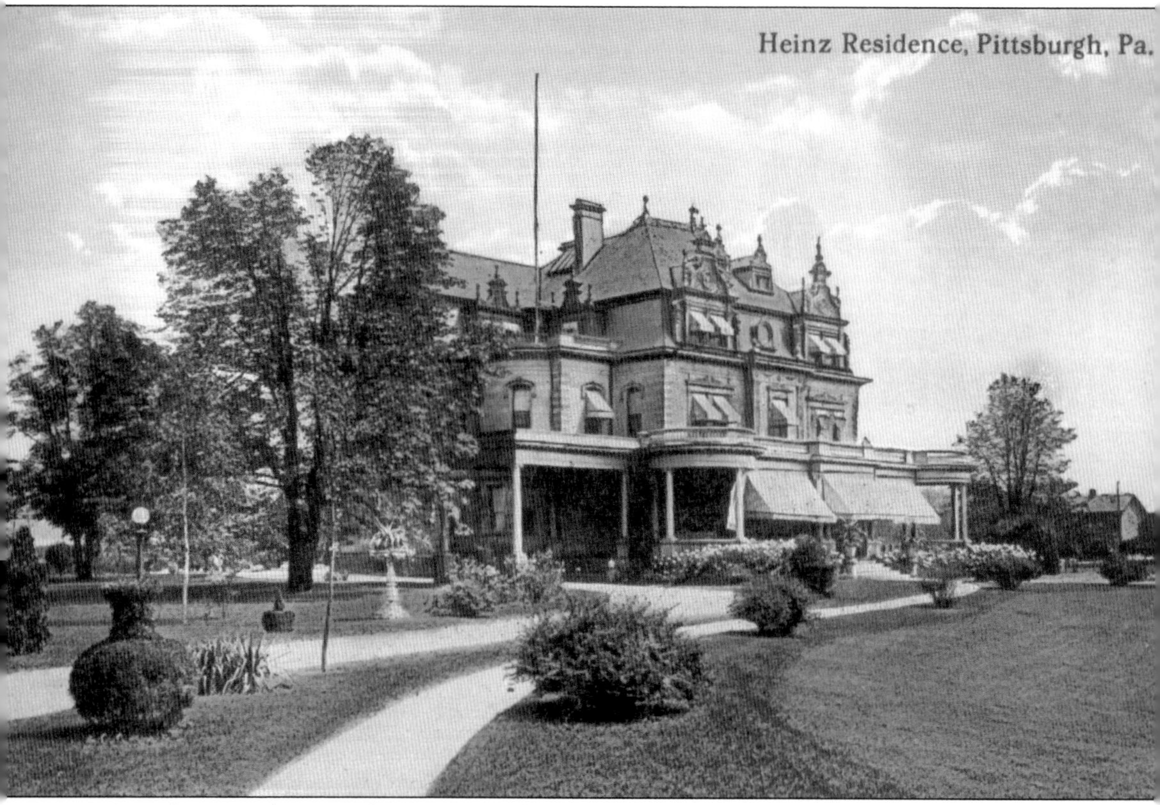

Greenlawn was home to the H.J. Heinz family of condiment fame. The property's Penn Avenue border was lined with an ornate wrought-iron fence, which is all that remains of the grand estate today. A period publication praised the house as "a beautiful mansion in the East end of Pittsburgh, furnished with a large library and many collections of quaint and interesting relics."

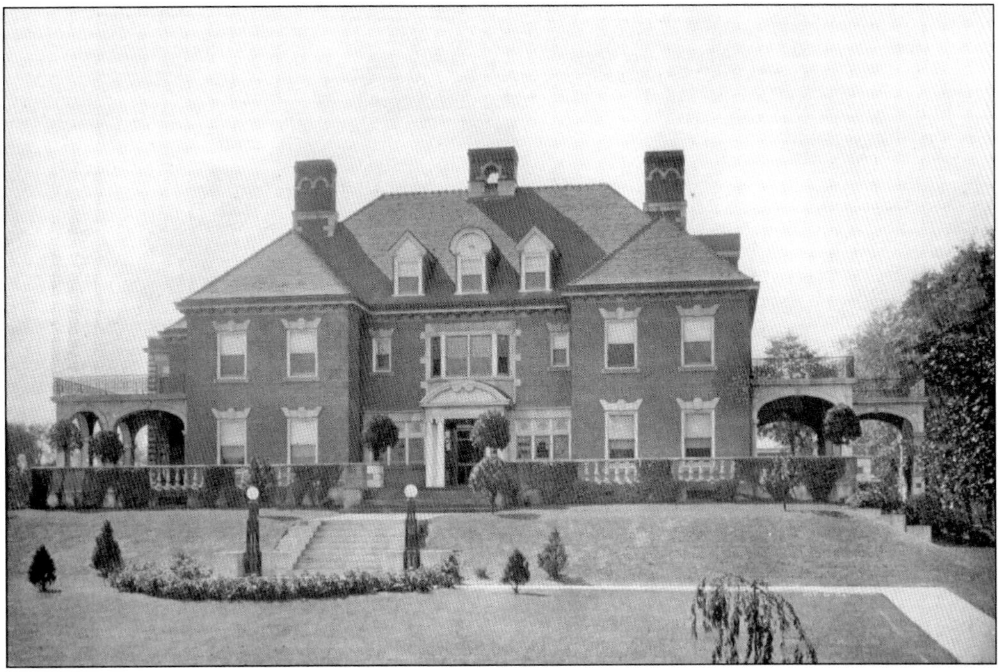

T.M. Armstrong's Penrose, designed by Alden & Harlow around 1905, stood at Penn Avenue and Murtland Street. The home had 21 rooms, including a billiard room and music room. The property also featured a two-story stable and carriage house, plus a gardener's cottage. Armstrong was the owner of Armstrong Cork Co. and sat on the board of directors for various banking and mining companies. The home was demolished in 1955.

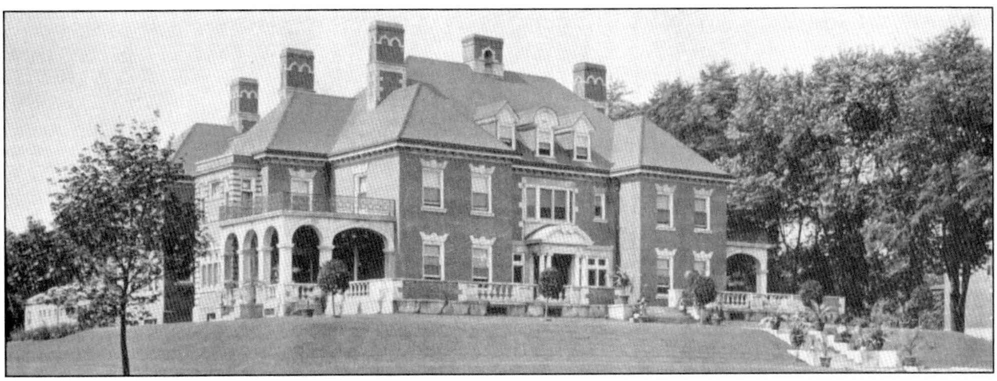

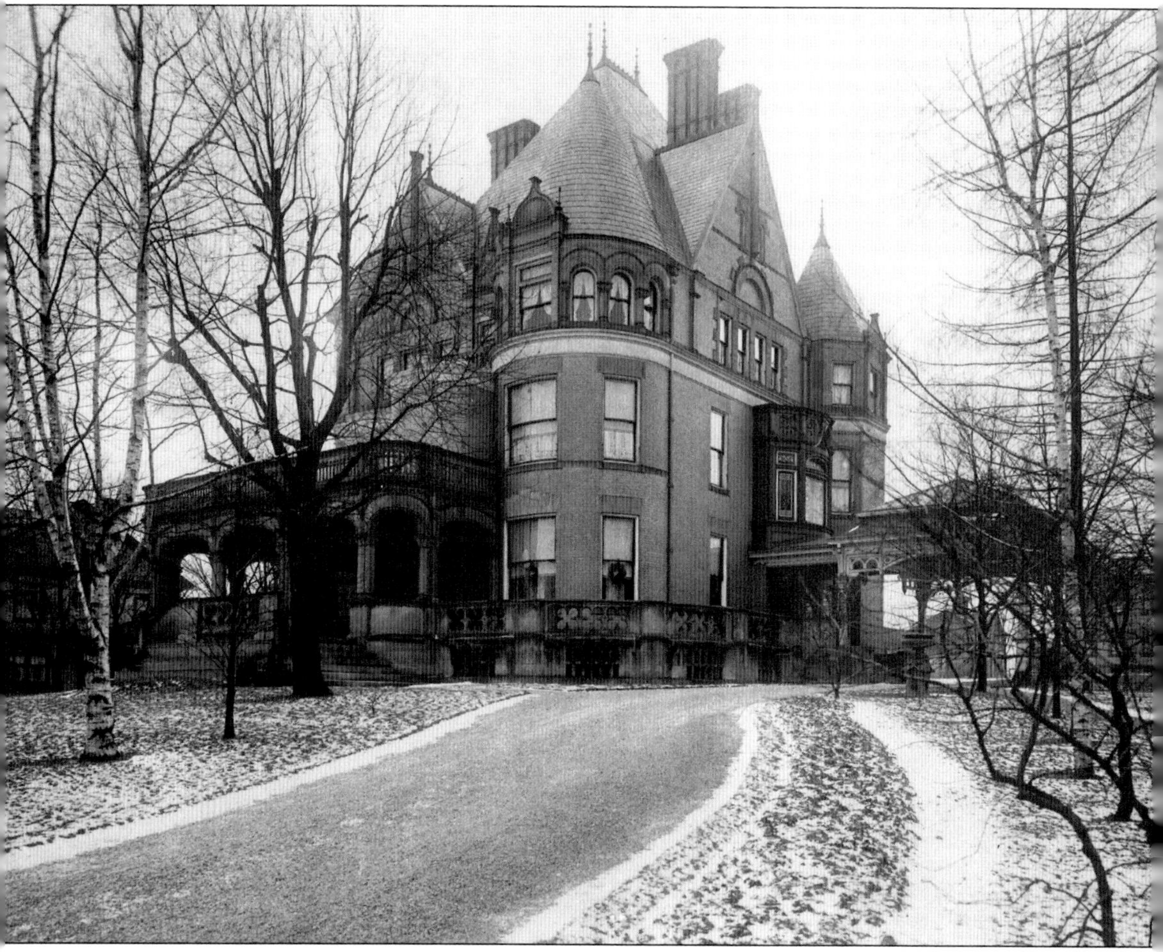

Clayton, the Point Breeze home of the Henry Clay Frick family, was built in 1870 as a two-story, 11-room Italianate structure at the corner of Penn and South Homewood Avenues. Andrew Peebles remodeled the home when the Fricks purchased it in 1882. A massive renovation overseen by Frederick J. Osterling in 1891–1892 transformed it into a châteauesque mansion. Alden & Harlow made later additions to the property. Today, Clayton is open to the public as a house museum. (Frick Collection/Frick Art Reference Library Archives.)

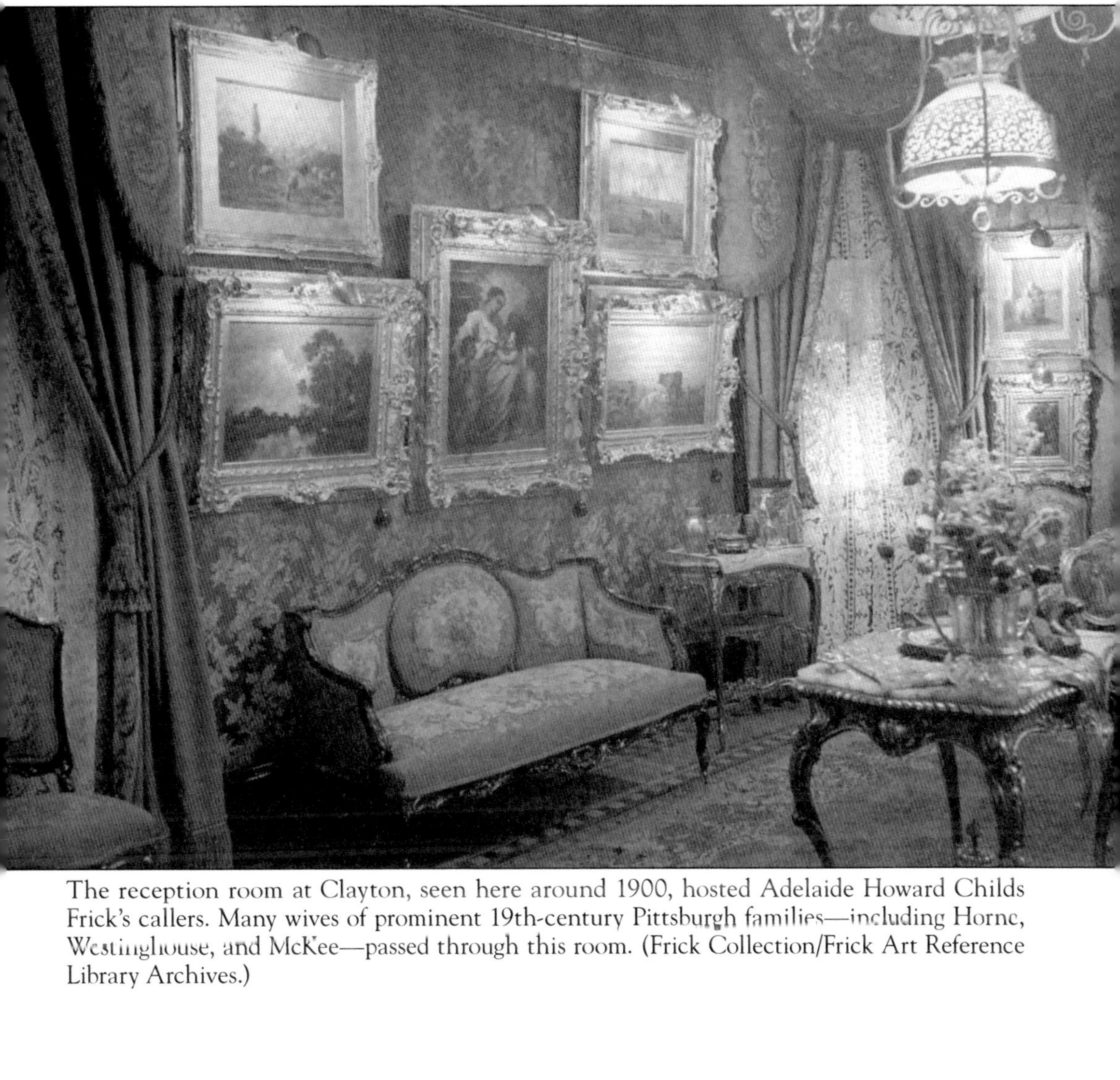

The reception room at Clayton, seen here around 1900, hosted Adelaide Howard Childs Frick's callers. Many wives of prominent 19th-century Pittsburgh families—including Horne, Westinghouse, and McKee—passed through this room. (Frick Collection/Frick Art Reference Library Archives.)

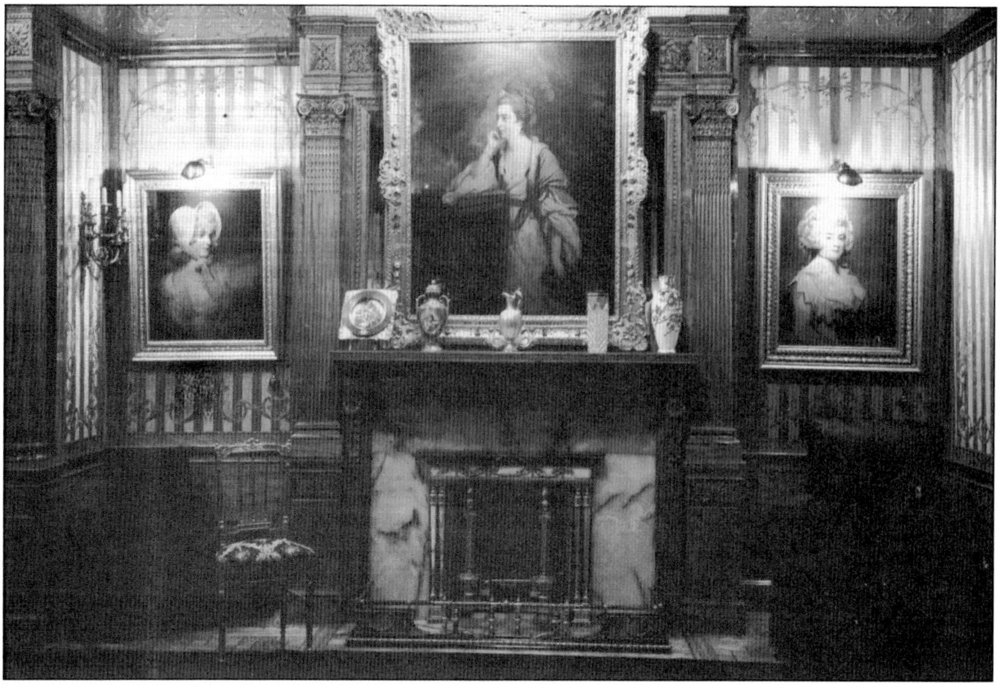

As Clayton did not have a gallery or similar space, the parlor was home to many of Henry Clay Frick's fine paintings over the years. To the left of the mantel is John Hoppner's *The Hon. Lucy Byng*, now in the Frick Collection in New York City. (Frick Collection/Frick Art Reference Library Archives.)

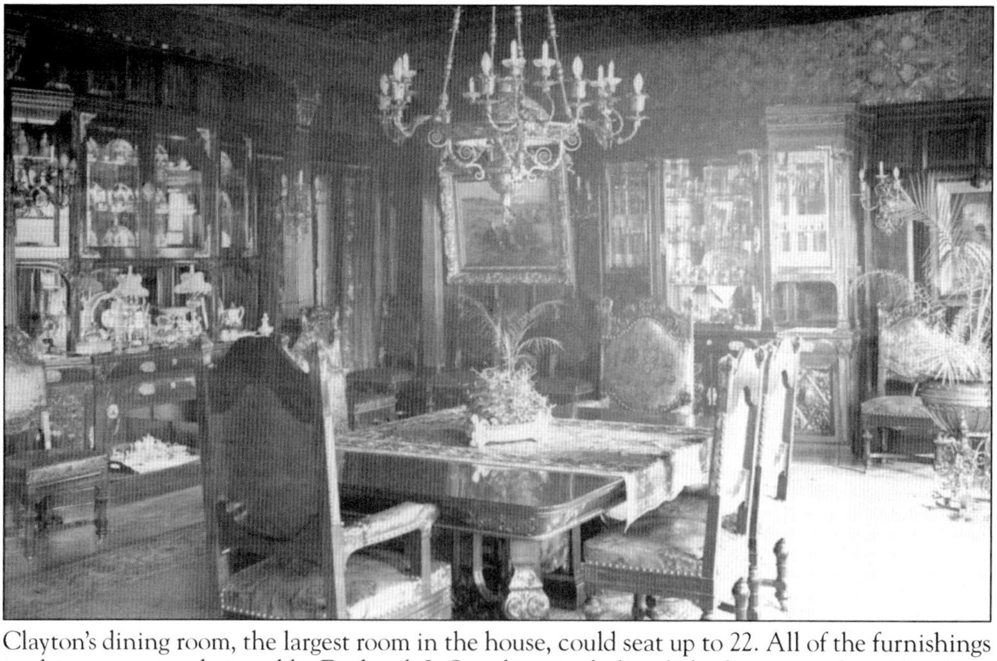

Clayton's dining room, the largest room in the house, could seat up to 22. All of the furnishings in this room were designed by Frederick J. Osterling, including light fixtures and textiles. Pres. Theodore Roosevelt lunched in this room during a visit to Pittsburgh on July 4, 1902. (Frick Collection/Frick Art Reference Library Archives.)

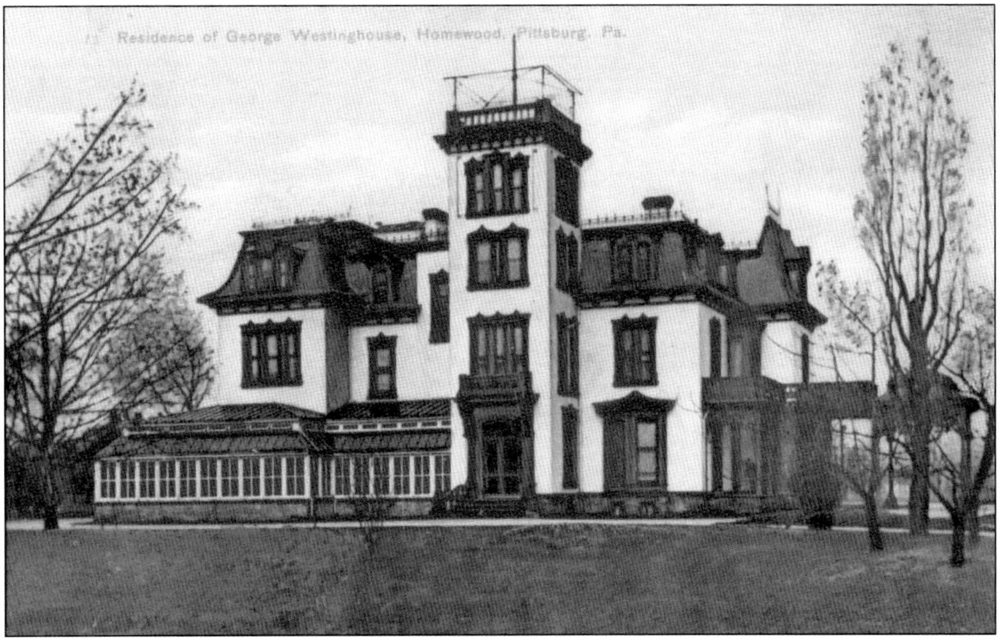

Solitude was the home of engineer and electrical pioneer George Westinghouse. Pres. William McKinley, then a congressman, once visited the house to confer with Westinghouse on railroad safety issues. Located close to the former Pennsylvania Railroad station in Point Breeze, the home was demolished in 1919 to make way for the public Westinghouse Park.

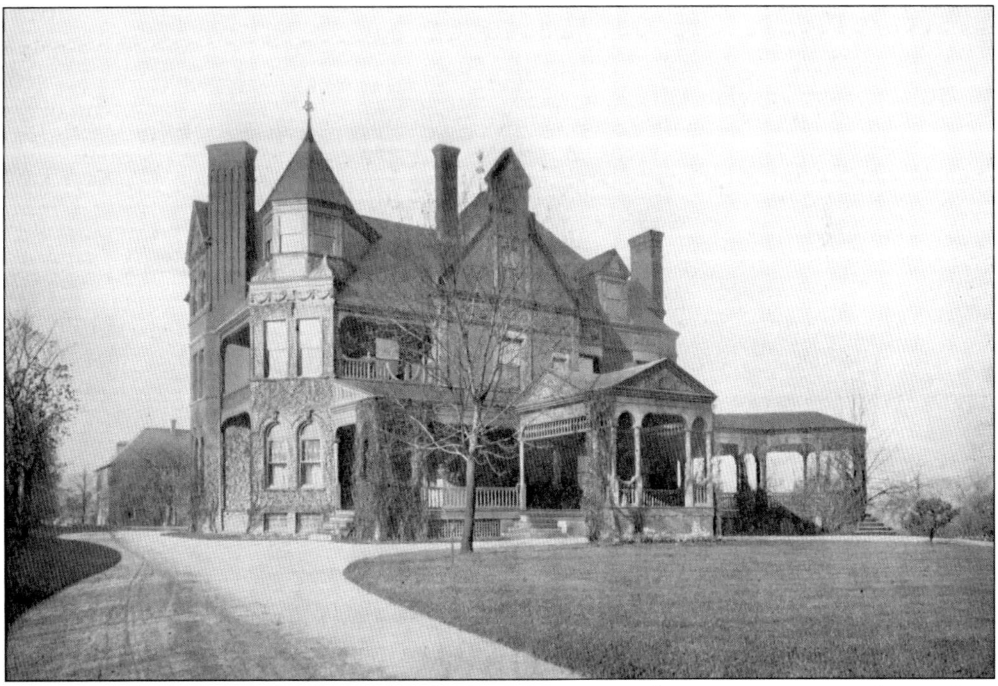

George Lauder Sr. was a first cousin of Andrew Carnegie and spent many years advising him and his associates on the board of Carnegie Steel Company. Lauder's home at 7403 Penn Avenue combines many elements of Victorian Revival architecture.

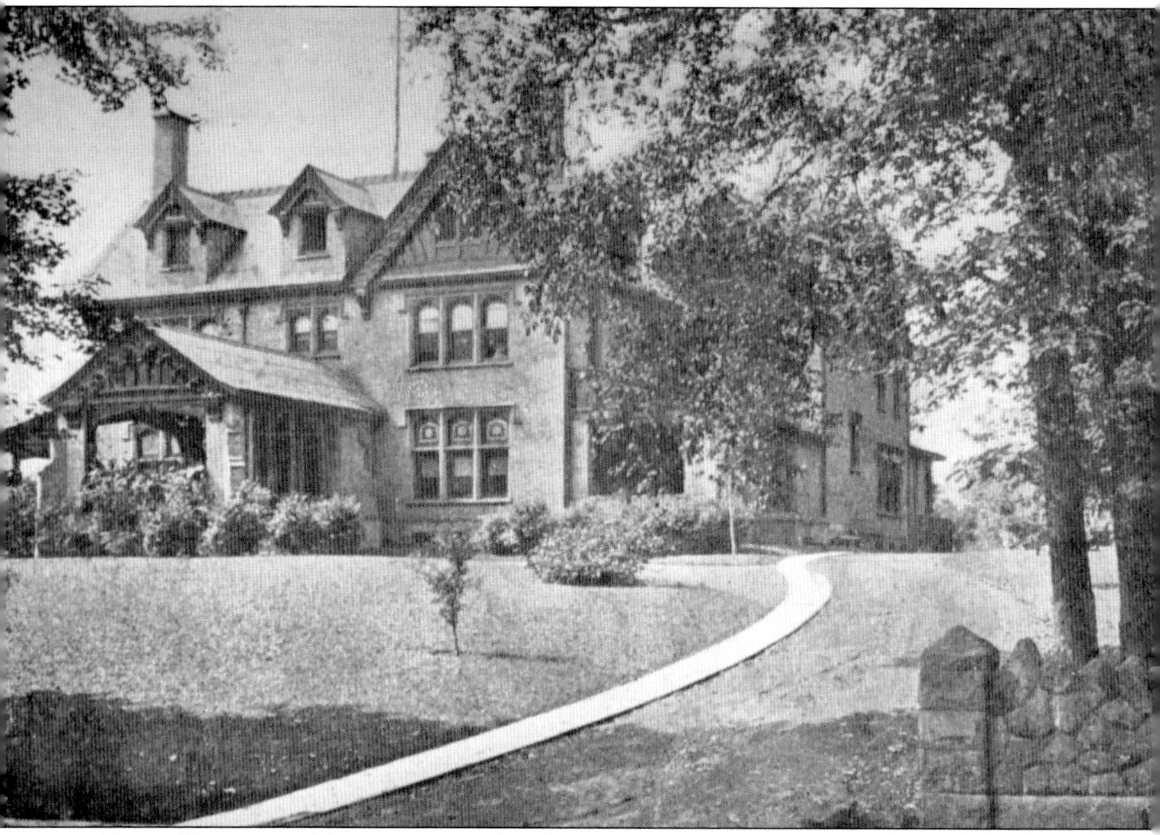

Durbin Horne, son of department store founder Joseph Horne, lived at The Gables on Penn Avenue. Horne became president of his father's company, whose flagship store stood at Penn Avenue and Stanwix Street in downtown Pittsburgh. The company was acquired by Federated Department Stores in 1994 and thereafter ceased to do business under the name "Horne's."

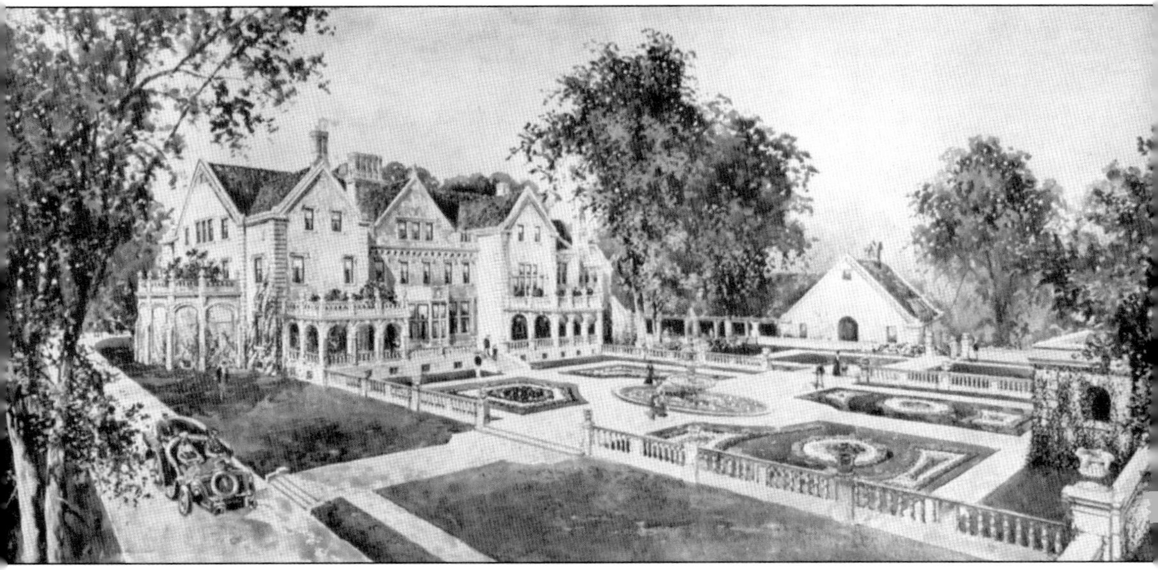

Edgehill, the sprawling estate of F.T.F. Lovejoy, stood at Braddock and Edgerton Avenues, at the very edge of Point Breeze. The home was designed by Alden & Harlow around 1905. During the infamous Homestead Steel Strike, Lovejoy, secretary and manager of Carnegie Steel Company, was selected by the board as the only official authorized to release information to the press. In protest of Andrew Carnegie's treatment of Henry Clay Frick during the dissolution of the "Ironclad Agreement" in 1895, Lovejoy resigned all of his board positions. (CMU.)

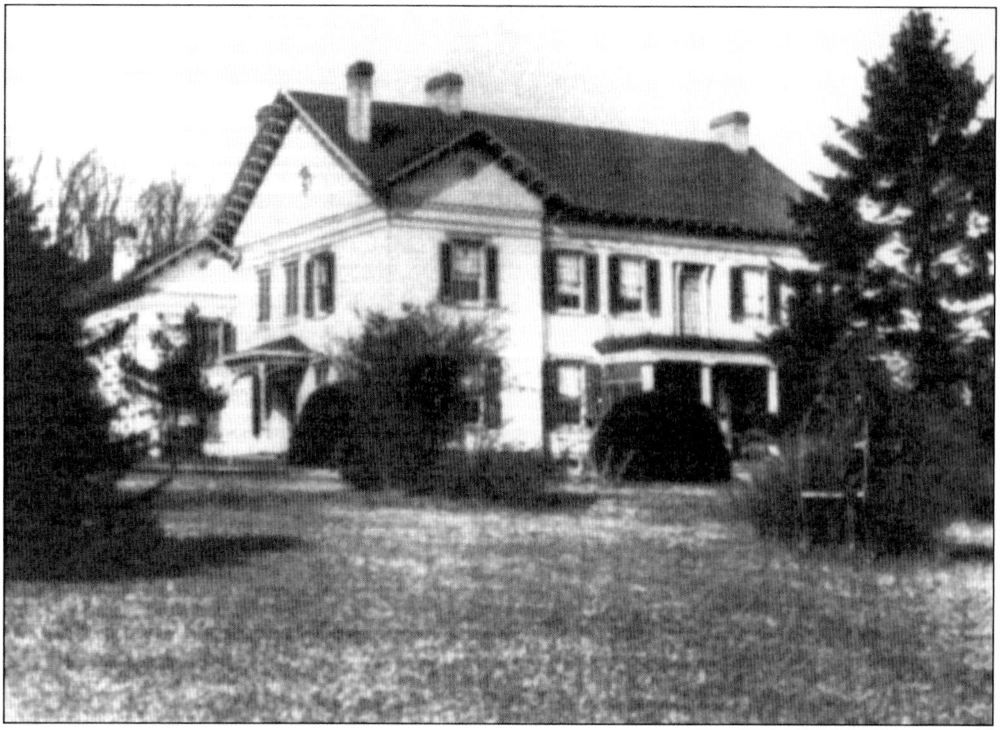

Judge Thomas Mellon was the patriarch of the vast Mellon clan, whose influence in the banking industry enabled many of the businessmen mentioned in this book to prosper. Mellon shared this 22-room North Negley Avenue home with his wife, Sarah Jane Negley. The property was demolished in 1955.

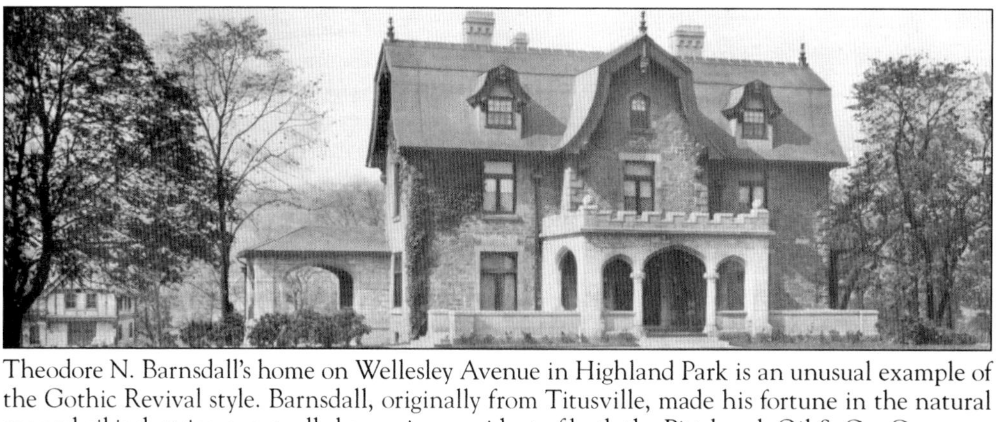

Theodore N. Barnsdall's home on Wellesley Avenue in Highland Park is an unusual example of the Gothic Revival style. Barnsdall, originally from Titusville, made his fortune in the natural gas and oil industries, eventually becoming president of both the Pittsburgh Oil & Gas Company and the Union National Gas Corporation. He died in 1917.

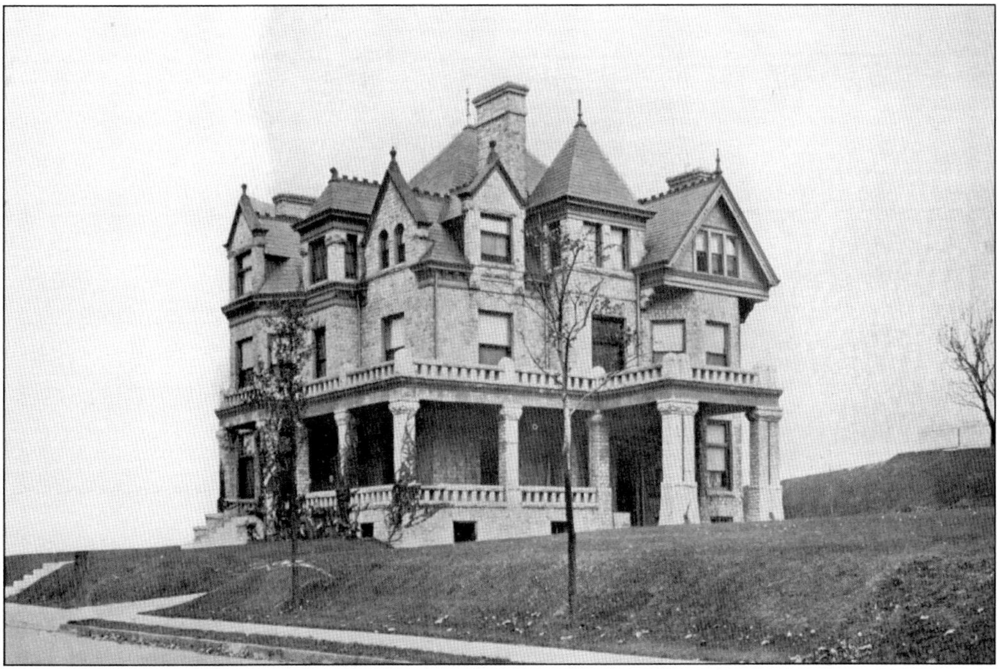

James T. Armstrong's Gothic Revival home stood at 5907 Callowhill Street in Highland Park. Armstrong served as the first secretary and treasurer of the Fidelity Title & Trust Company.

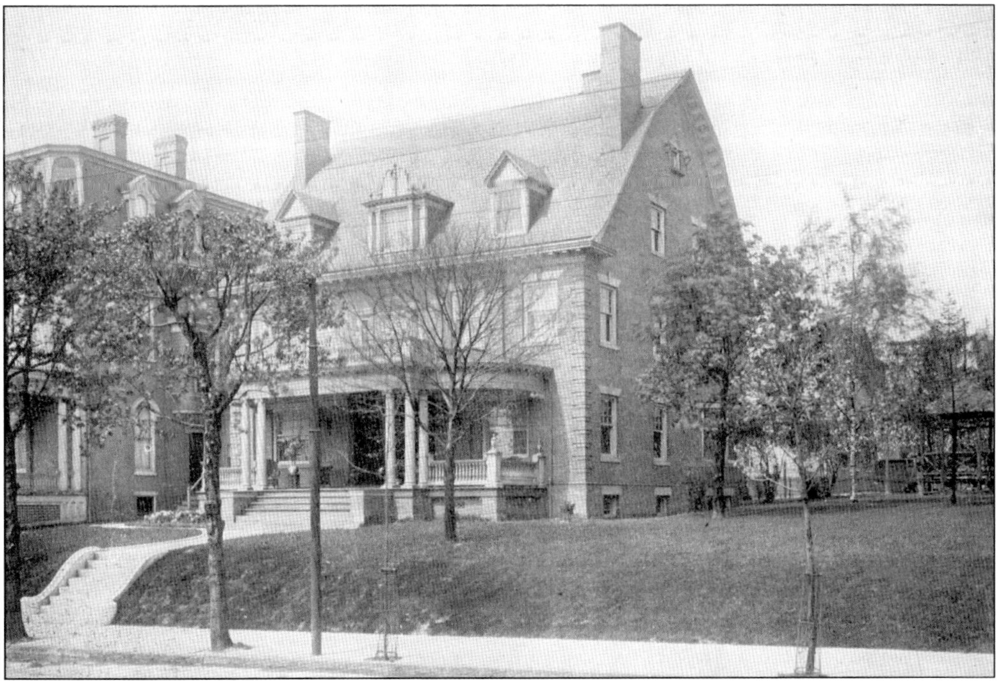

Sam F. Sipe was a well-respected jeweler and importer of diamonds and precious stones. His home at 737 North Highland Avenue long ago gave way to the wrecking ball and is now the site of a nursing home. Sipe died in 1922.

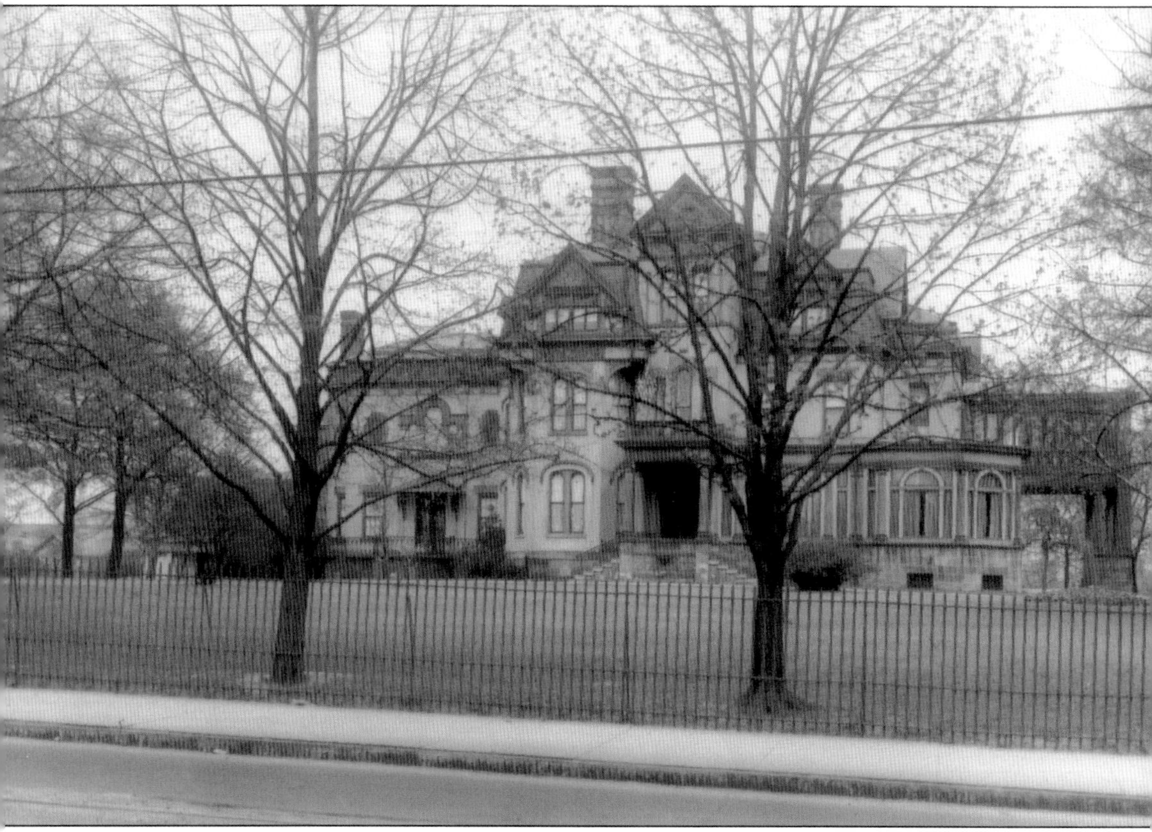

Charles Lockhart's mansion stood at 608 North Highland Avenue, on property that now houses the Pittsburgh Theological Seminary. Like many of his contemporaries, Lockhart was a Scottish immigrant, and he made his fortune in the oil industry. His home was demolished in 1952. (Pittsburgh City Photographer Collection, Archives Service Center, University of Pittsburgh.)

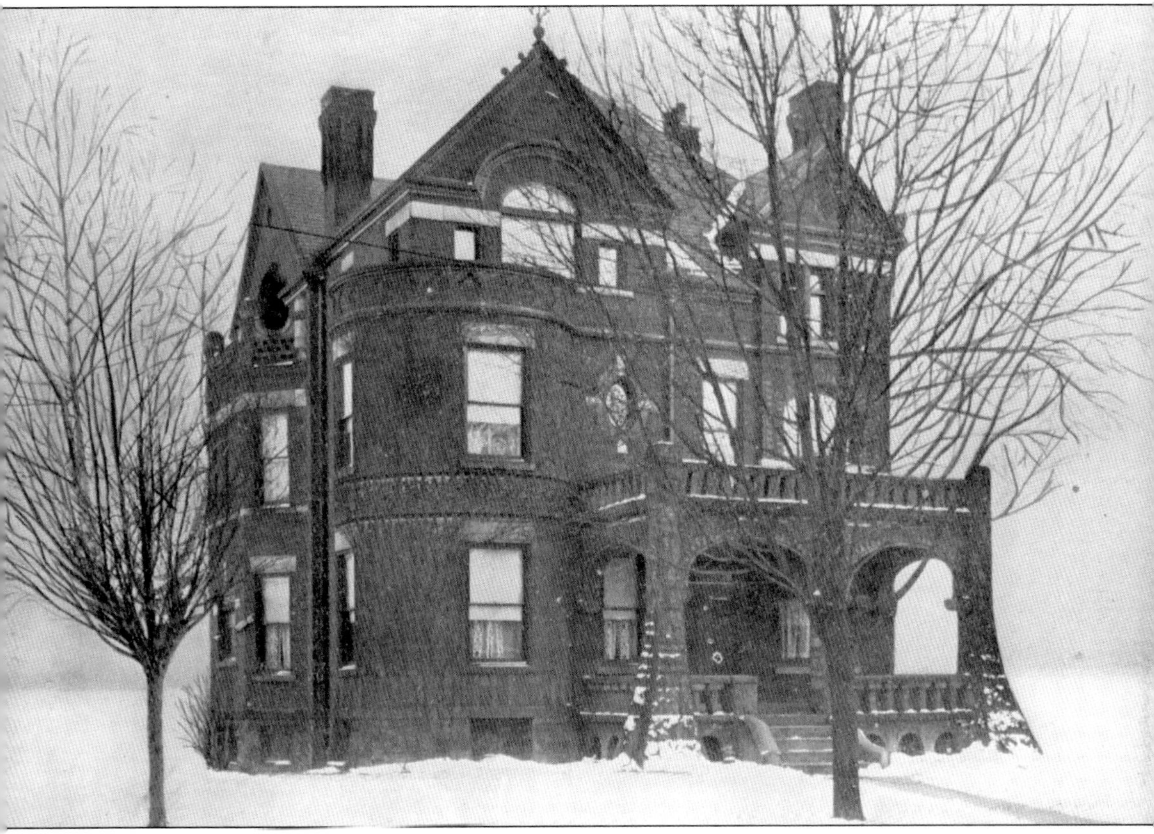

Henry A. Lappe was president of J.C. Lappe Tanning Co. on Spring Garden Avenue in Allegheny City, now Pittsburgh's North Side. His Romanesque home at 812 North Highland Avenue appears rather modest compared to the houses of many of his Highland Park neighbors.

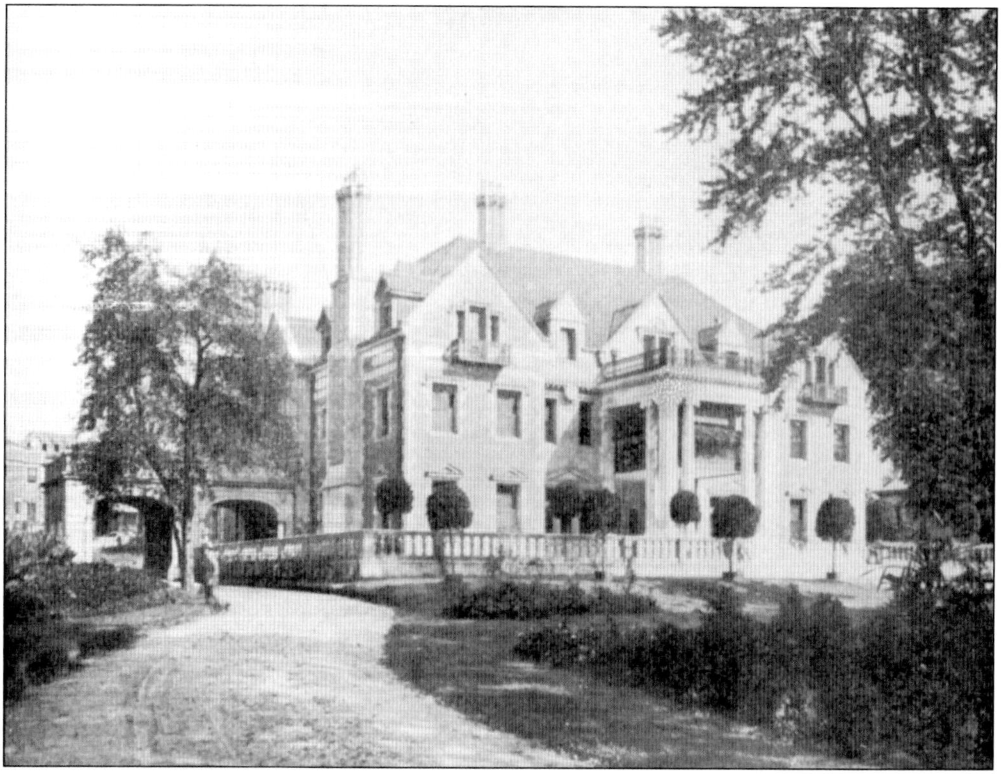

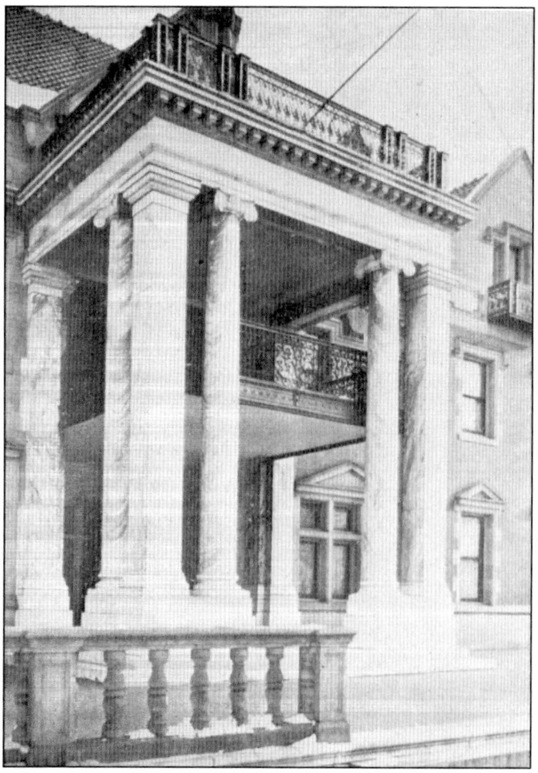

Alexander R. Peacock's Rowanlea occupied a large plot of land in Highland Park, essentially covering what is now an entire city block along Highland Avenue. Peacock was on the board of directors of Carnegie Steel Company and reaped massive benefits upon its absorption into U.S. Steel. The home, designed by Alden & Harlow around 1901, displays both Jacobean Revival and Neoclassical elements, as seen by the Ionic columns of the porch and the pediments above the first-floor windows. (CMU.)

Thomas Morrison's massive Rhu-Na-Craig was located at 1400 North Highland Avenue. The home's name roughly translates as "point of the hill" in Scottish Gaelic. Morrison, the general superintendent of the Edgar Thompson Works, also had glass and coal interests.

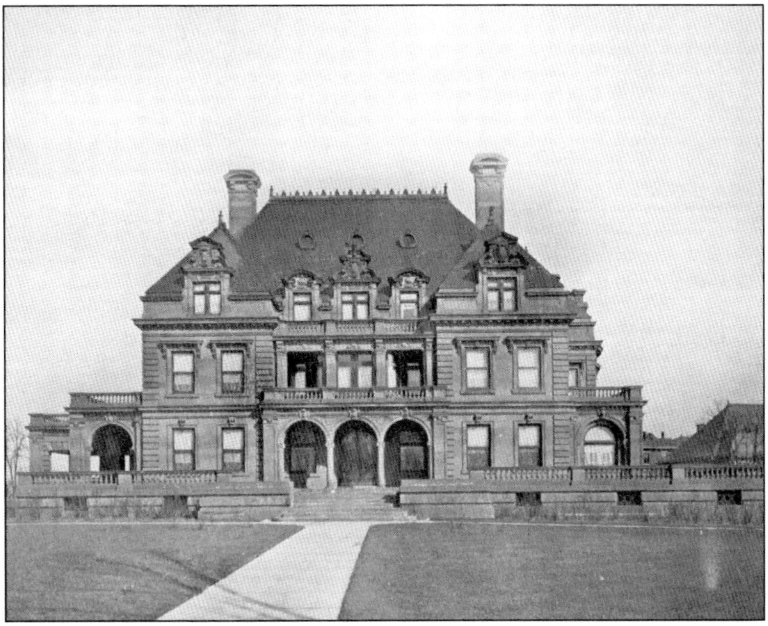

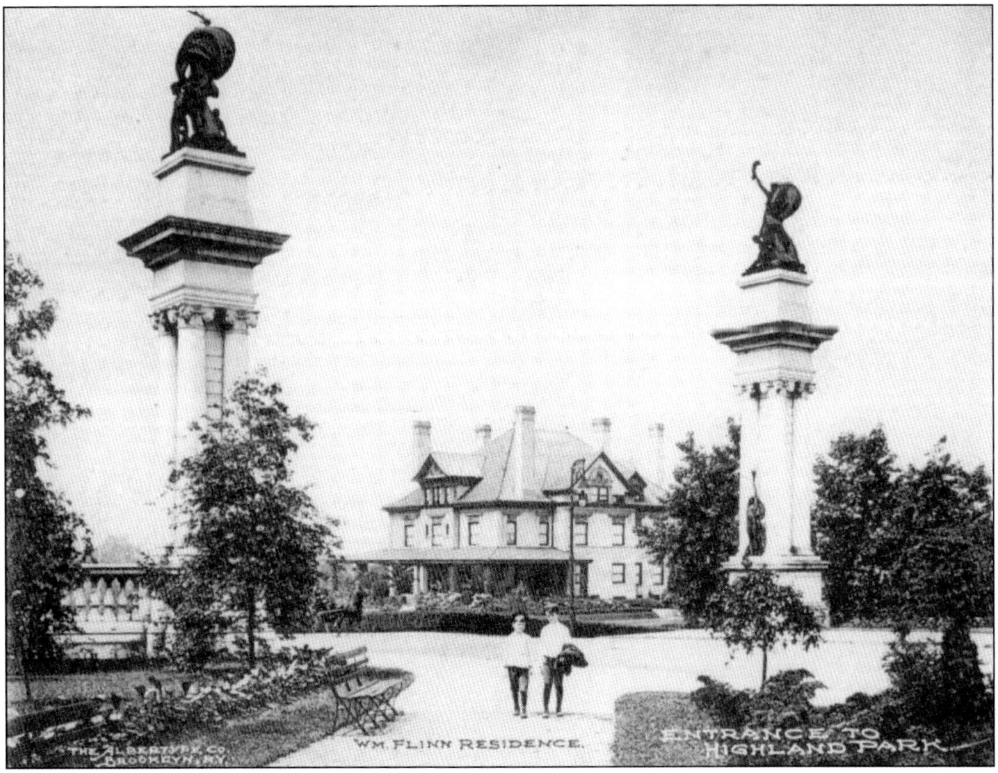

Originally from Manchester, England, William Flinn immigrated with his family as an infant. His home on North Highland Avenue was situated immediately outside the grand entrance to Highland Park. Flinn was a prominent player in Republican politics both locally and nationally. He served as a state senator and was an active member of Theodore Roosevelt's Bull Moose Party. The home, named Braemar, was demolished in 1924.

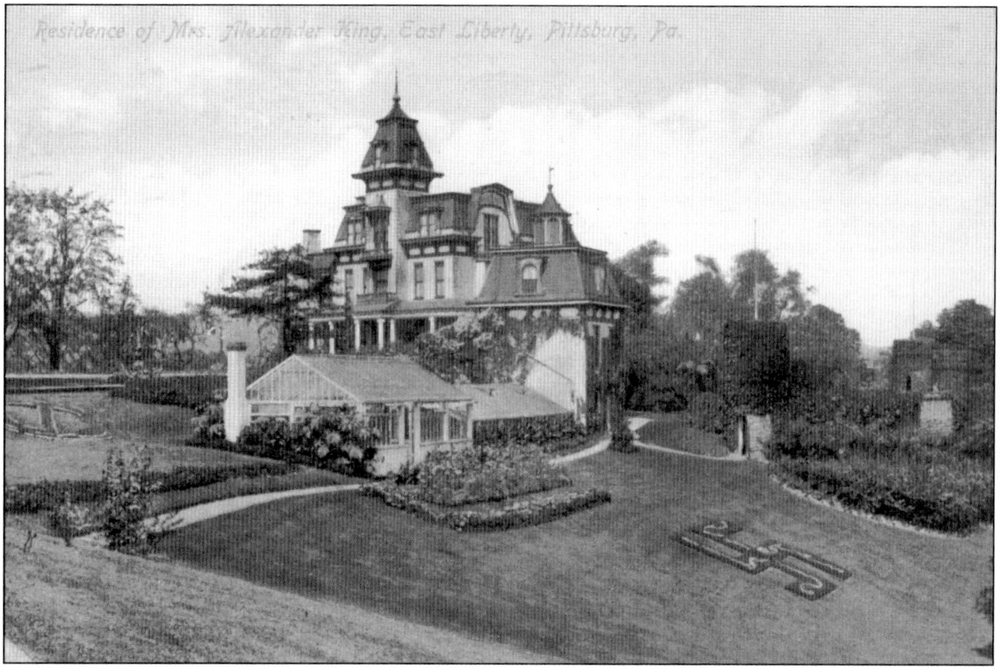

The King family owned Baywood, a white-painted brick Italianate home. Here, Alexander and Cordelia King raised four children. After a descendant left the home to the city of Pittsburgh in 1954, the building played host to generations of children who took art classes in its rundown yet still impressive rooms. By 1994, the home was back in private hands and has been handsomely restored.

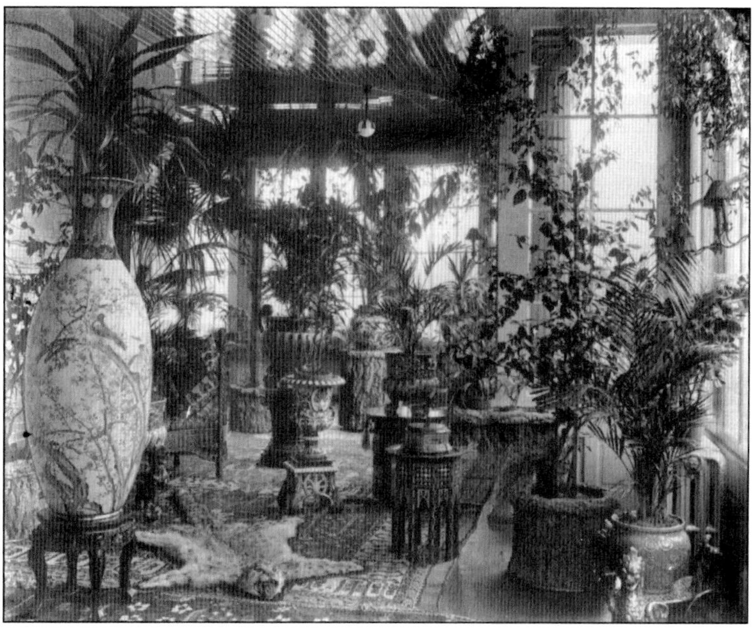

Cordelia King enjoyed the use of her sun porch, which was glassed in during the colder months, for both plants and butterflies. Her husband, Alexander King, had made his fortune in the glass manufacturing industry. (Frank and Maura Brown.)

The trophy room at Baywood was part of a later addition to the house. The room displays what appears to be a variety of Asian decorative motifs. Seen here are Cordelia King and her son Robert Burns King. (Frank and Maura Brown.)

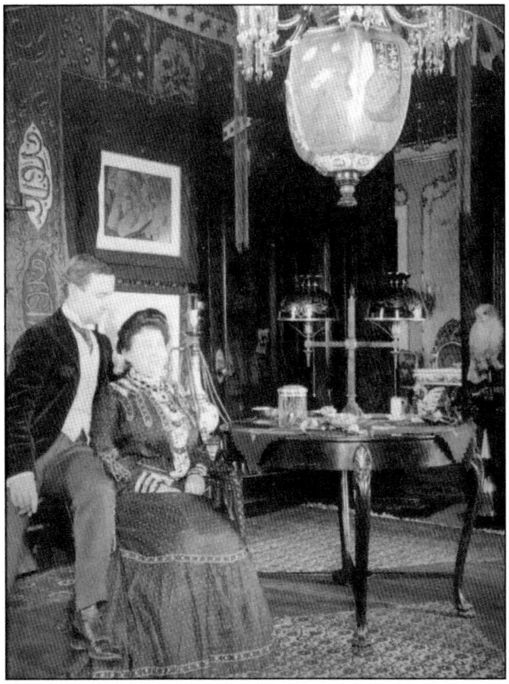

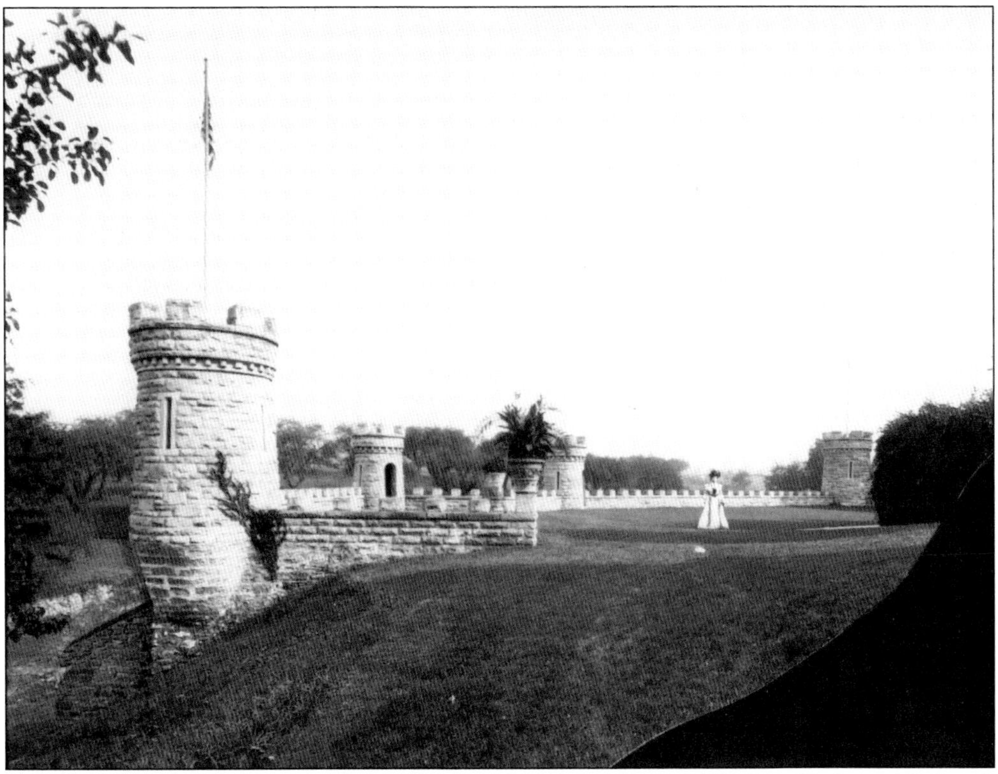

The King estate occupied a large parcel of land in what is now the city's Highland Park neighborhood. The property included formal gardens, a large greenhouse, and, seen in this photograph, a castle-like folly. A small portion of the folly still stands today. (Frank and Maura Brown.)

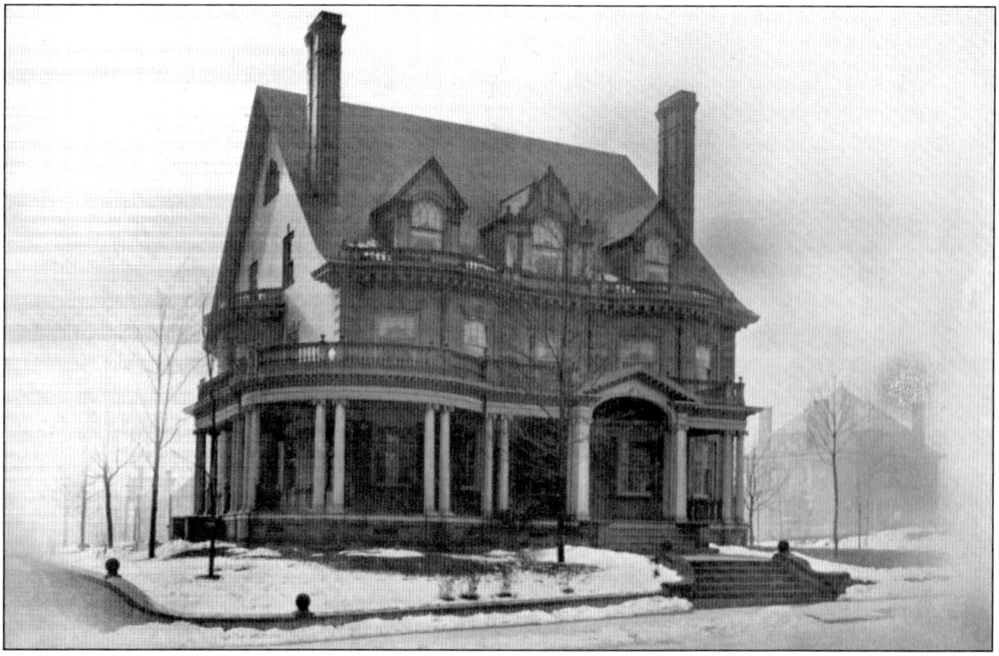

Capt. Alfred Hicks was a Civil War veteran and former member of the 76th Pennsylvania Infantry, known as the Keystone Zouaves. Hicks lived at Baum Boulevard and Graham Street with his wife, Mary Lewis Hicks, and their three children. Hicks held coal interests and was involved in area veterans' affairs. (HHC.)

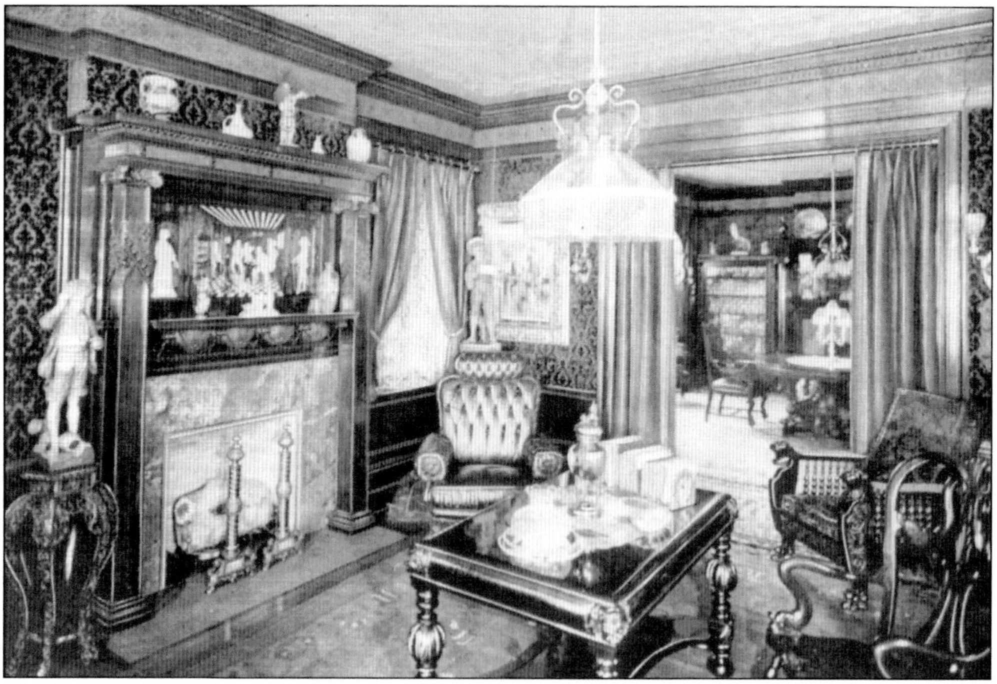

The living room of the Hicks home displays the overstuffed interior typical of Victorian homes. Elaborately carved furniture, flocked wall coverings, and portières give way to the dining room, seen on the right. (HHC.)

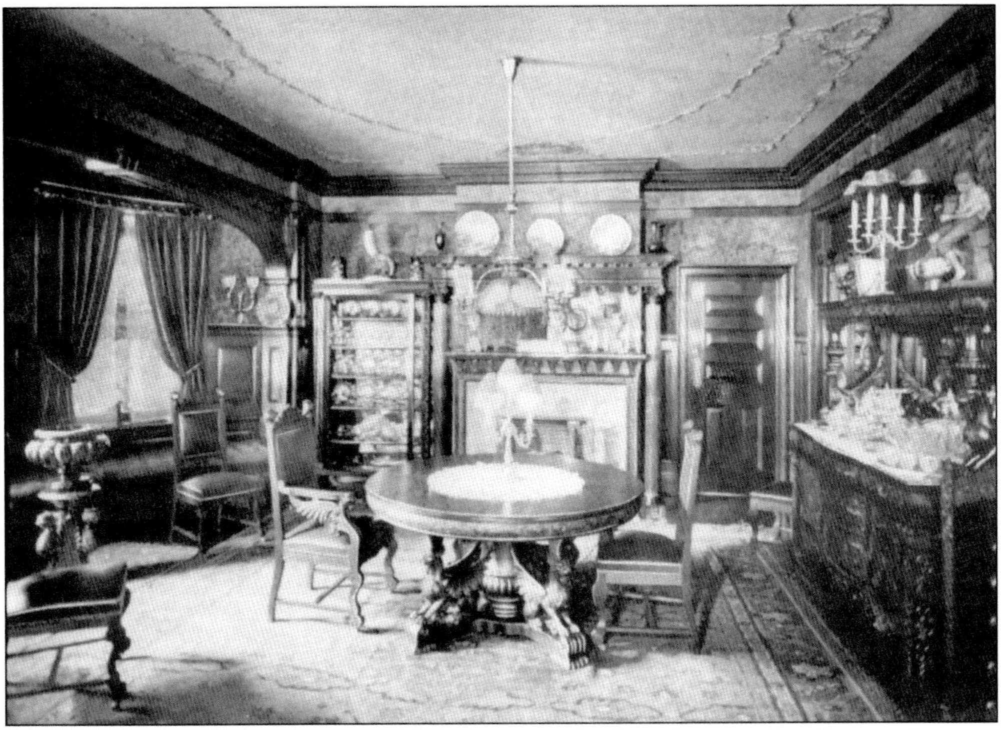

The dining room displays rather unusual furniture, much of it with a carved griffon motif, seen in the sideboard, pedestal table, and one of the chairs. Dual gas-electric fixtures are further evidence of the Hicks family's wealth, as electricity was an expensive new technology. (HHC.)

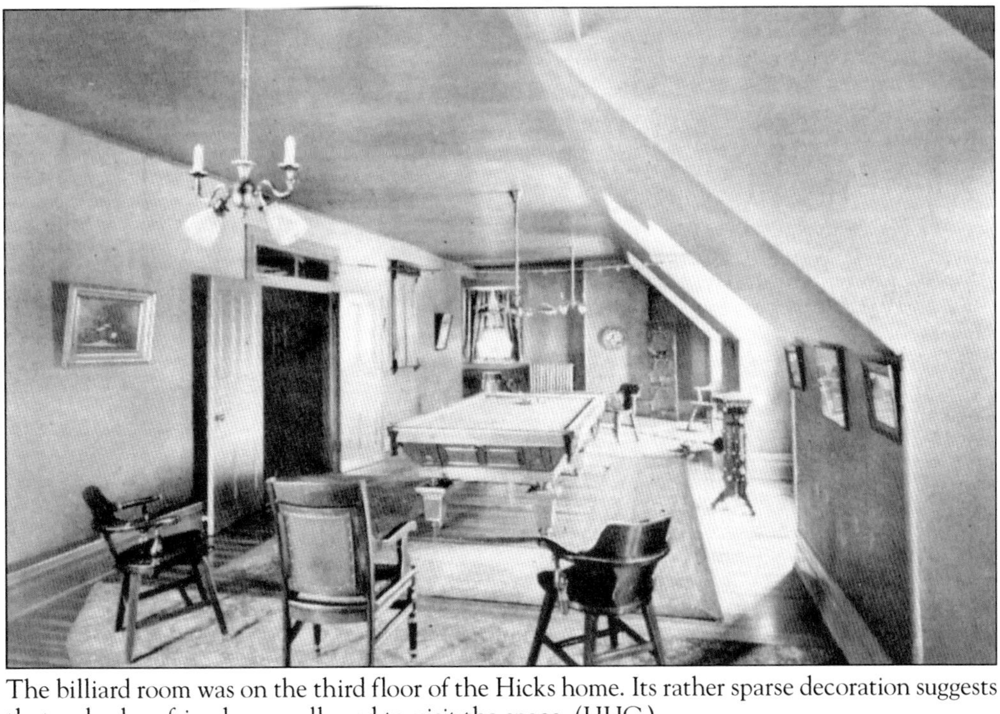

The billiard room was on the third floor of the Hicks home. Its rather sparse decoration suggests that only close friends were allowed to visit the space. (HHC.)

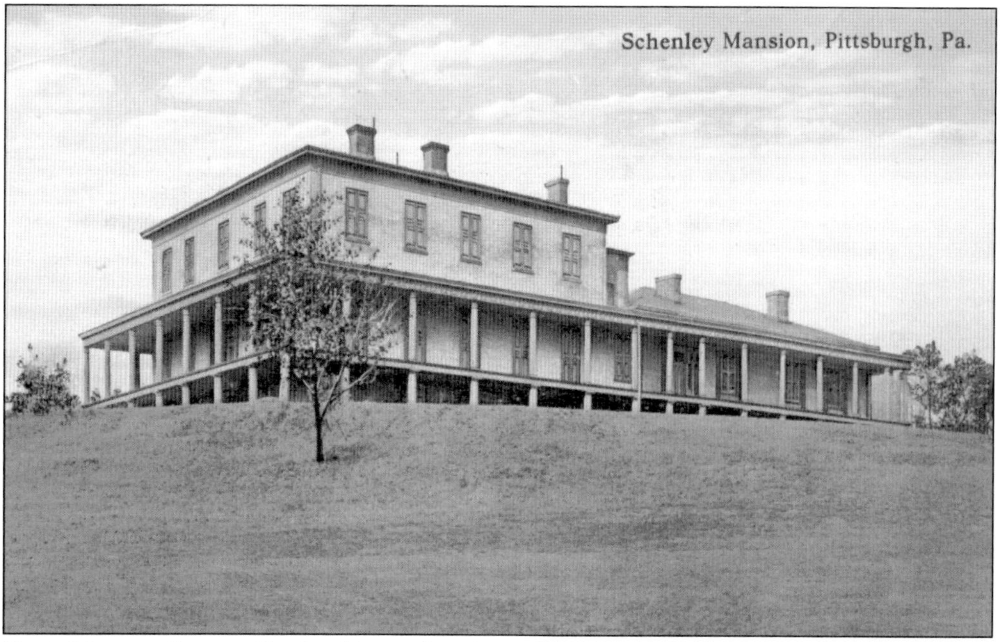

Picnic House in Stanton Heights (then referred to as Black Horse Hill) was one of Pittsburgh's first mansions. It was also the childhood home of philanthropist Mary Croghan Schenley, who shocked her father and Pittsburgh society when she eloped in 1842 at age 16 with the much older Capt. Edward Schenley. William Croghan enlarged the home to 29 rooms in an effort to lure his only daughter back from England, but the couple returned to Europe shortly after his death in 1850.

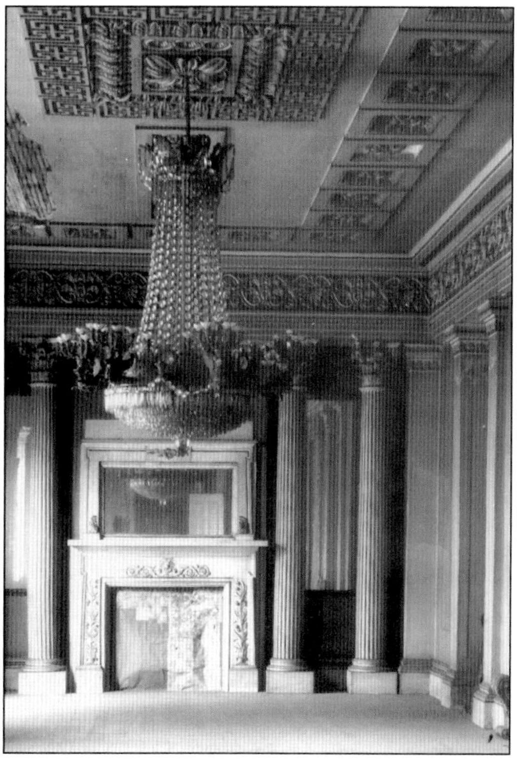

Though Picnic House was demolished in the 1950s, two of its interiors were preserved in the University of Pittsburgh's Cathedral of Learning. The Ballroom (shown here) and Oval Room had to be adjusted to fit the lower ceilings in their new home. The reconstructed Ballroom incorporated many fixtures original to the mansion, including Corinthian columns, elaborately carved cornices, and a gold-plated crystal chandelier. A suite of furniture from the Oval Room can now be seen in the Carnegie Museum of Art's collection. (HCC.)

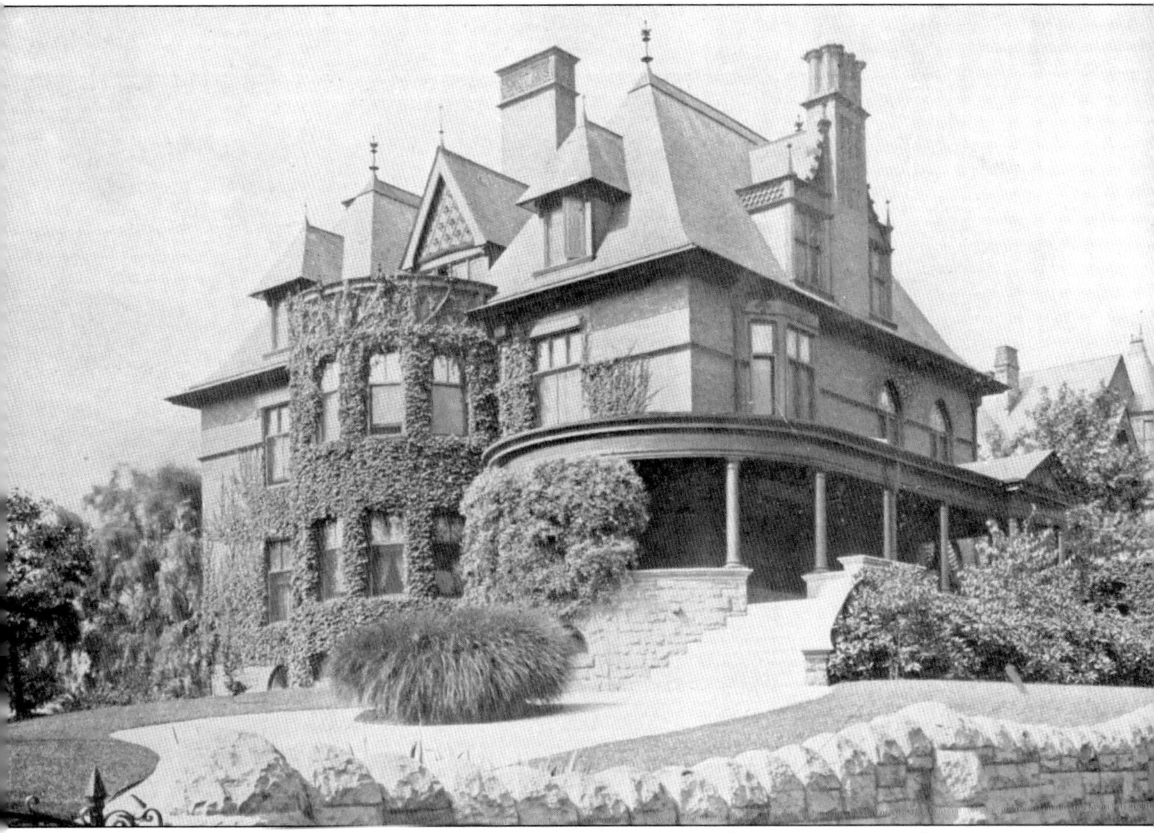

Wesley S. Guffey lived at Liberty and Atlantic Avenues at the intersection of modern-day Bloomfield, Friendship, and Shadyside. His home displays an eclectic style, drawing on elements of Jacobean Revival, Queen Anne, and Romanesque architecture. Guffey was a partner in Guffey & Queen, producers of petroleum and natural gas.

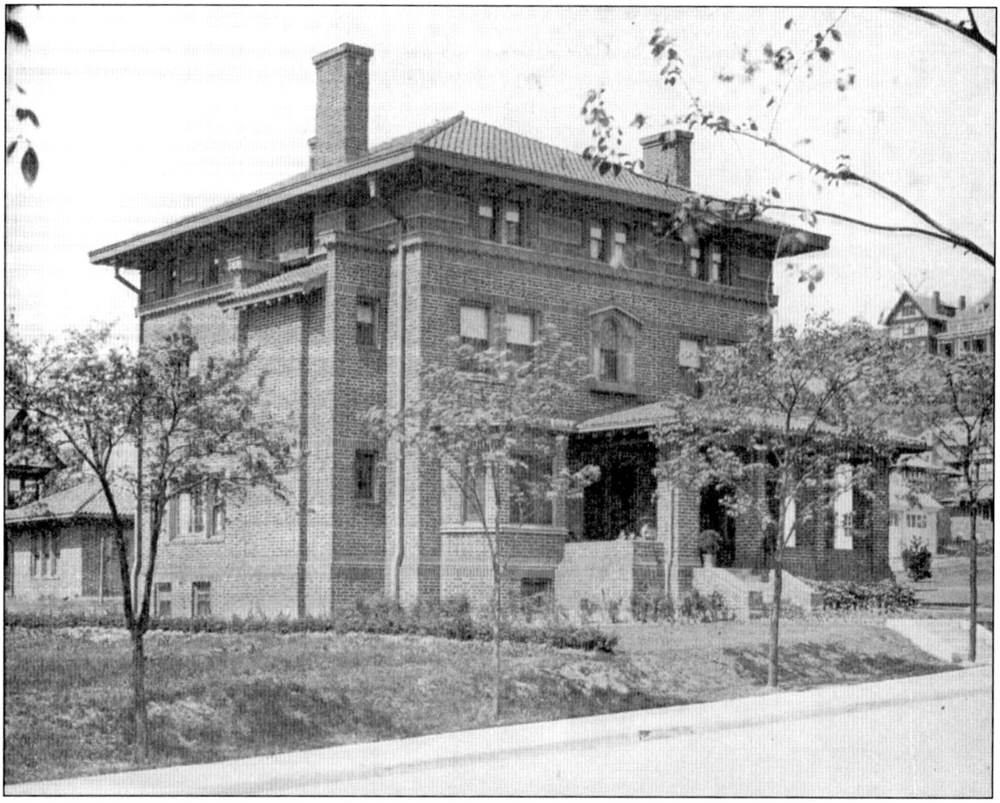

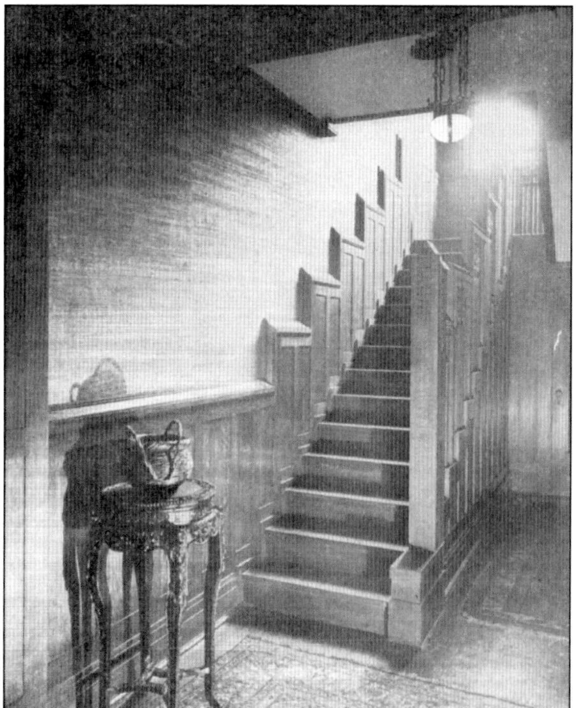

Mrs. Godfrey Stengel lived in this Arts and Crafts–style home in Oakland, designed around 1915 by Kiehnel & Elliott. Stengel's late husband owned a steel-wire and tool manufacturing company, and the couple were benefactors of the South Side Hospital. Godfrey Stengel's father, the renowned Dr. Alfred Stengel, was among the medical students depicted in Thomas Eakins's 1889 painting *The Agnew Clinic*. (CMU.)

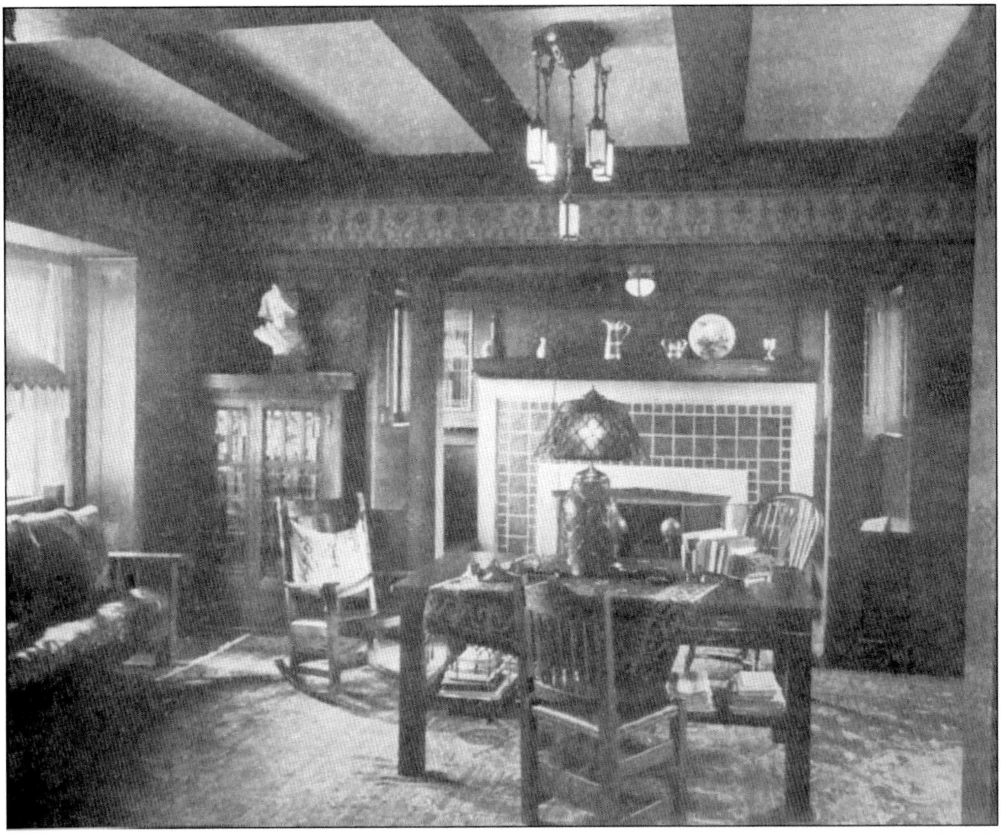

The interior of the Stengel home further reflects the Arts and Crafts style, which prized hand-produced decorative elements. The living room furnishings, seen above, include a decorative frieze, wrought-iron light fixture, fireplace surround, and Mission-style chairs. The home's sun porch (below) could be used year-round thanks to its fireplace. (CMU.)

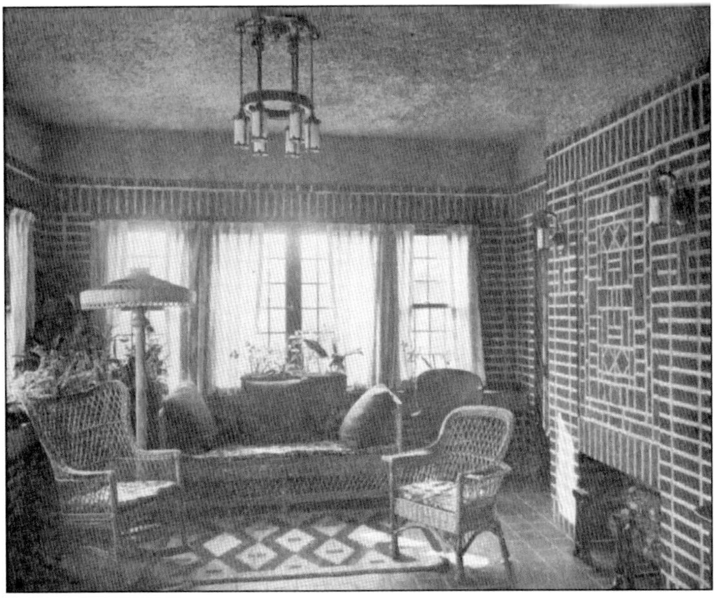

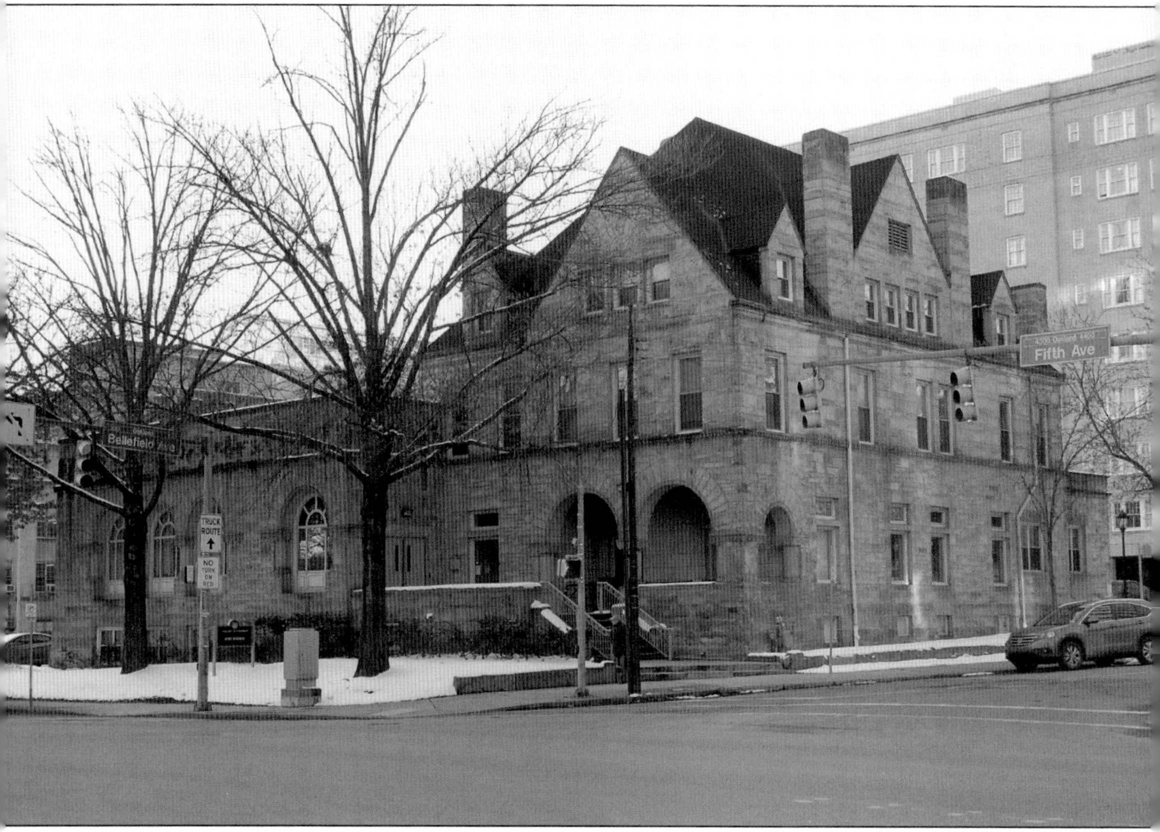

William J. Holland, born in Jamaica in 1848, lived at Fifth and Bellefield Avenues with his wife, Carrie T. Moorhead, in a home designed by Longfellow, Alden & Harlow. Holland was chancellor of the University of Pittsburgh from 1891 to 1901, during which time the school became coeducational. He was also a noted zoologist and paleontologist. His former home now houses the university's music department.

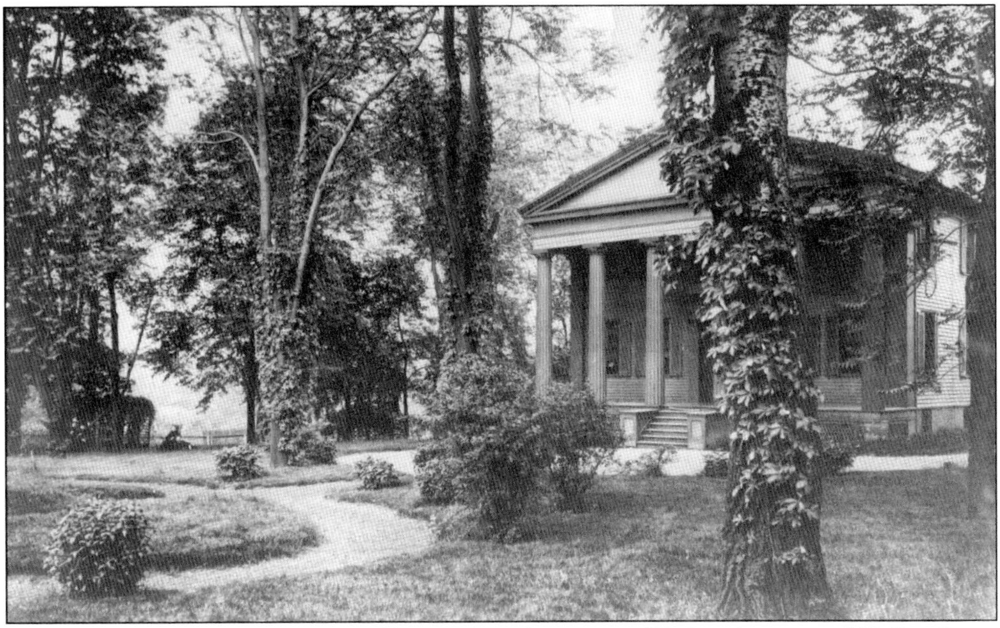

Pennsylvan, the estate of Asa P. Childs, stood on the corner of Forbes Avenue and Halket Street in Oakland. Childs was a founder of the Third Presbyterian Church, a leather-goods merchant, and father of Adelaide Howard Childs, later Mrs. Henry Clay Frick. Childs's original property extended unbroken up to Fifth Avenue before Forbes Avenue was laid out. The home was later owned by Christopher Magee. (Frick Collection/Frick Art Reference Library Archives.)

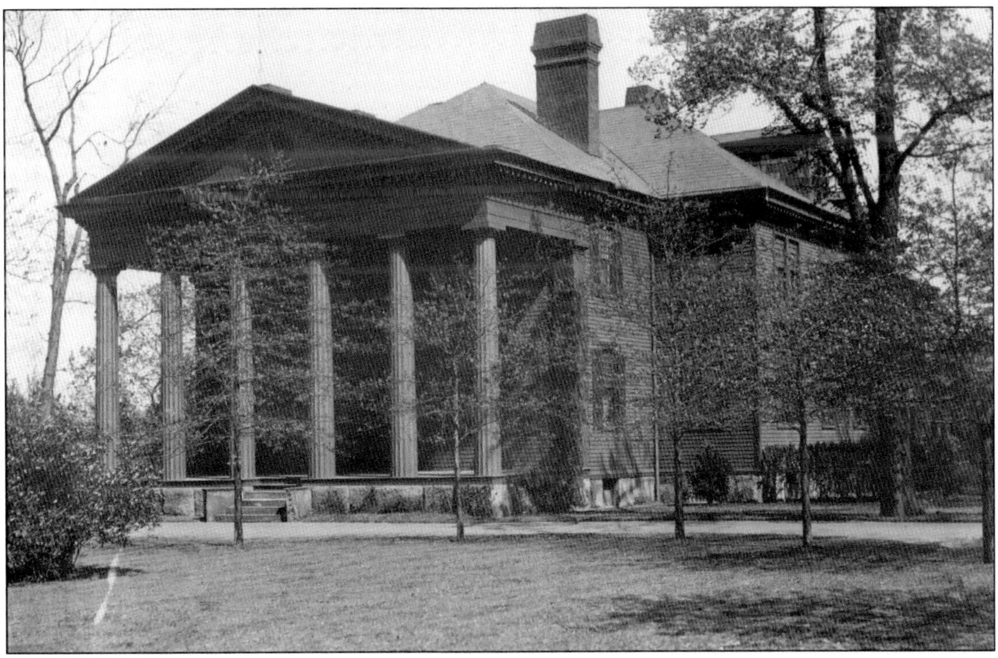

After state senator Christopher L. Magee purchased the former Asa P. Childs estate, he had the house enlarged and renamed it The Maples. Magee and his wife, who did not have any children, eventually donated their home in memory of the senator's mother as the first structure housing Elizabeth Steel Magee Hospital, now Magee-Women's Hospital of UPMC. (HHC.)

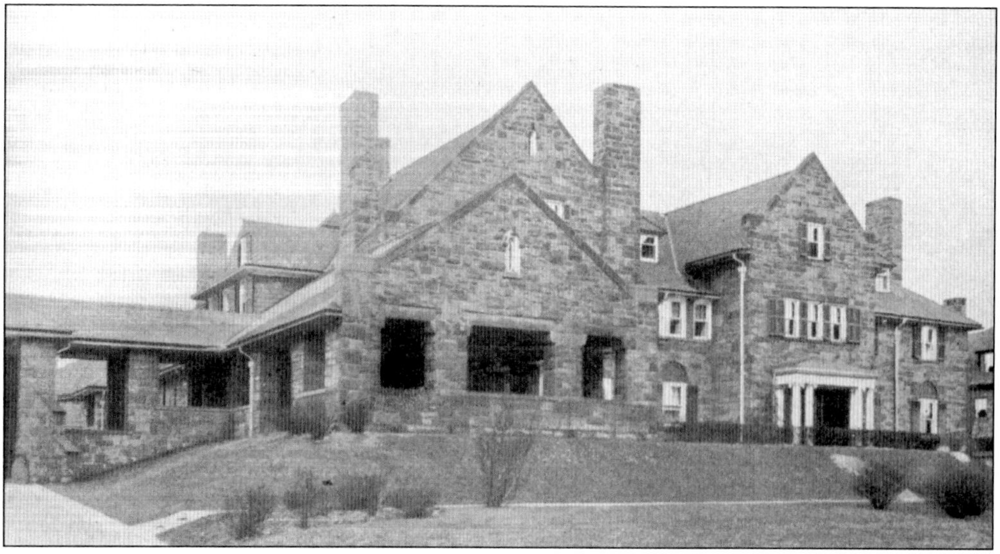

Julian Kennedy was the owner of this home, designed by George Orth around 1907. Kennedy was an engineer and inventor who was associated with almost every important steel concern in America and Europe. He was a former general superintendent for Carnegie, Phipps & Co. at their Homestead plant from 1885 to 1888. An inventor, he developed an automatic device for charging ingots and tabling them. (CMU.)

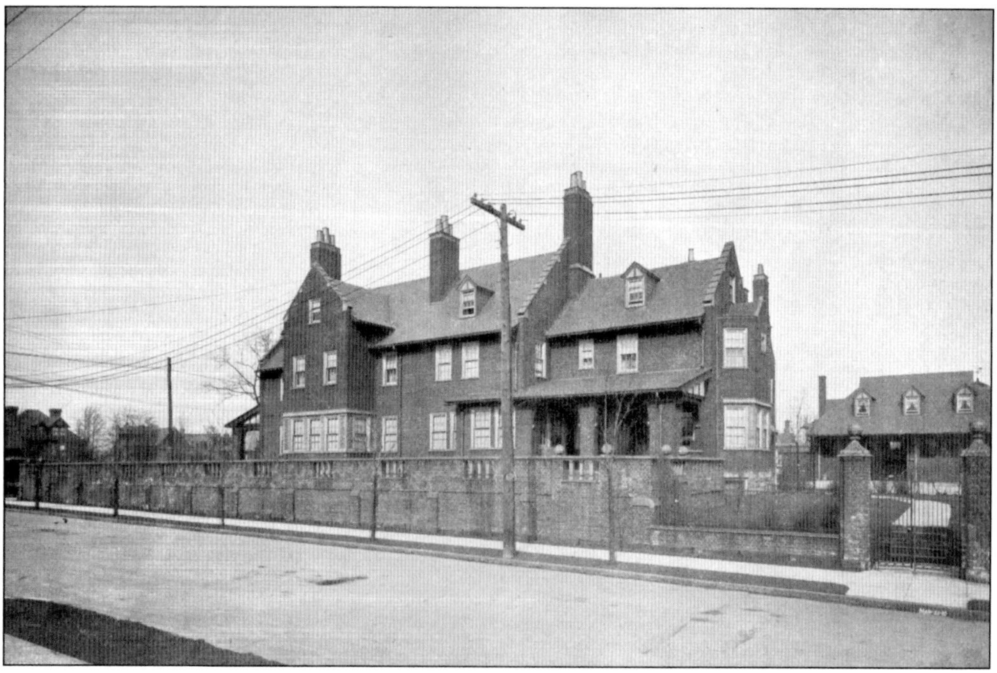

Willis L. King's home was designed by George Orth around 1911. King, who served on the executive committee of Jones & Laughlin Steel Company, was the nephew and successor of company founder B.F. Jones of Allegheny City. (CMU.)

Two

Shadyside and "Millionaire's Row"

Shadyside was initially conceived in the 1860s by Thomas Aiken as a planned suburb to allow Pittsburgh businessmen an easy commute to downtown. Though the area later became distinguished by the city's "Millionaire's Row" along Fifth Avenue, the neighborhood was home to residents of varied socioeconomic backgrounds from the start, a state that continues to the present.

Shadyside's Millionaire's Row was not the only one in Pittsburgh, though it became the best known and at present still displays the most reminders of its former days. Other area streets that held this distinction included Penn Avenue in Point Breeze and Ridge Avenue in Allegheny City, also known as "Allegheny's gold coast." The building of Fifth Avenue's mansions took place from about 1850 to 1925.

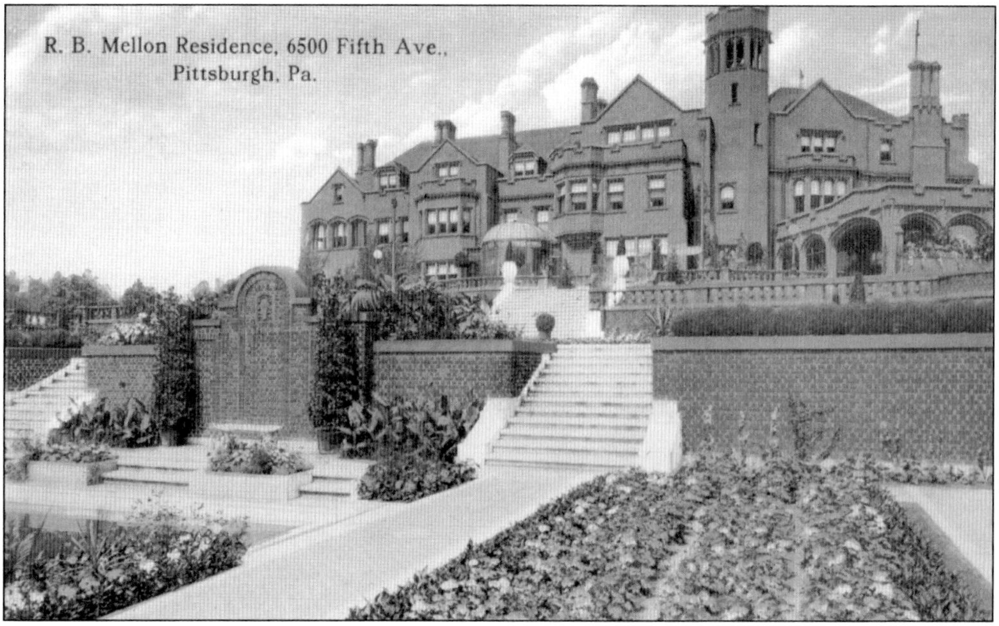

One of the grandest of Pittsburgh's Gilded Age mansions was the estate of Richard Beatty Mellon and Jennie King Mellon, which sat atop a hillside along Fifth Avenue. Designed by Alden & Harlow in 1911, the 65-room home featured a stained-glass Tiffany mural at the head of its grand staircase, part of which is in the collection of the Carnegie Museum of Art. The home was demolished in 1940 after being donated to the city of Pittsburgh and today is the site of Mellon Park.

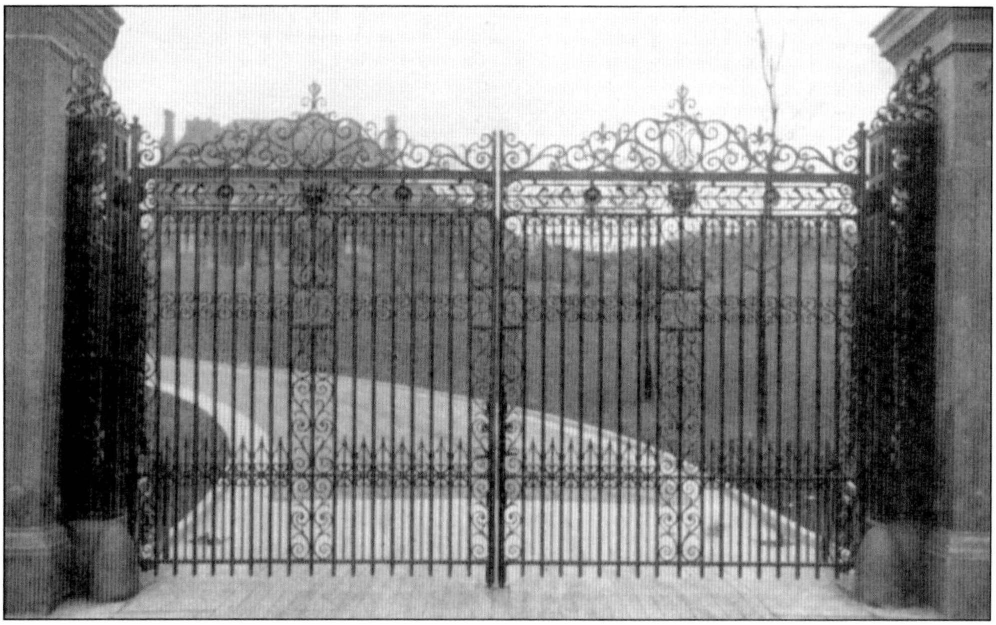

The elaborate iron gates leading to the Mellon estate, designed by Samuel Yellin, still stand today as the entrance to Mellon Park. The park features remnants of the estate's formal gardens, which were originally designed by Vitale & Geiffert and Gilmore D. Clarke in the late 1920s. In 1927, when daughter Sarah Cordelia Mellon married Alan Magee Scaife, the wedding breakfast, reception, and dance were held in the gardens. (Carnegie Mellon University Libraries.)

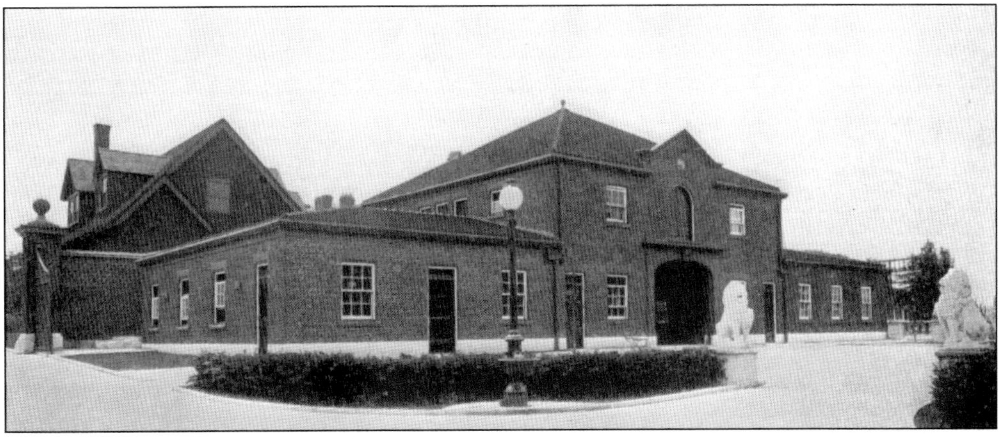

The garage and carriage house of Richard Beatty Mellon's estate is now known to Pittsburghers as Phipps Garden Center, formerly the Pittsburgh Civic Garden Center. Additions were made for classroom and event space once the building became a community center in Mellon Park. It is now the only building that remains of the former estate. (Carnegie Mellon University Libraries.)

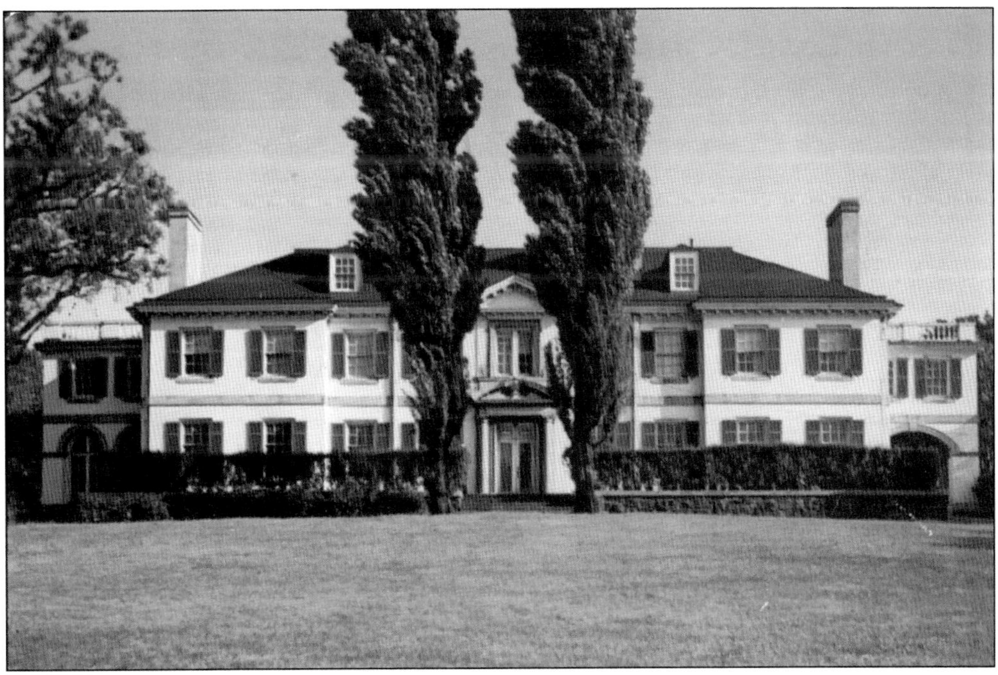

Charles D. Marshall, a construction magnate, commissioned this home adjacent to the Richard Beatty Mellon estate in 1911. It was donated to the city of Pittsburgh in 1943 and formally opened as part of the Arts & Crafts Center of Pittsburgh (Now Pittsburgh Center for the Arts) in 1945. (Charlotte Cohen.)

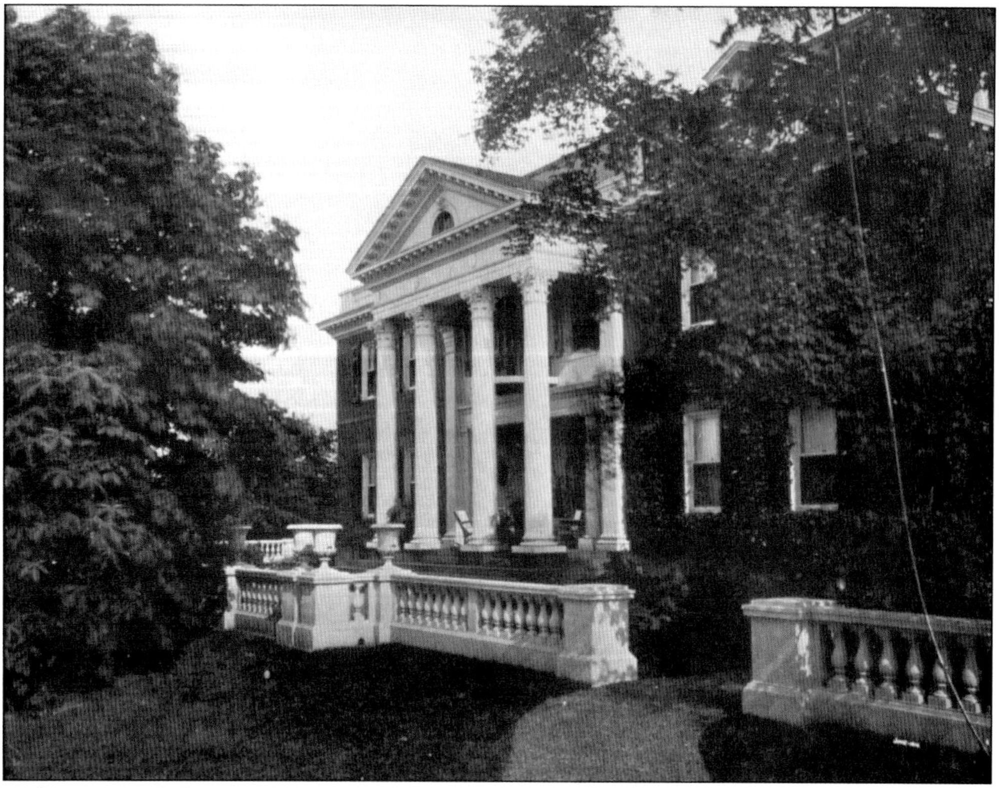

William Nimick Frew's Georgian Revival mansion, Beechwood Hall, was designed by Alden & Harlow around 1913. The house was an immediate neighbor of the Richard Beatty Mellon estate along Fifth Avenue. Frew was a member of the board of directors of Mellon National Bank, Union Trust Company, and the Carnegie Institute. After the home was demolished, the land on which it stood became part of present-day Mellon Park. (Above, CMU.)

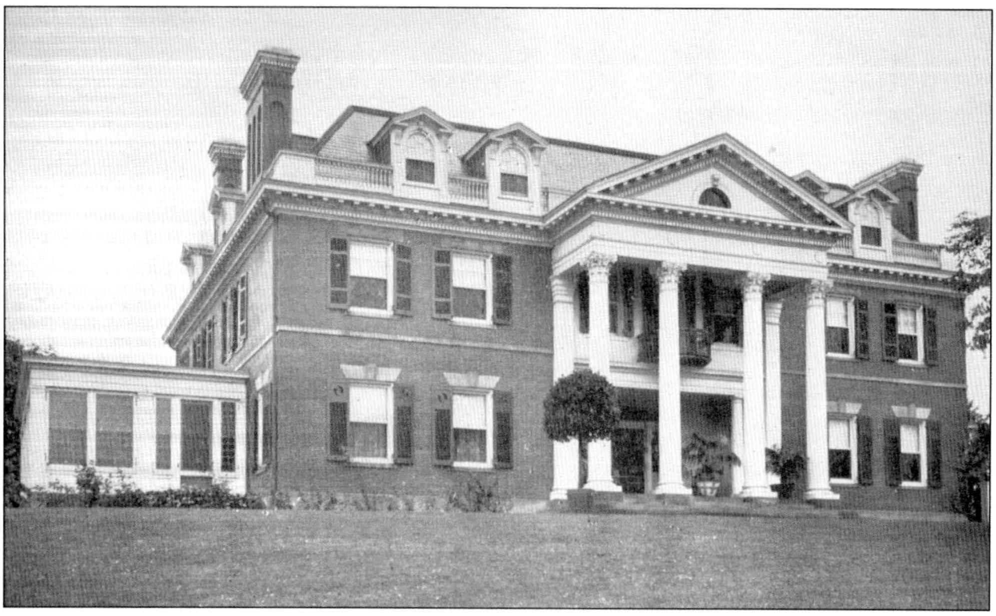

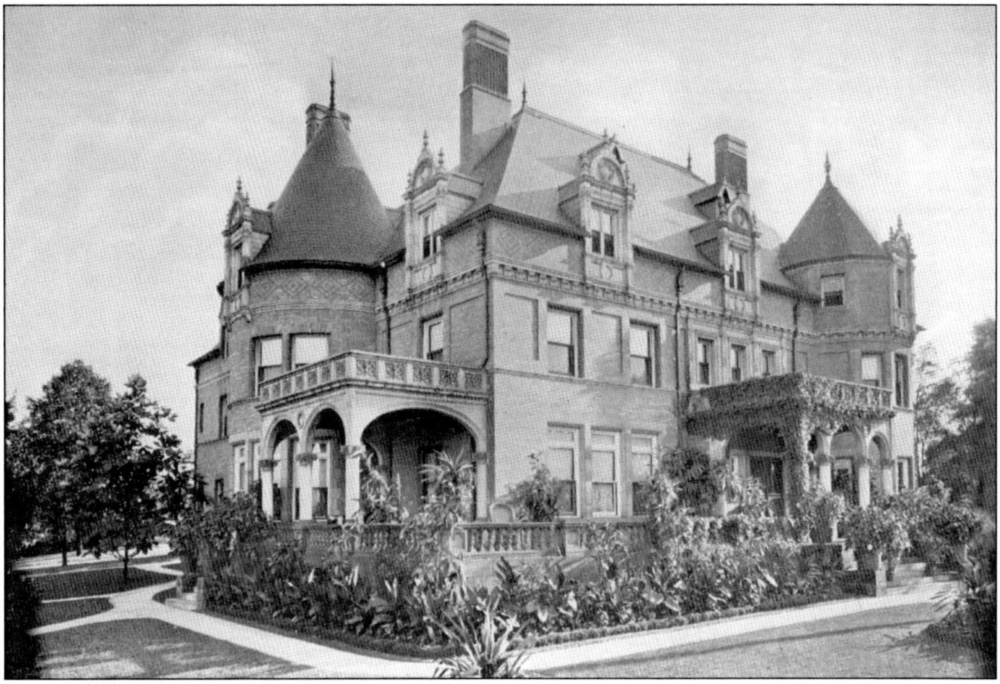

Daniel M. Clemson, owner of Highmont at Fifth and Shady Avenues, was president of the Carnegie Natural Gas Company. The entire operation of the company's Pennsylvania and West Virginia gas fields was under his direction. He later ran a fleet of lake steamers for U.S. Steel.

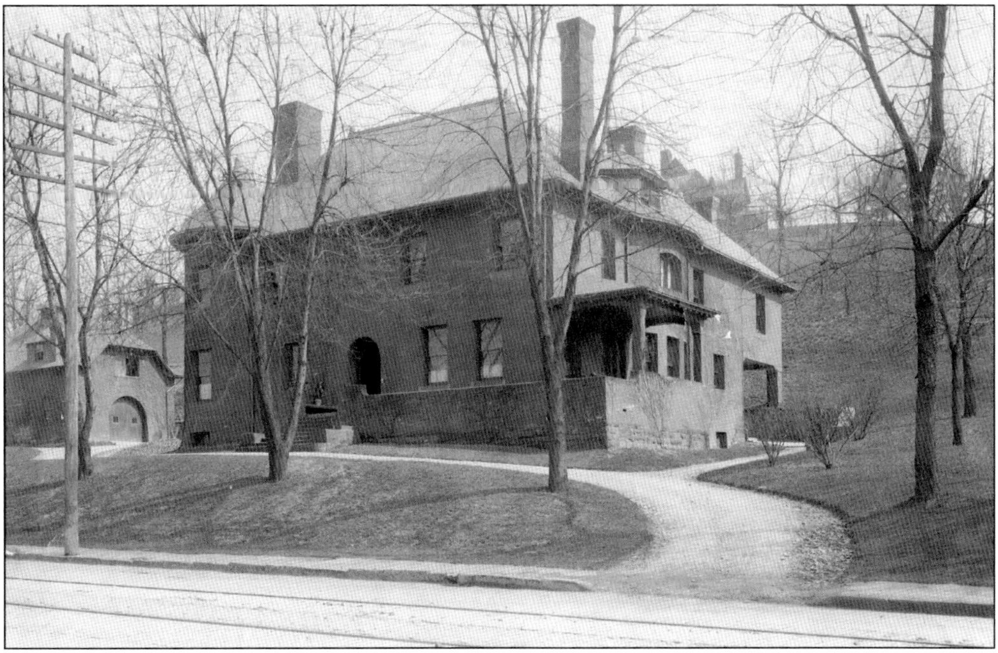

Sunnyledge, designed by Longfellow, Alden & Harlow around 1888, was the home of physician James McClelland. Dr. McClelland practiced homeopathic medicine from his office in the house's turret. Patients included members of the Frick, Mellon, and Scaife families. Today, the house is a boutique hotel bearing the same name. (HHC.)

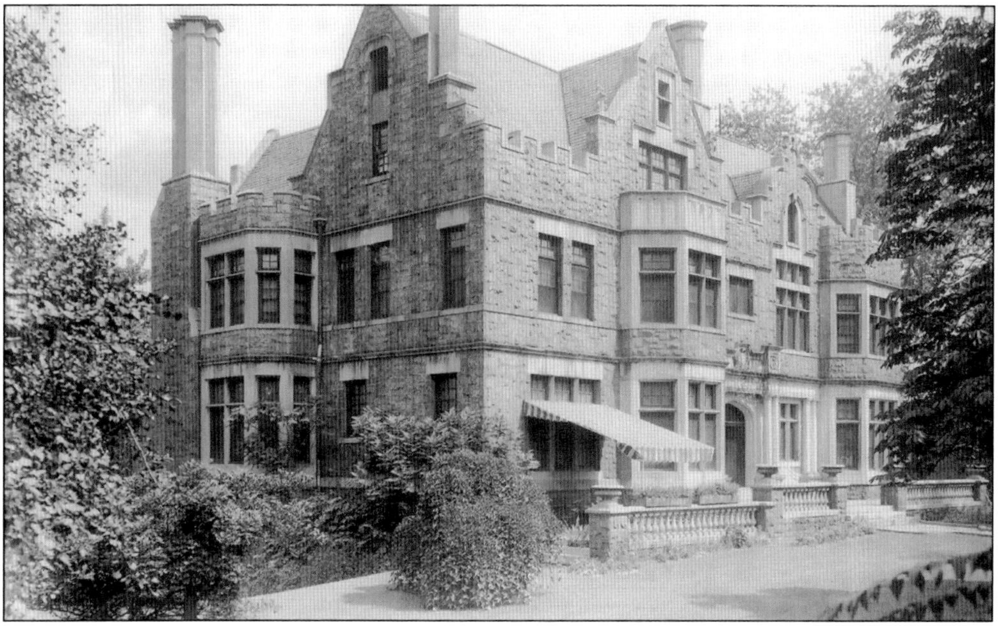

Willis F. McCook commissioned his enormous Jacobethan Revival mansion from Carpenter & Crocker around 1905 as a home for himself, his wife, Mary, and their 10 children. A corporate lawyer, McCook successfully represented Henry Clay Frick against Andrew Carnegie during the "Ironclad Agreement" proceedings in the late 1890s. The home is now part of the Mansions on Fifth, a boutique hotel. (Jack Carpenter.)

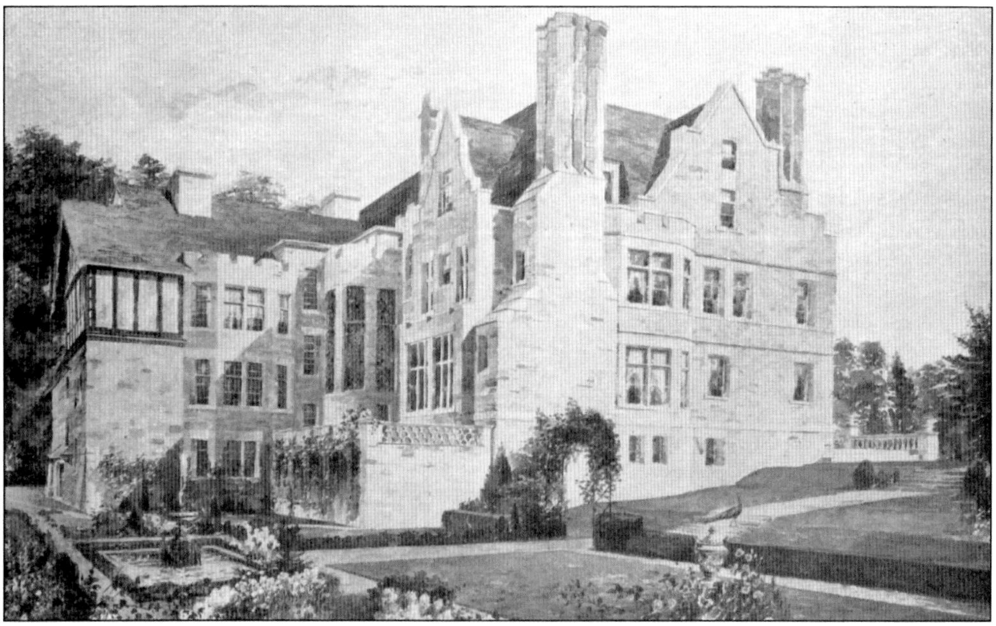

This rendering of the rear of the McCook mansion offers a glimpse of the home that has never been visible to onlookers. It reveals a half-timbered Elizabethan Revival element as well as a back terrace. This view has been blocked since before the mansion's completion due to the construction next door of a home for Bessie McCook Reed, Willis McCook's eldest daughter, as a wedding present. The second home was completed in 1905, a year before McCook's own. (CMU.)

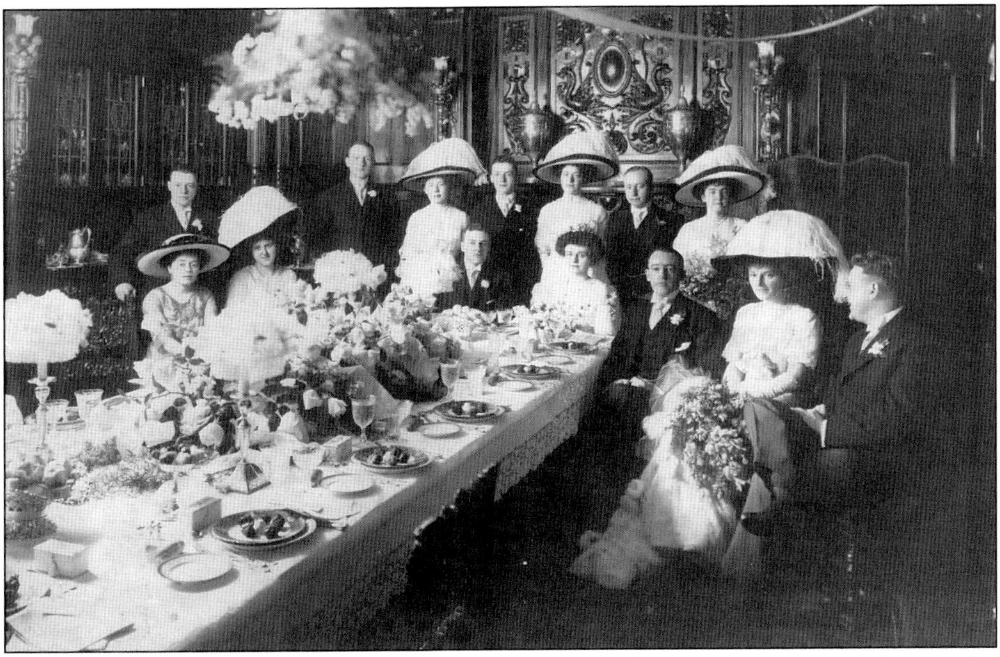

The McCook mansion has played host to many weddings during its history. Seen here in the home's dining room is the reception of Katharine McCook and Harry Miller (seated at head of table) of New York City in 1910. The *New York Times* proclaimed Katharine McCook "one of several daughters, all popular members of Pittsburg's smart society." (Mansions on Fifth.)

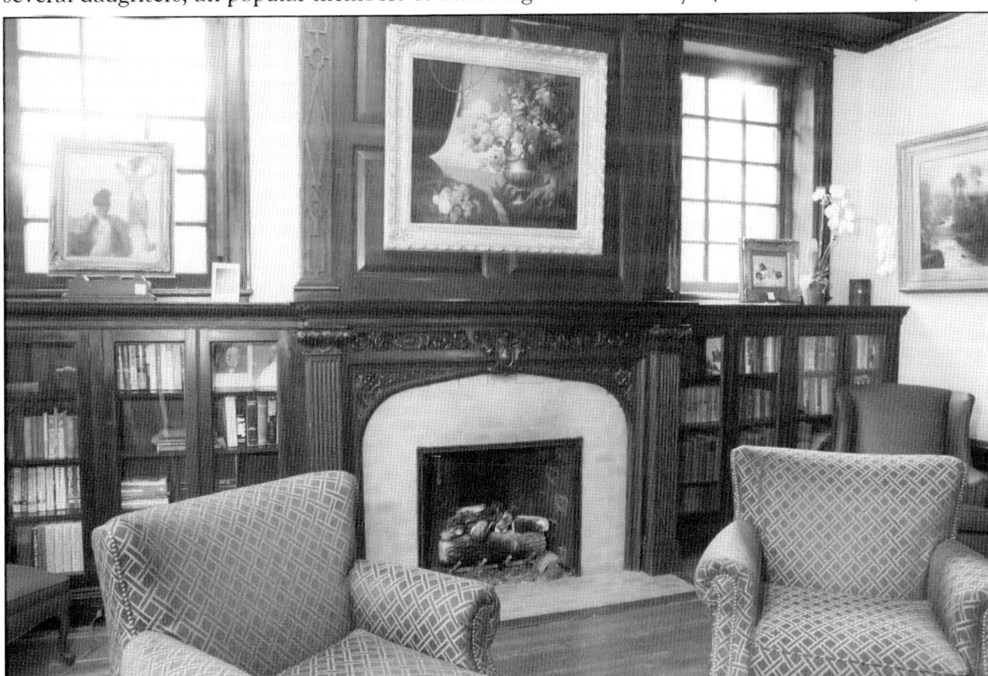

The McCook library, seen here following the home's extensive restoration, features original woodwork and built-in bookcases. The fireplaces throughout the home are once again regularly lit and enjoyed by visitors. (Annie O'Neill.)

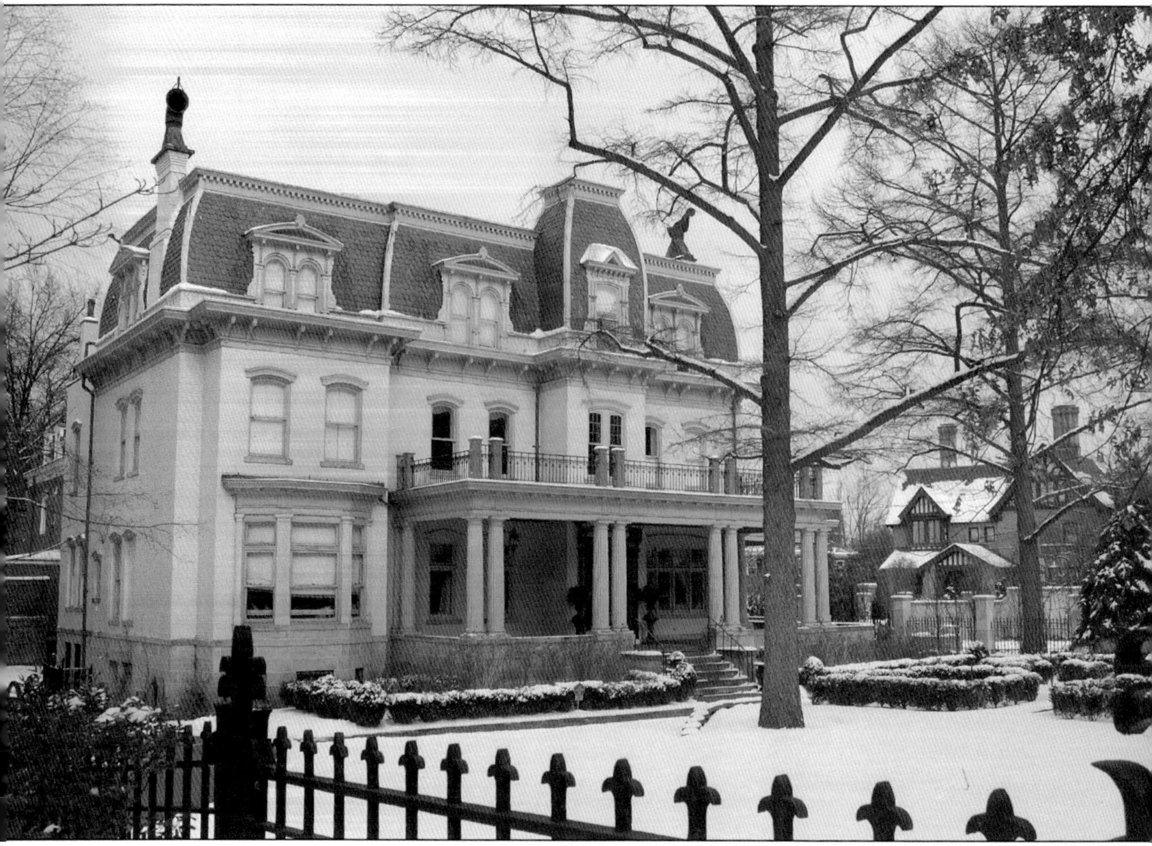

This large Second Empire house at 5061 Fifth Avenue with its mansard roof was originally built for William B. Negley in 1871. After stonemason Edward Gwinner purchased the home in 1911, he commissioned Frederick J. Osterling to design an addition to it, and later brought the architect back to renovate several interior spaces. Today, the home is known as the Gwinner-Harter House, after its second and third owners.

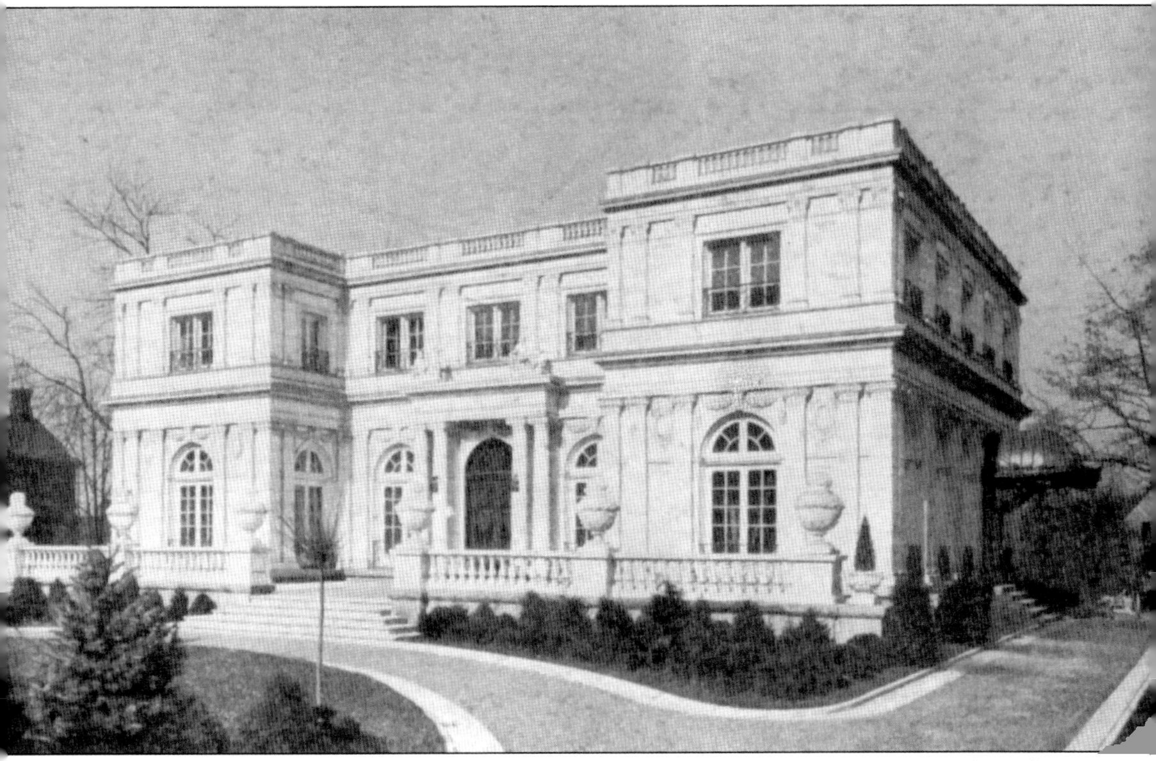

The Moreland-Hoffstot House at 5057 Fifth Avenue, designed by Paul W. Irwin in 1914, echoes the design of the Grand Trianon of France. Clad in white terra-cotta tile, a popular façade treatment at the time, the mansion is also reminiscent of Rosecliff, a home owned by the family of Andrew Moreland's wife. Moreland held iron interests; the home's later owner, Henry Phipps Hoffstot, was heavily involved in the steel industry. (CMU.)

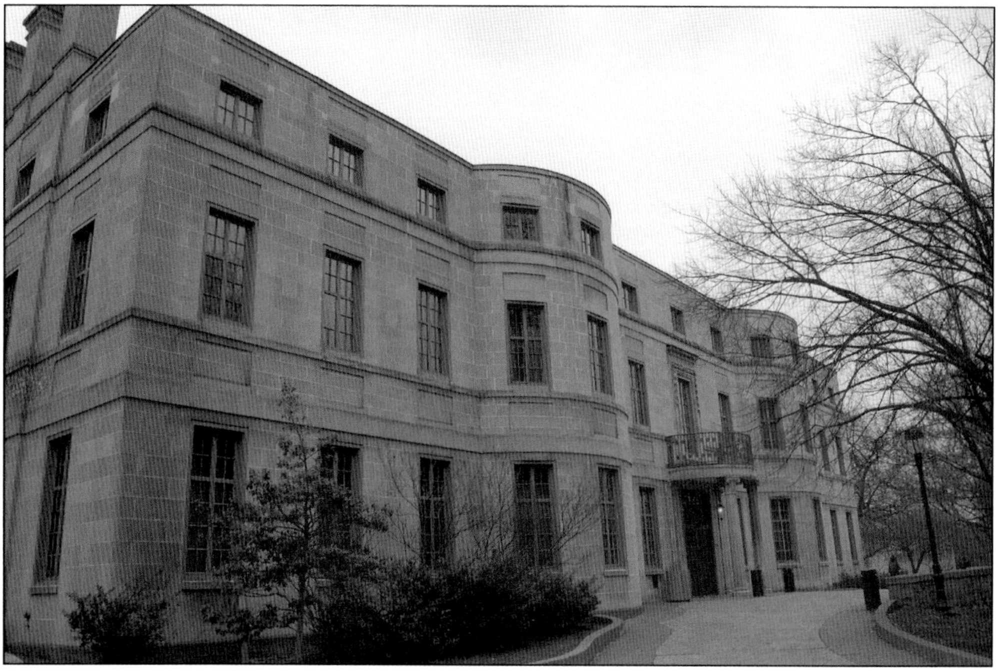

Edmund Webster Mudge, a pig iron and coke magnate, commissioned his limestone-clad house at 1000 Morewood Avenue in 1924. The house was designed by Henry Gilchrist. The Mudge family donated the home to Carnegie Mellon University in the 1950s, and the house's two upper floors were converted into student rooms.

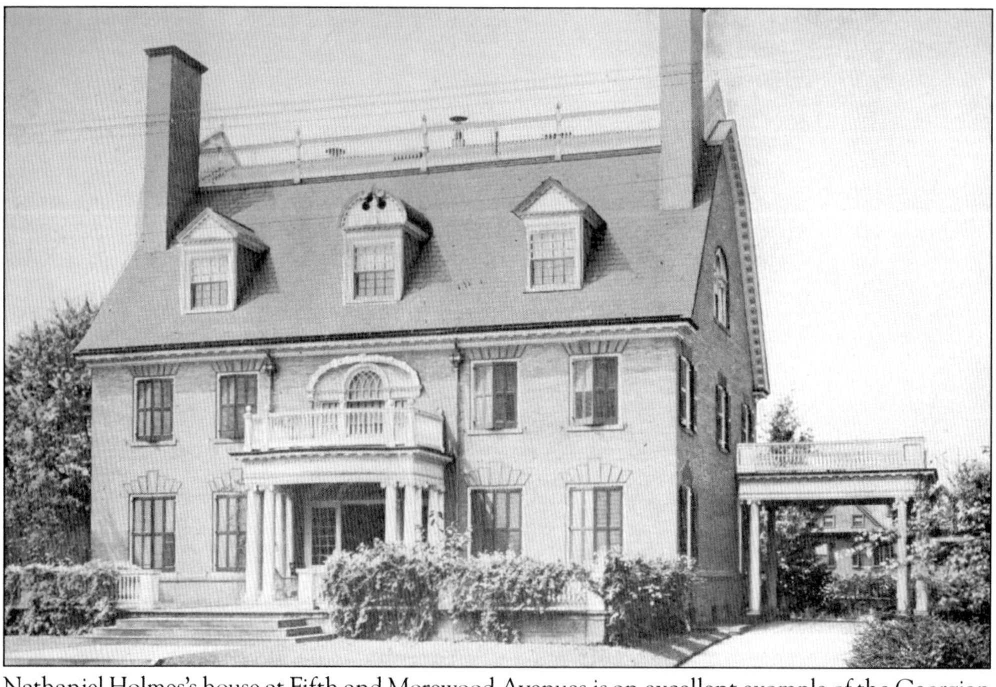

Nathaniel Holmes's house at Fifth and Morewood Avenues is an excellent example of the Georgian Revival style. Holmes was part of the third generation of his family's involvement in Pittsburgh's banking industry.

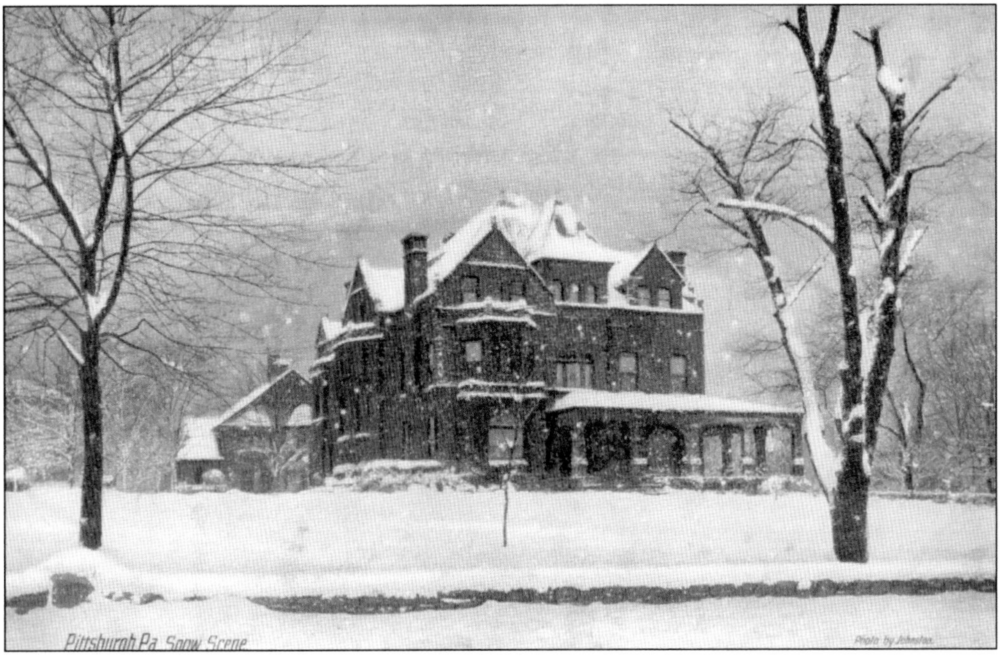

Dr. William S. Huselton lived at 4936 Fifth Avenue, near Morewood Avenue and across the street from Henry Hornbostel's Rodef Shalom synagogue. Huselton was a physician and a member of the Allegheny County Medical Society. His Jacobean Revival home was the subject of a picture postcard (above) identified only as "Pittsburgh, Pa. Snow Scene."

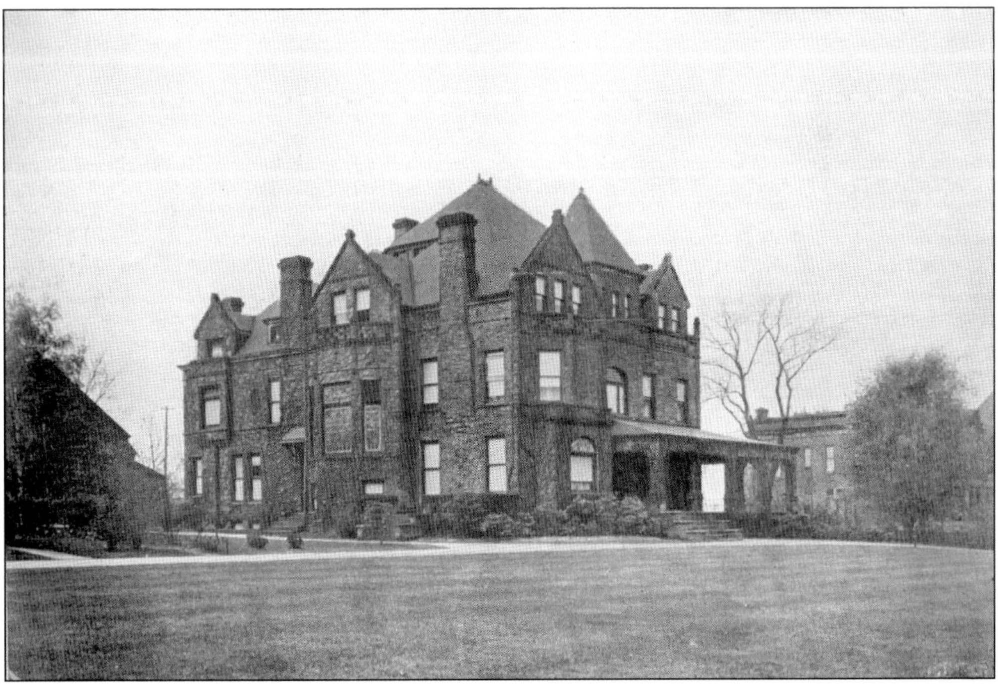

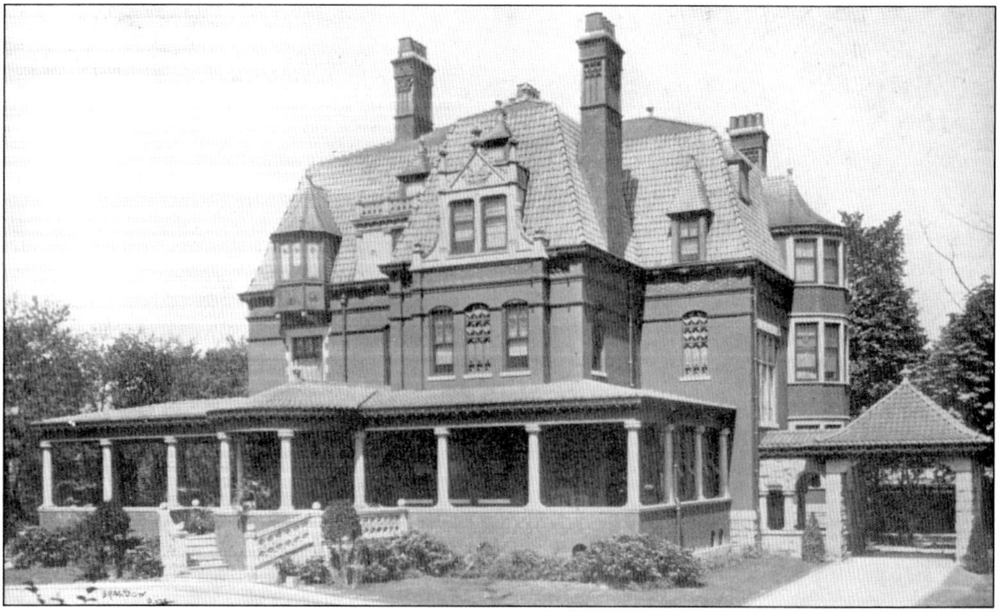

Col. James McClurg Guffey lived with his wife and three children at 5025 Fifth Avenue, a home designed by George Pearson around 1903. Guffey was heavily invested in oil fields and wells and leased territory for drilling. At one time, he was the largest individual producer of oil and gas in the country. A town, Guffey, located about 30 miles from Cripple Creek, Colorado, was named after him. The dining room (below) of the Guffey residence was used in period advertisements for the woodworking company that constructed the room. (CMU.)

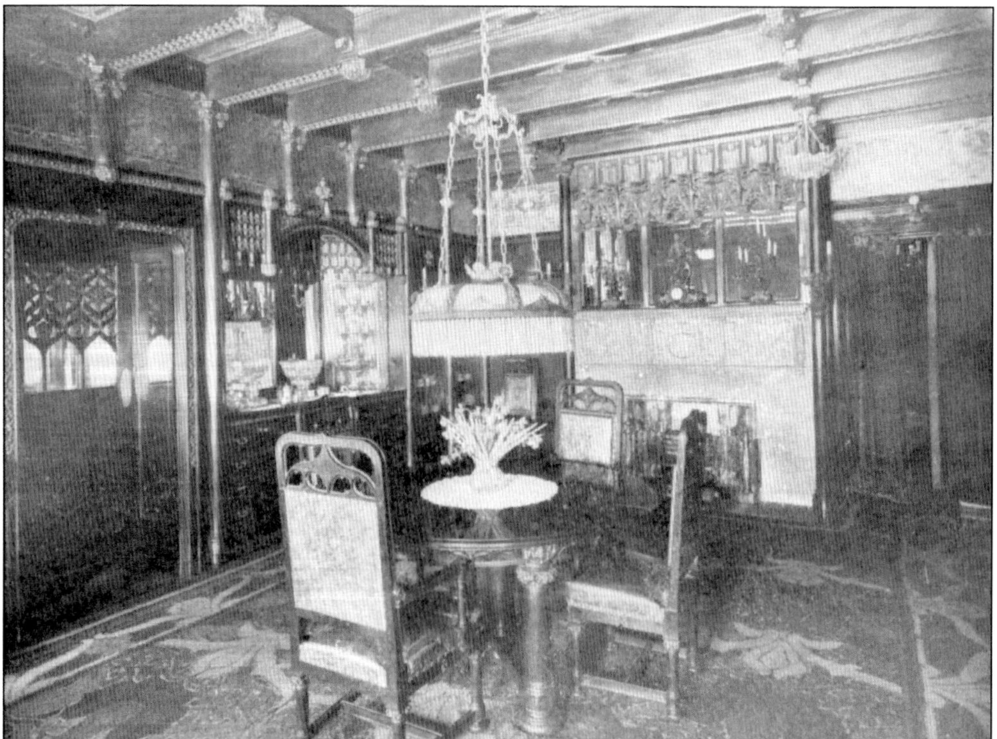

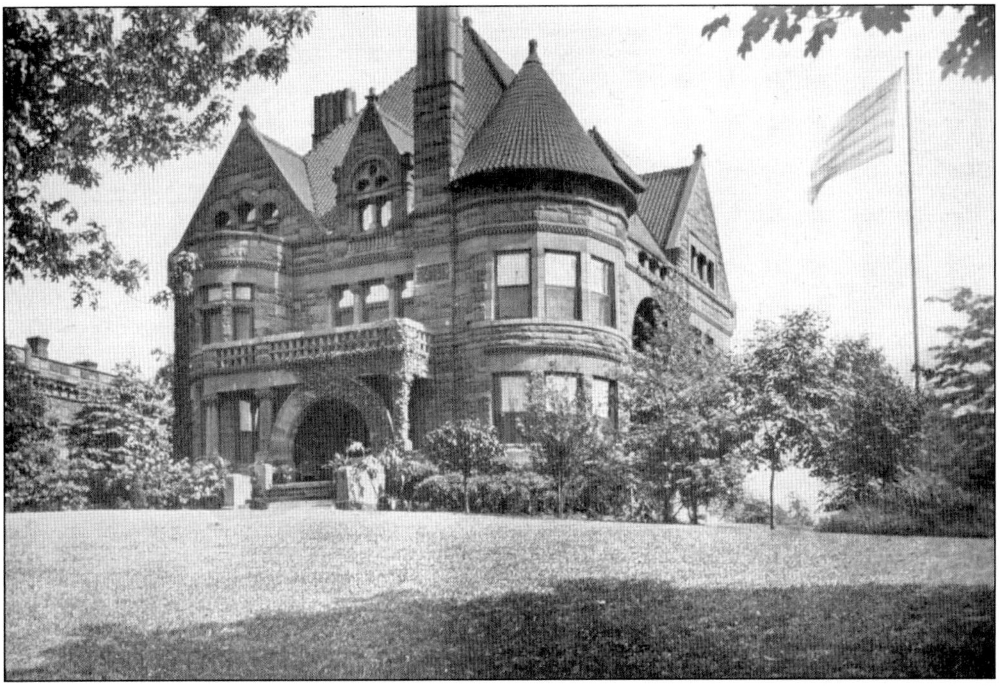

D. Herbert Hostetter's Romanesque home stood near the intersection of Fifth Avenue and Bidwell (now Devonshire) Street. He was originally from Allegheny City. The family's fortune came from Hostetter's grandfather, who developed Hostetter's Bitters, a medical tonic marketed for various ailments of the day.

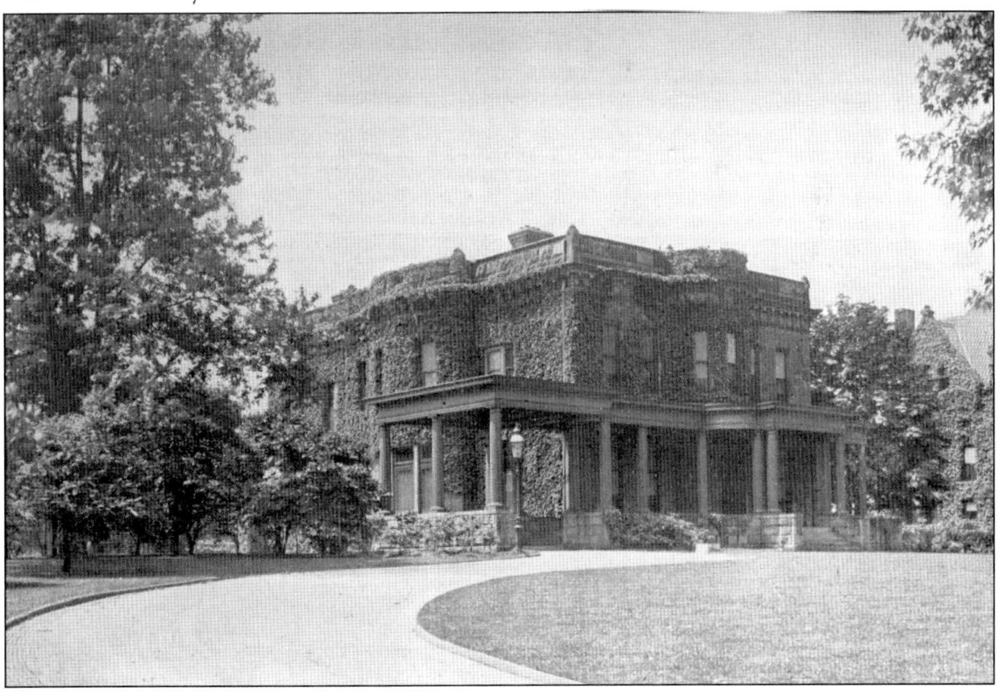

Ivy House, Reuben Miller's aptly named home at 4900 Fifth Avenue, was situated near Bidwell (now Devonshire) Street. Miller held interests in steel manufacturing and banking.

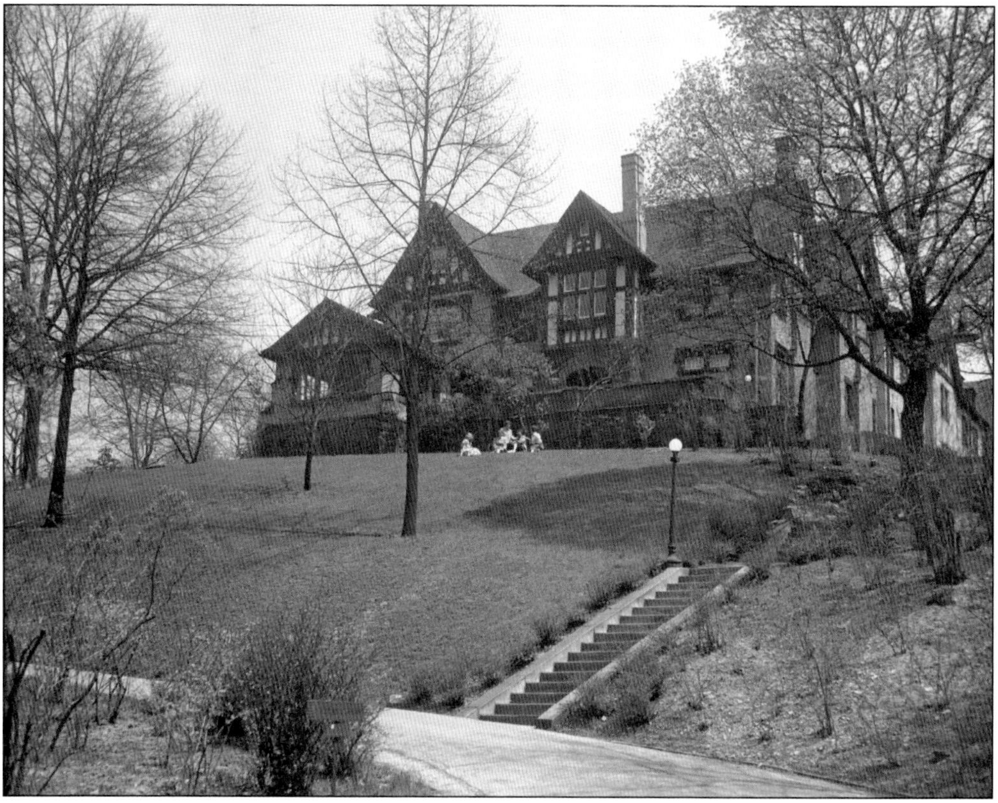

The Elizabethan Revival home of Edwin Stanton Fickes, his wife, Marguerite Knapp, and their three children was built in 1927. Fickes was chief engineer for Alcoa. Following Fickes's death in 1943, the home was donated to what is now Chatham University and was used as a dormitory. (Chatham University Archives.)

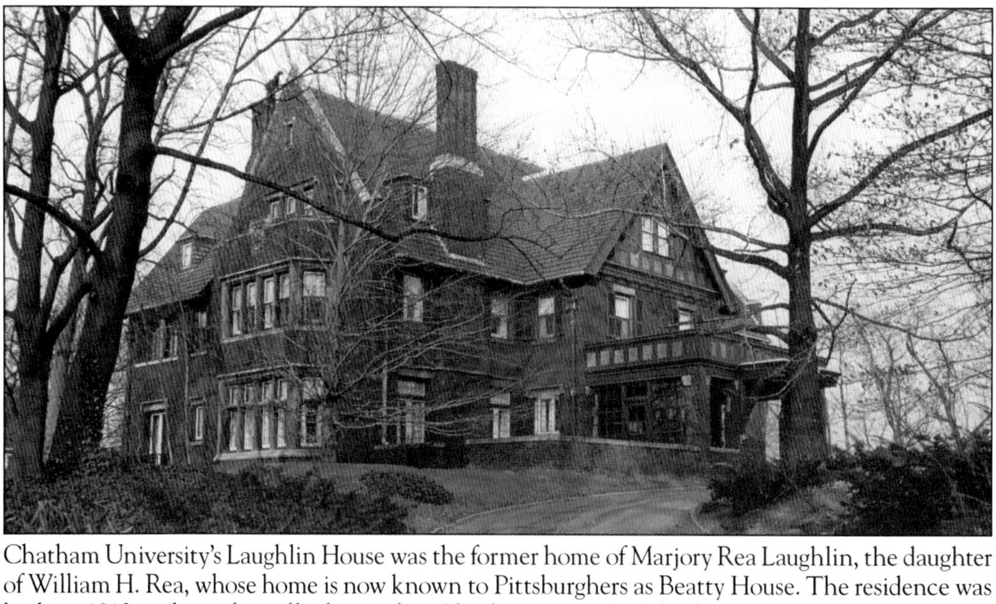

Chatham University's Laughlin House was the former home of Marjory Rea Laughlin, the daughter of William H. Rea, whose home is now known to Pittsburghers as Beatty House. The residence was built in 1913 and was formally donated to Chatham in 1967. (Chatham University Archives.)

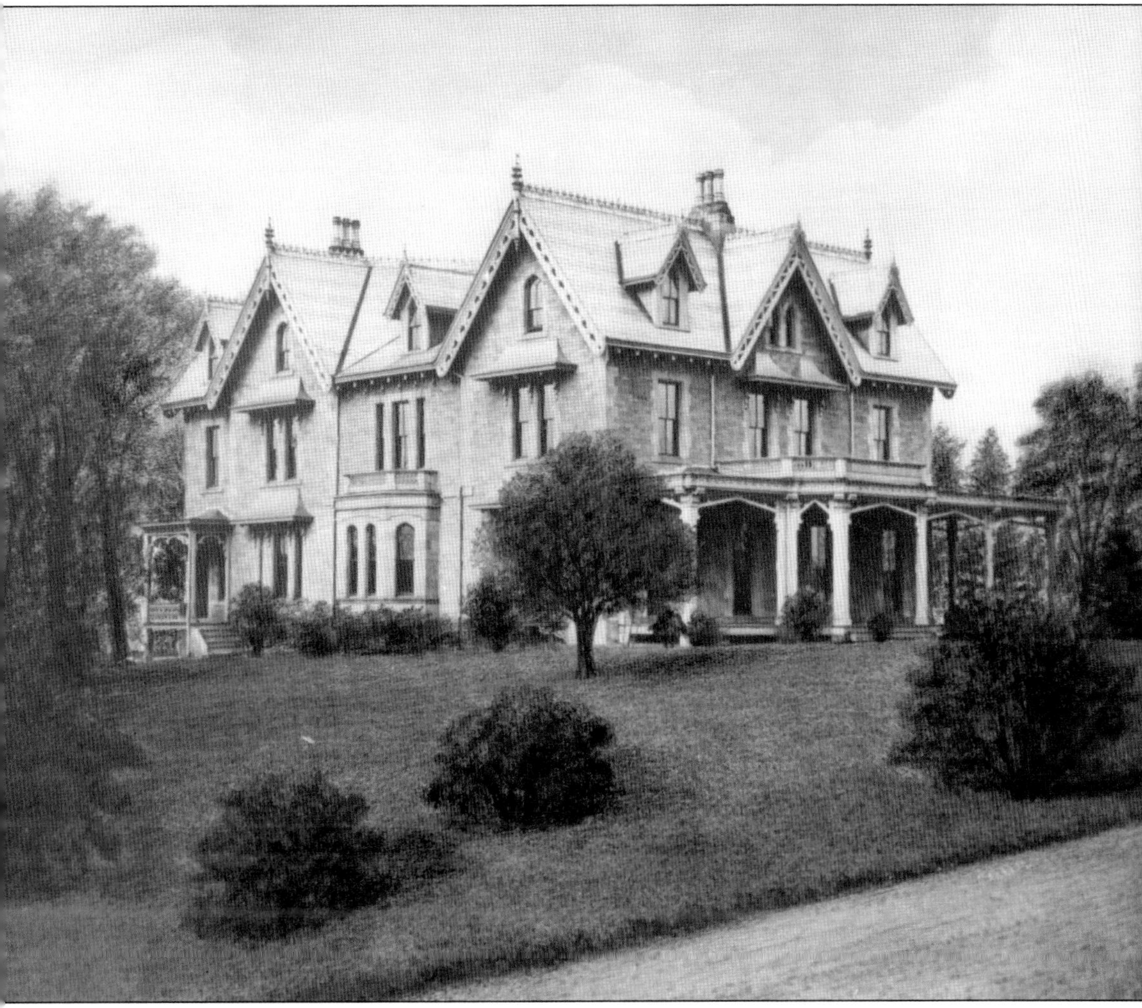

Thomas Marshall Howe's stick style mansion, known as Greystone, sat high above Fifth Avenue. Built around 1860, the estate housed a natural spring whose water was made available to the public through a springhouse. While a springhouse labeled "Howe Springs" still stands along Fifth Avenue today, it is not in the same location as the original. (Paul Slantis Photograph Collection, Archives Service Center, University of Pittsburgh.)

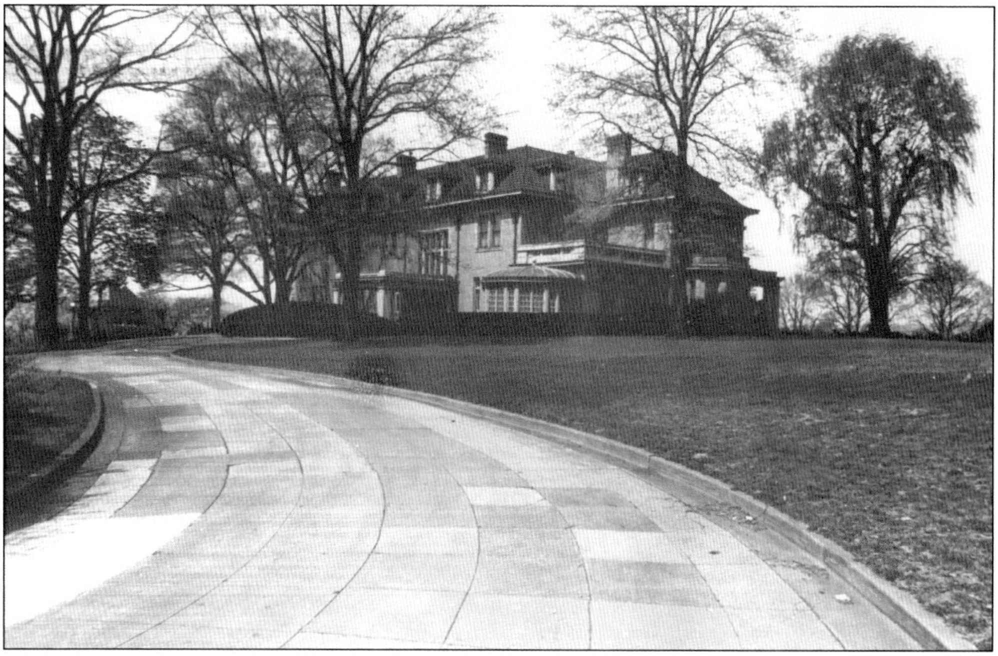

Michael L. Benedum bought the original Greystone in 1911 and demolished it, building in its place an elaborate mansion designed by W.H. Vantine in 1915, also dubbed Greystone. At Benedum's death, the home was donated to Chatham College (now Chatham University) and used as Benedum Hall until the building was sold in the late 1980s.

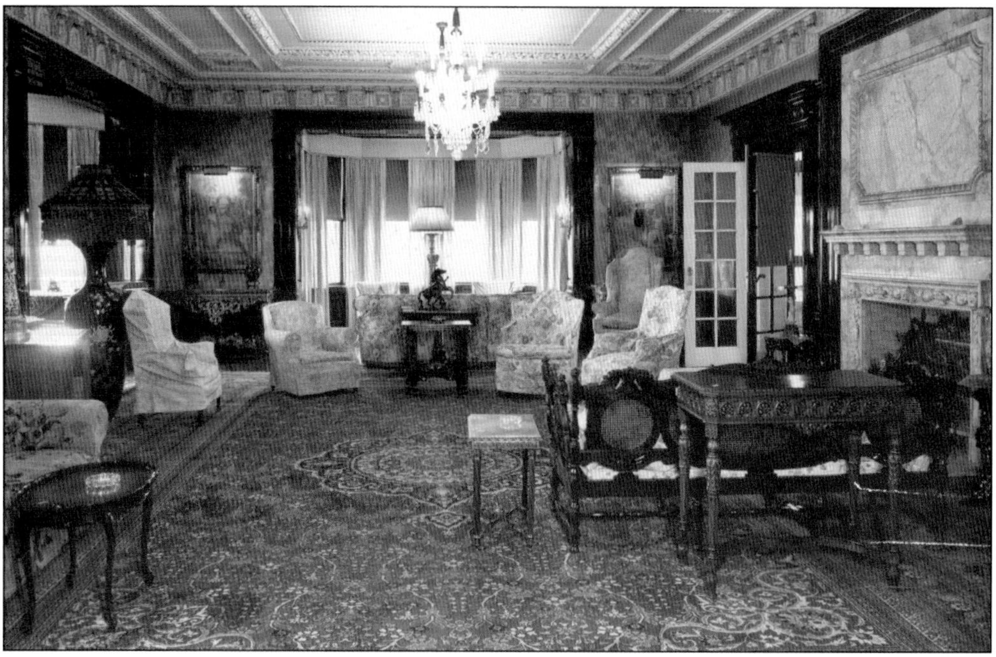

The interior of Michael L. Benedum's Greystone reflected an 18th-century English style. Decorative plasterwork on the ceilings, a marble fireplace, and silk wall coverings were just some of the furnishings left behind by the Benedum family when the home became a dormitory for young women in the 1960s. (Chatham University Archives.)

Benedum Hall featured a marble solarium, or winter garden, with an original, hand-carved fountain and other marble fixtures. (Chatham University Archives.)

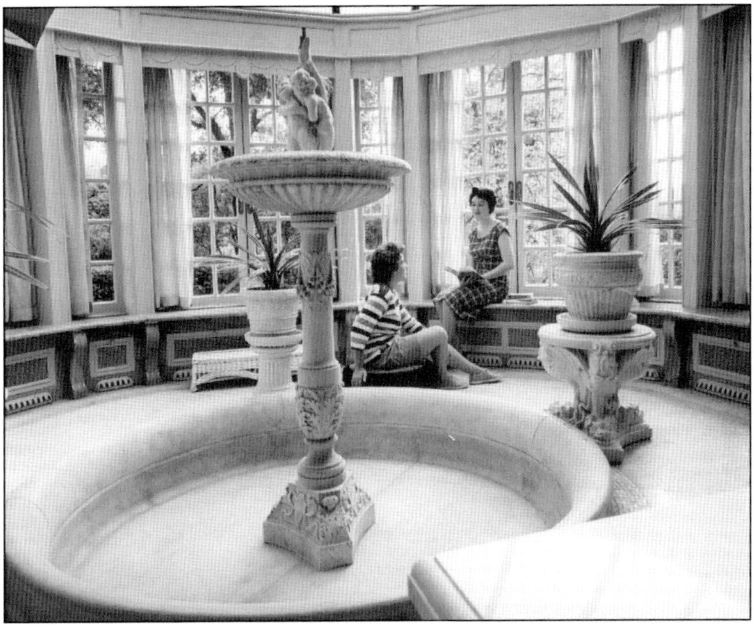

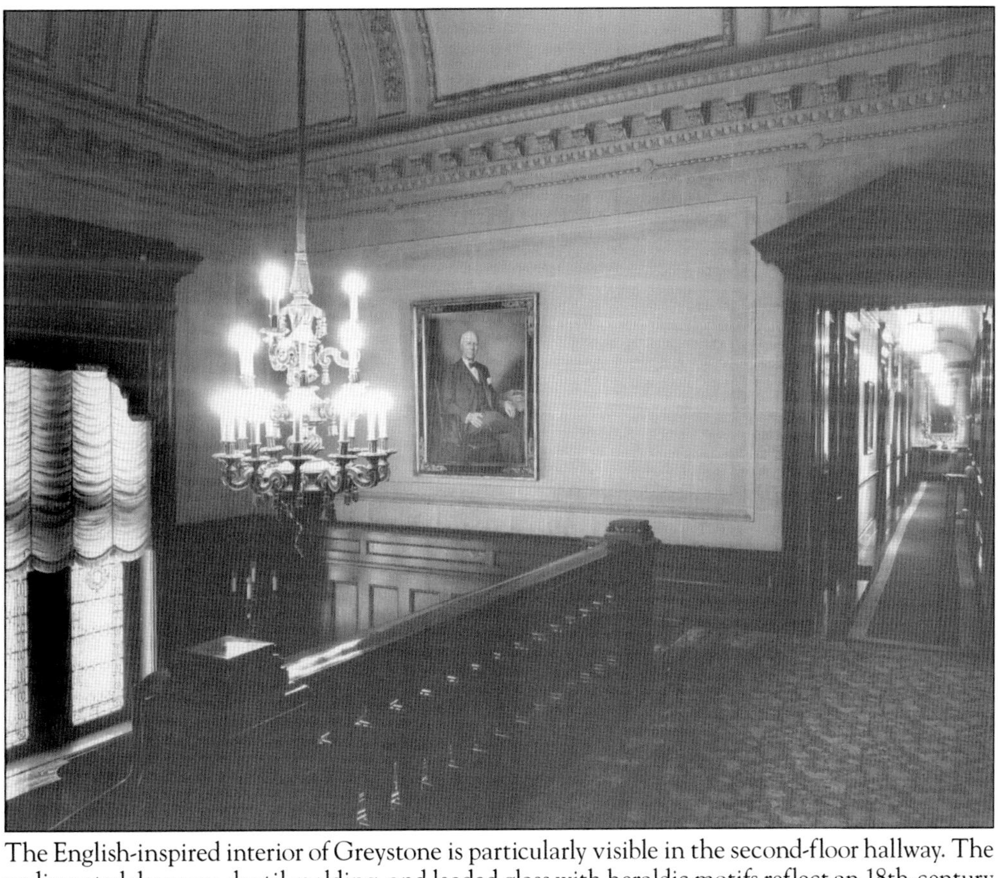

The English-inspired interior of Greystone is particularly visible in the second-floor hallway. The pedimented doorway, dentil molding, and leaded glass with heraldic motifs reflect an 18th-century English style. (Chatham University Archives.)

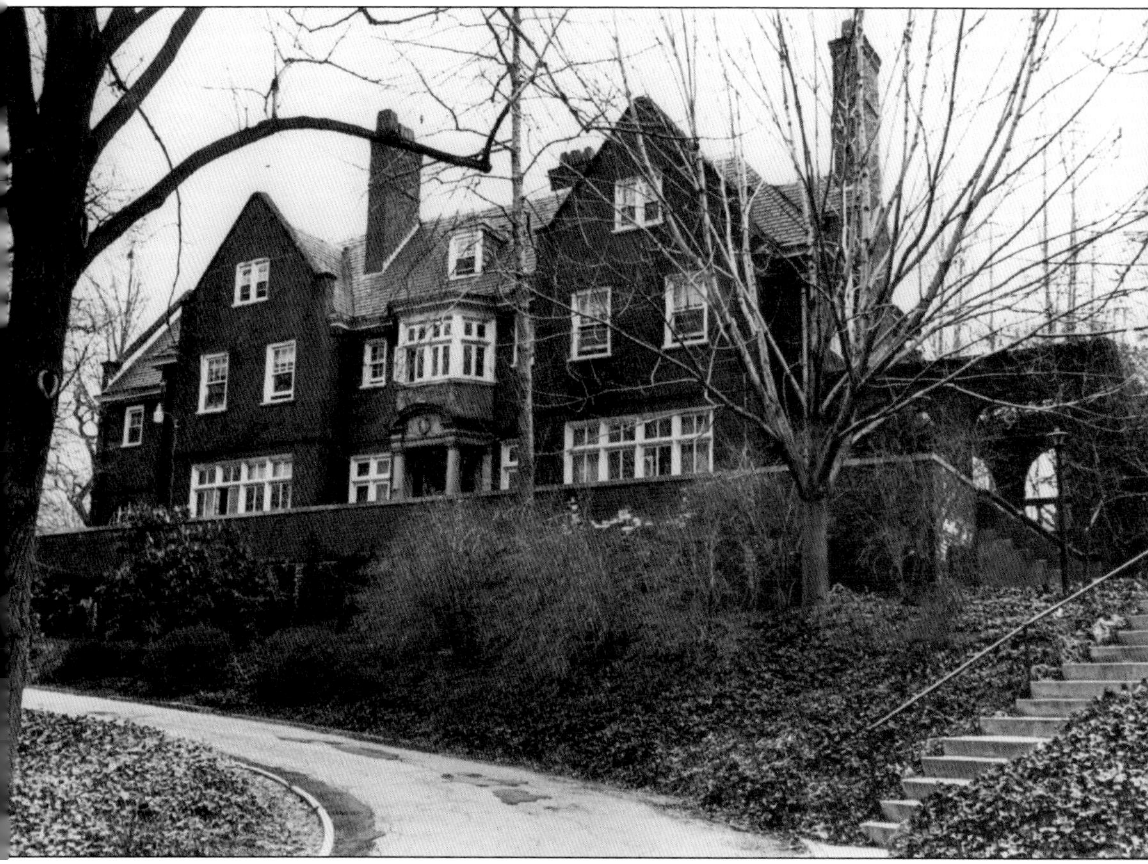

Rea House, the former home of Julia and James Rea, was donated to Chatham College in 1965. The Reas had resided in the 23-room Jacobean Revival–style home with their eight children. It opened as a student dormitory in 1967. (Chatham University Archives.)

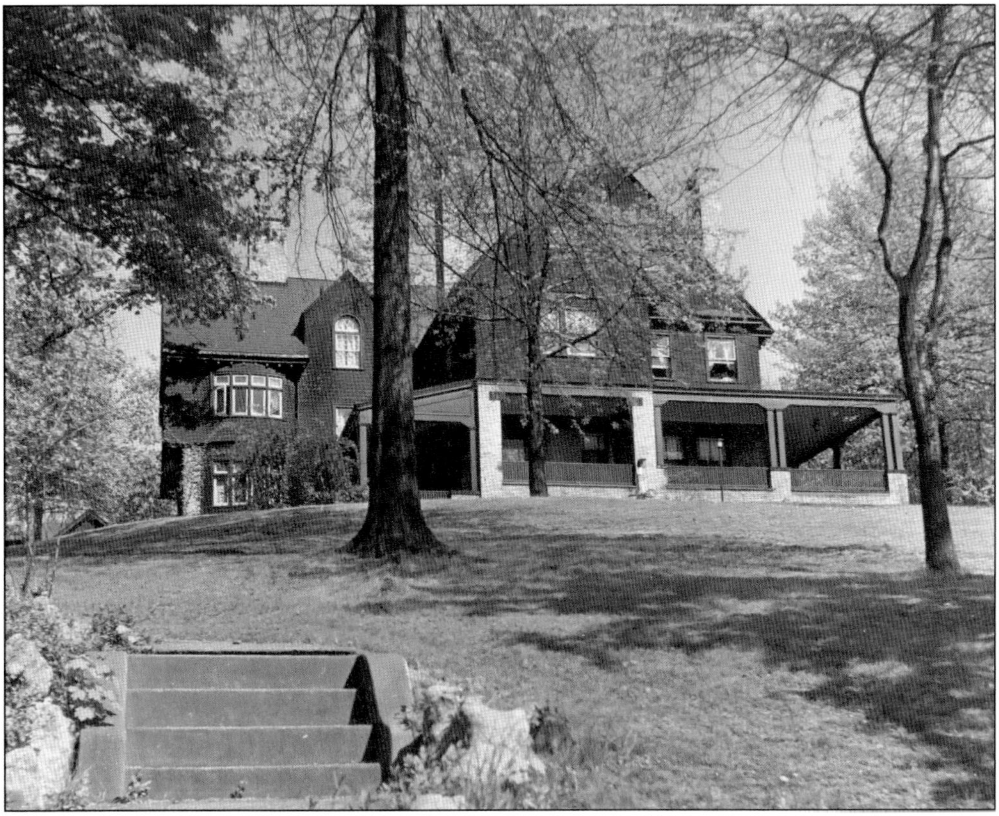

This shingle-style house was built in 1896 for William H. Rea and his wife, Mary. After the mansion, then known as Sunset Hill, was donated to what is now Chatham University, the school renamed it Beatty House in honor of the Reverend William Trimble Beatty. Beatty was a founder of the Pennsylvania Female College, the precursor to Chatham. (Chatham University Archives.)

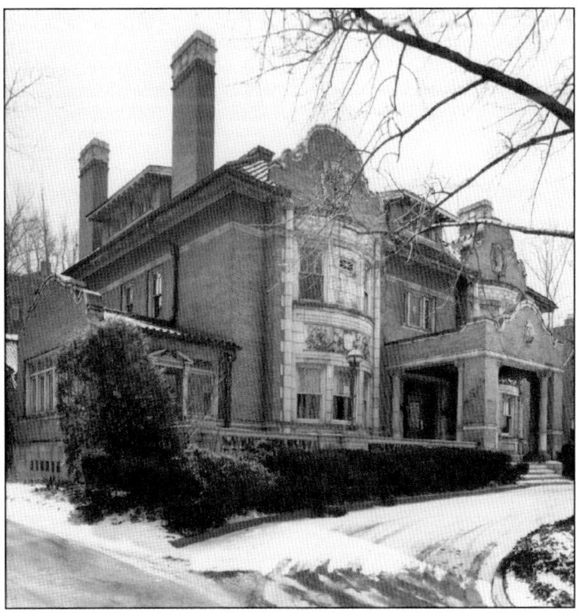

Grenville House, the former home of Lewis W. Hicks, was purchased by Chatham College in 1967. Hicks was an incorporator of the West Leechburg Connecting Bridge Company. After its sale to Chatham, Grenville House served as a temporary library while the current Jennie King Mellon Library was being built. (Chatham University Archives.)

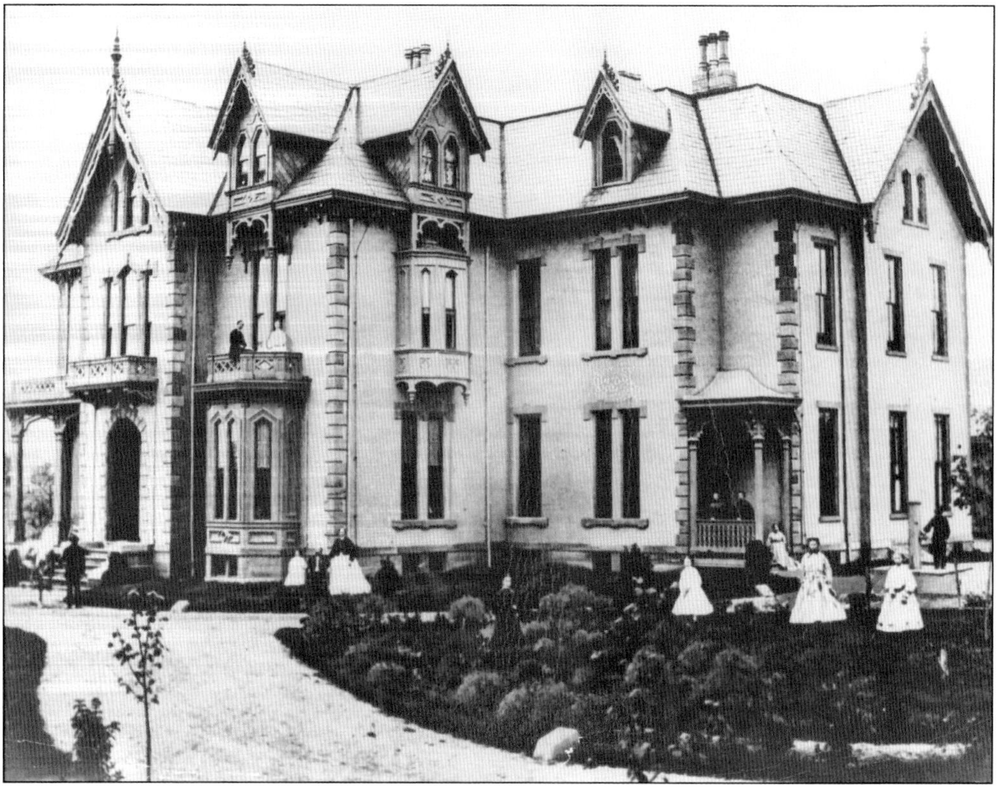

George A. Berry was one of the largest benefactors of Pennsylvania Female College (now Chatham University). He served as president of the Pittsburgh Clearing House Bank and Citizens' National Bank, and held many other business interests. Seen above posing with other members of his family in front of their home, Berry donated his Gothic Revival mansion and ten and a half acres of land to the school. The home, by that time known as Berry Hall, was demolished in 1953 to make way for administrative offices, and another nearby home was purchased to serve as the new Berry Hall. (Chatham University Archives.)

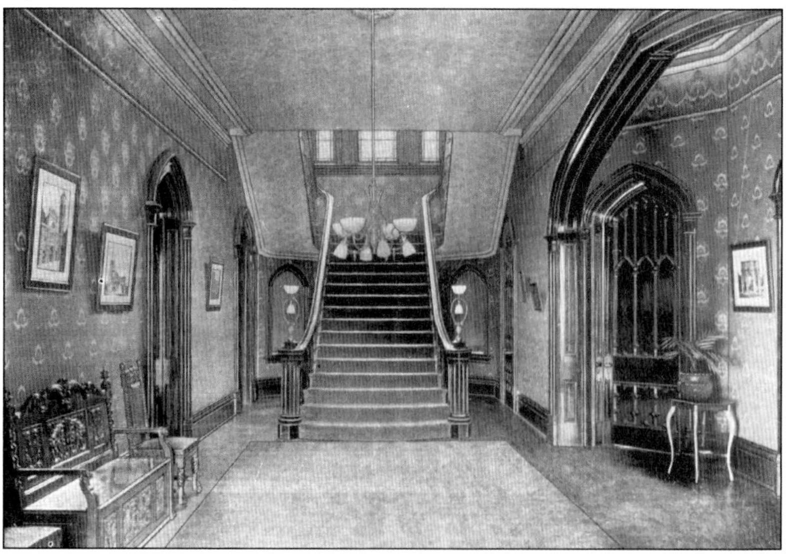

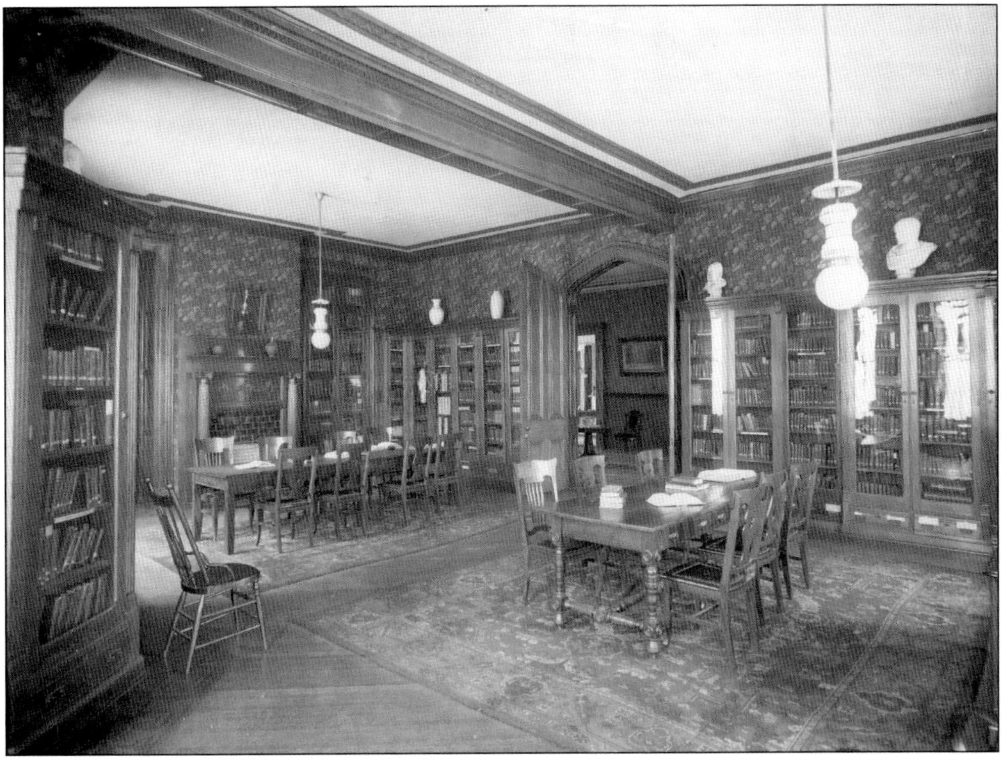

For many years following its acquisition, George A. Berry's mansion served as the flagship building of what is now Chatham University. It contained a library, classrooms, living and dining areas, and housing for the school's students, faculty members, and administrators. The school made several additions to the house over the years, including a large tower and a fourth floor. (Chatham University Archives.)

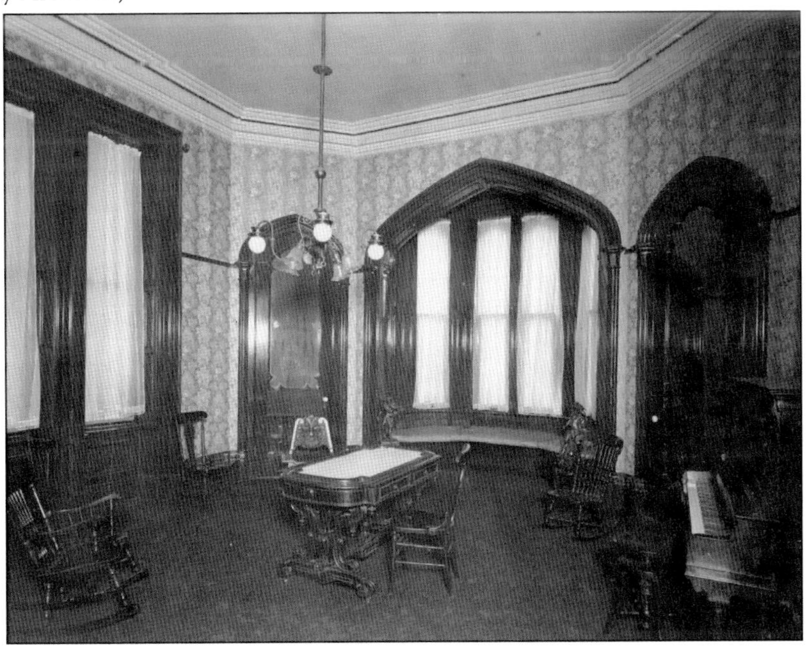

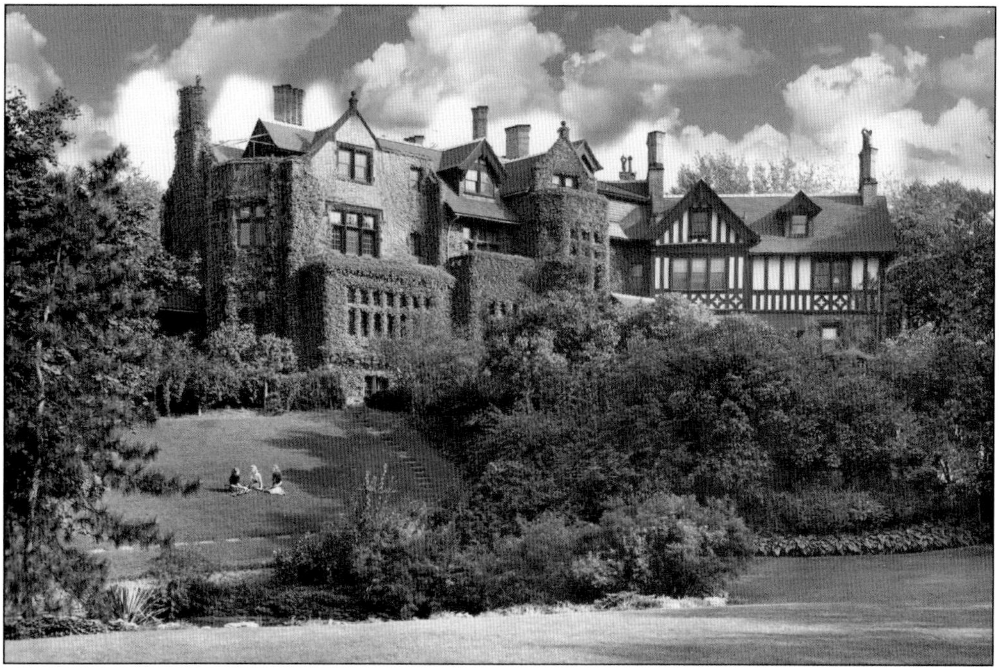

Lenmarkee, estate of banker Andrew W. Mellon, was originally the home of steel baron George Laughlin. Mellon's son, Paul, donated the home and its surrounding acreage to Chatham University in 1940. The edifice remains in use as Mellon Hall. (Chatham University Archives.)

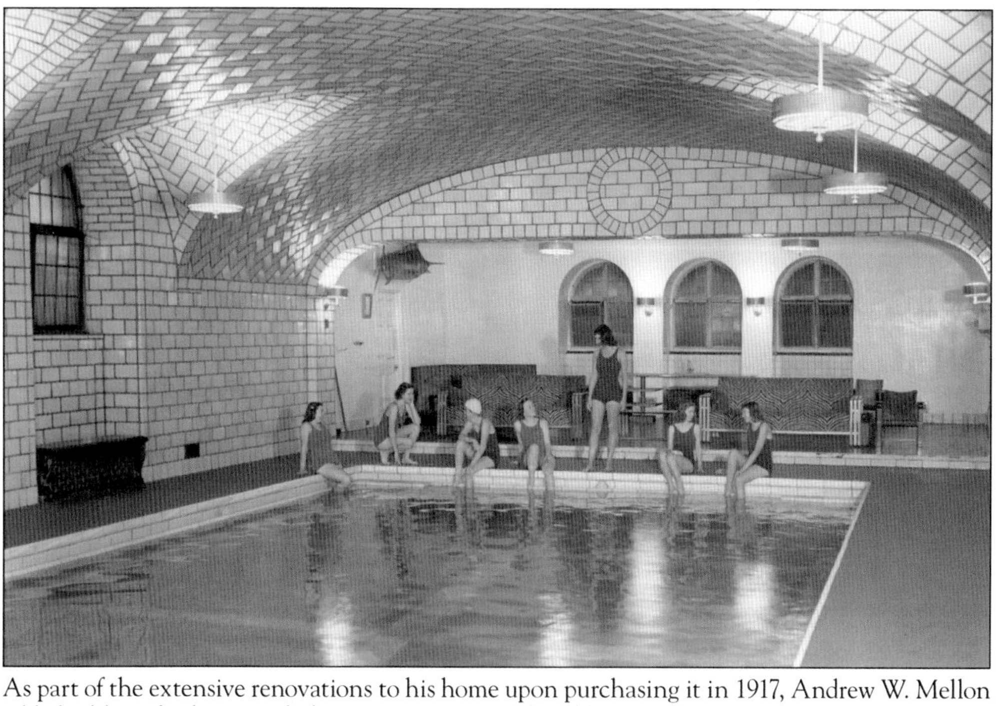

As part of the extensive renovations to his home upon purchasing it in 1917, Andrew W. Mellon added athletic facilities, including a swimming pool and bowling alley. The pool has since been filled in and is now used as a boardroom for Chatham University's trustees, though it retains the Gustavino fireproof tiles on the walls and ceiling. (Chatham University Archives.)

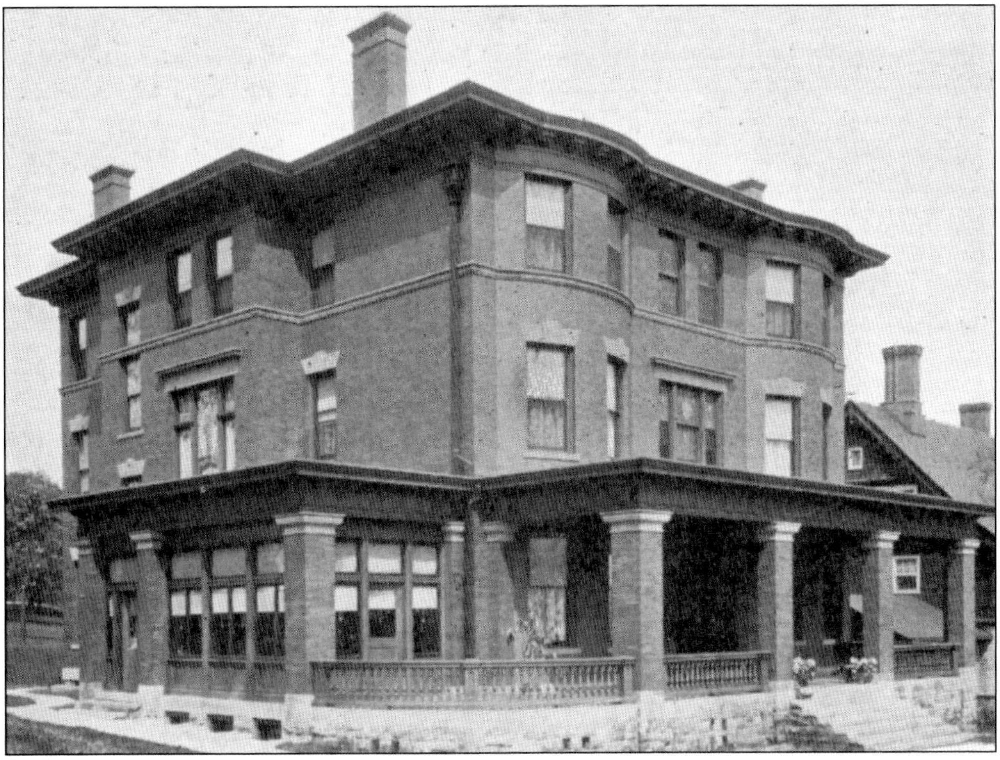

Gregg House is the current residence of Chatham University's presidents. Built around 1908 for John R. and Anna M. Gregg, the house was designed by Thomas Hannah. The Greggs donated the home to Chatham and it has housed the school's presidents since 1945. (CMU.)

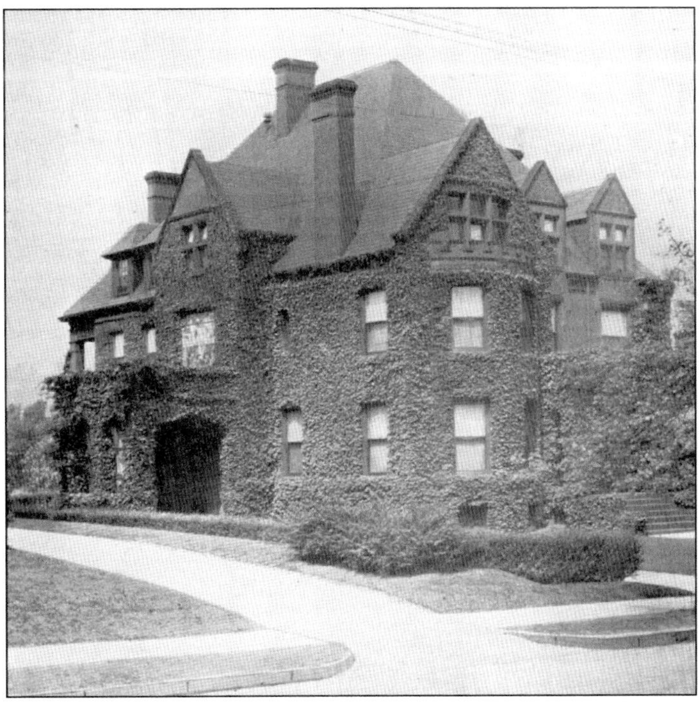

Henry S. Atwood Stewart, originally from Steubenville, Ohio, began his business career in the Pennsylvania oil industry, eventually selling his interests to Standard Oil in 1874. Stewart was also involved in area banking concerns. His home, shown here, stood at 800 Morewood Avenue.

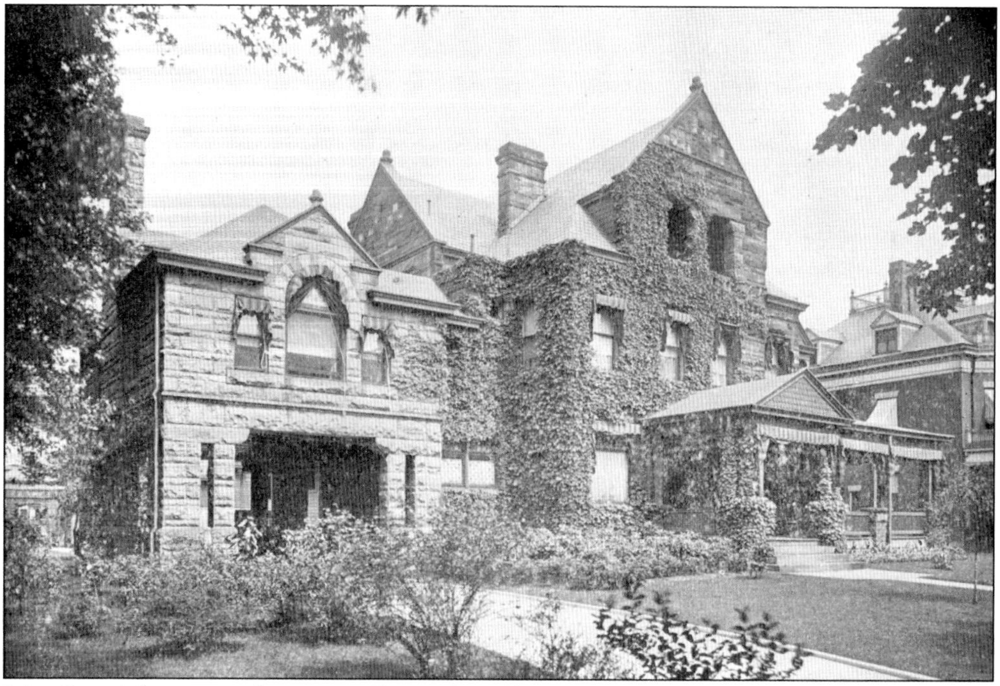

John Eaton's home on what is now Devonshire (formerly Bidwell) Street combines elements of the Romanesque and Jacobean Revival styles. Eaton, whose fortune was made in the oil industry, was president of the Pittsburgh Chamber of Commerce and sat on the board of the Kingsley Association. He was also a Civil War veteran.

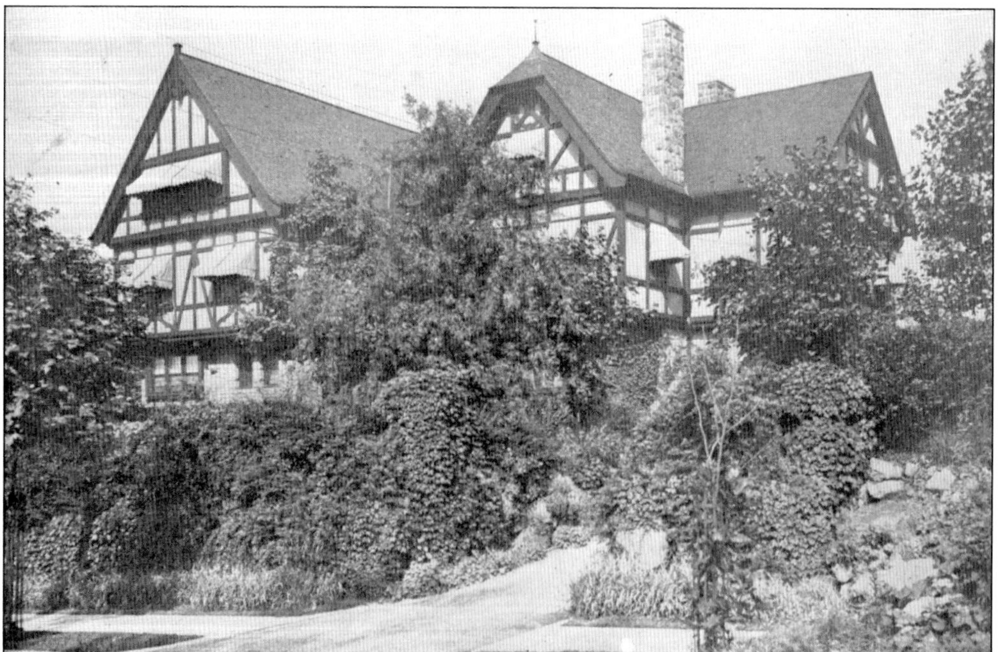

E.H. Utley lived in this Elizabethan Revival home on Shady Avenue. He was the general manager of the Bessemer & Lake Erie Railroad's Pittsburgh division.

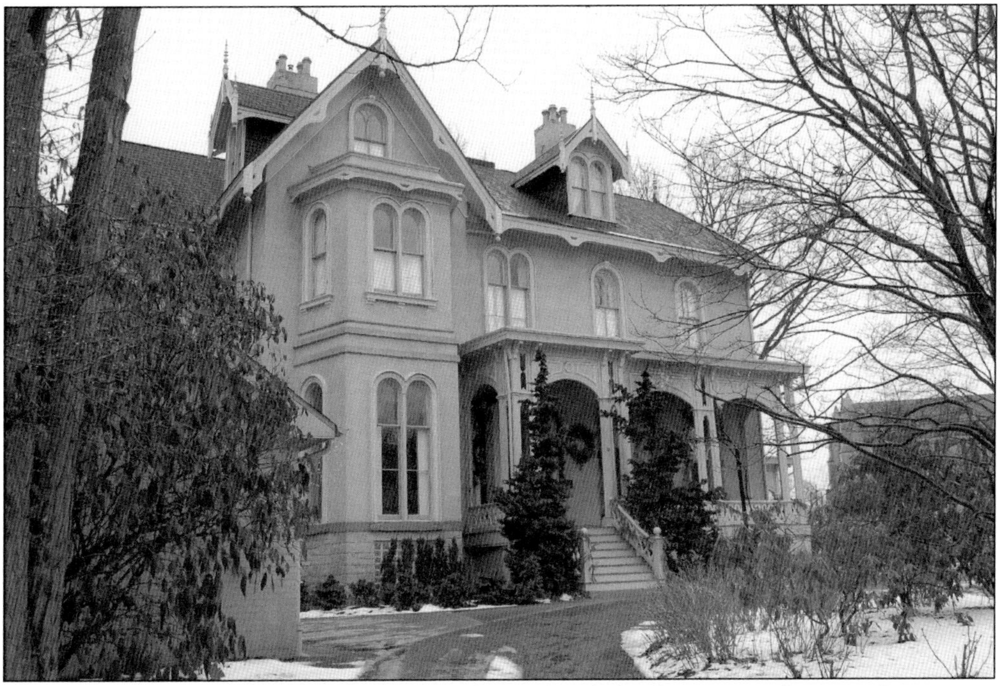

The Carnahan-Sellers House was built around 1858 for wholesale grocer and meatpacking owner Francis Sellers. The home, at the corner of Shady Avenue and Walnut Street, was later sold to Jay W. Carnahan, a boot and shoe merchant and director of Diamond National Bank. The home later served as the rectory of neighboring Calvary Episcopal Church and is now a privately owned residence.

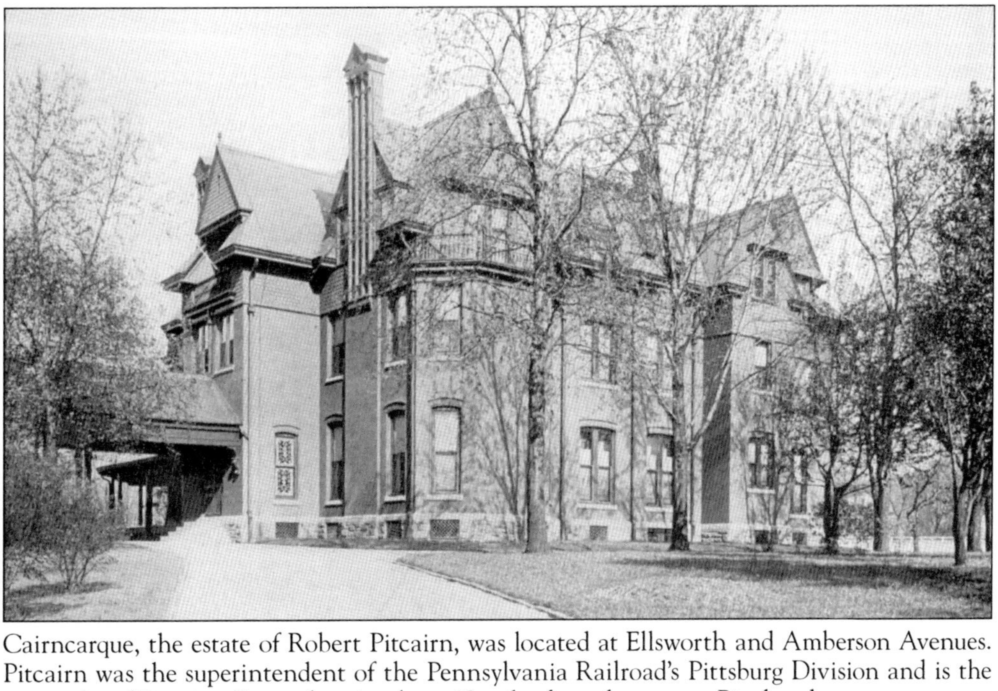

Cairncarque, the estate of Robert Pitcairn, was located at Ellsworth and Amberson Avenues. Pitcairn was the superintendent of the Pennsylvania Railroad's Pittsburg Division and is the namesake of Pitcairn, Pennsylvania, about 18 miles from downtown Pittsburgh.

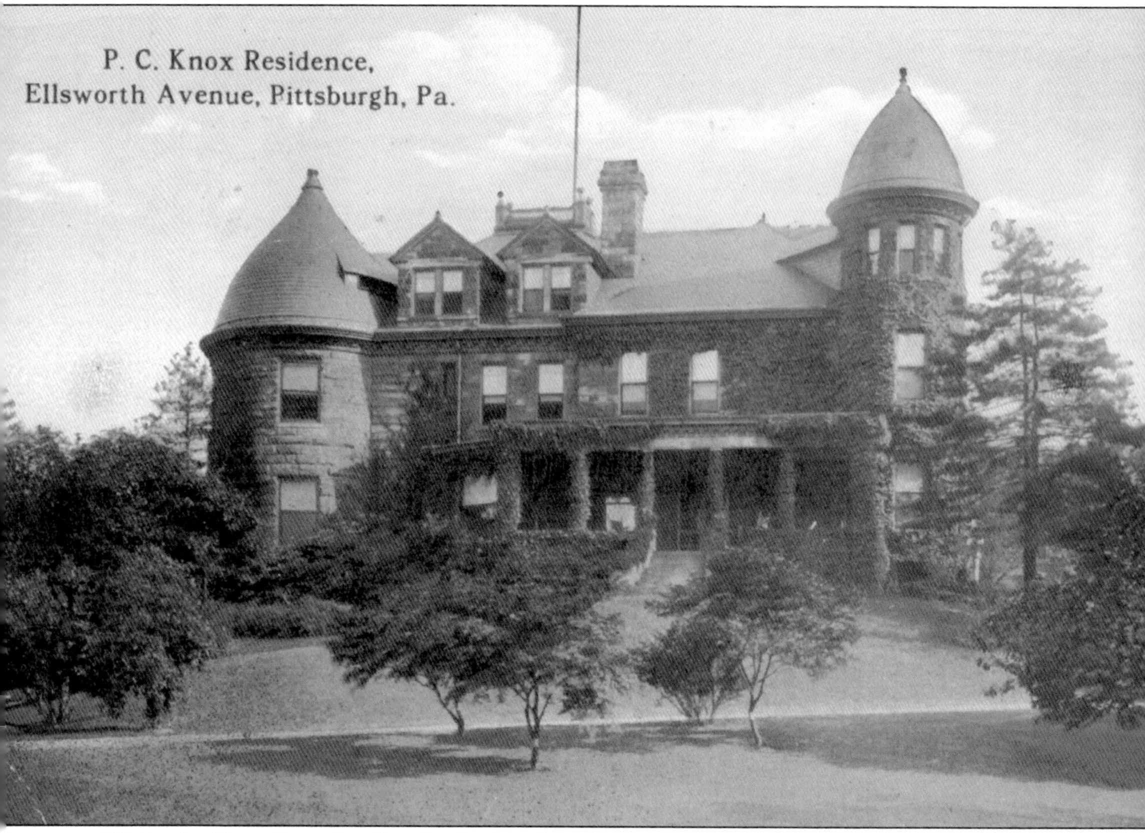

Philander Chase Knox lived in this home, with its curious Queen Anne and Romanesque elements, on Ellsworth Avenue. Knox, a lawyer, was appointed attorney general under the McKinley and Roosevelt administrations. He also served as a US senator and was later appointed secretary of state by Pres. William Howard Taft.

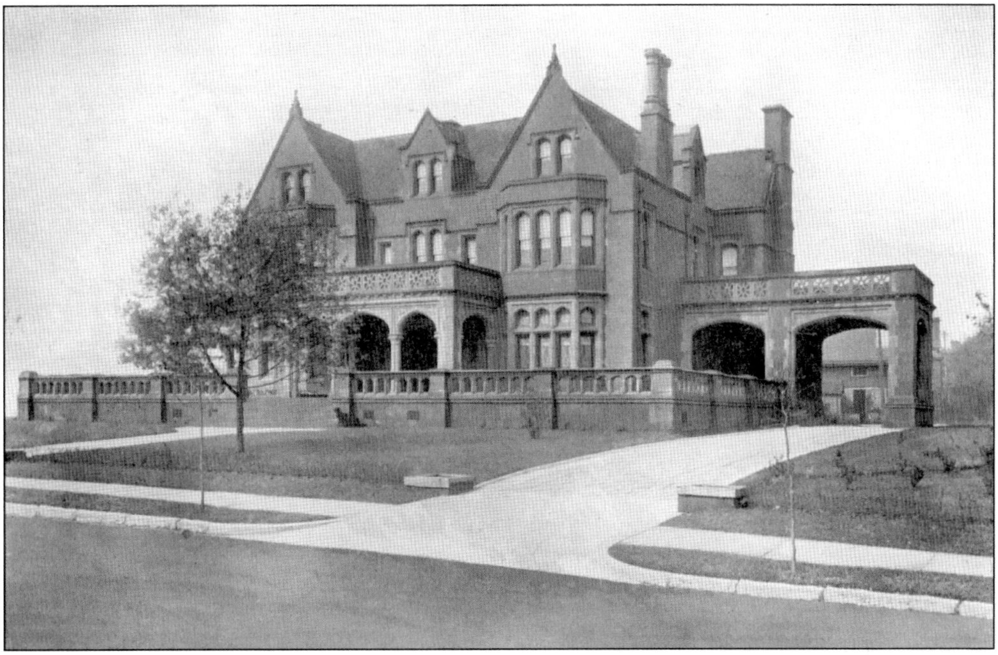

Wallace H. Rowe, president of the Pittsburgh Steel Company, lived on Morewood Avenue in this Jacobean Revival home. Originally from St. Louis, Rowe was also the founder of the Braddock Wire Company, which was later incorporated into the Consolidated Steel & Wire Company of Chicago and eventually became part of U.S. Steel. At one time, Rowe was in charge of all the company's Pennsylvania interests. (CMU.)

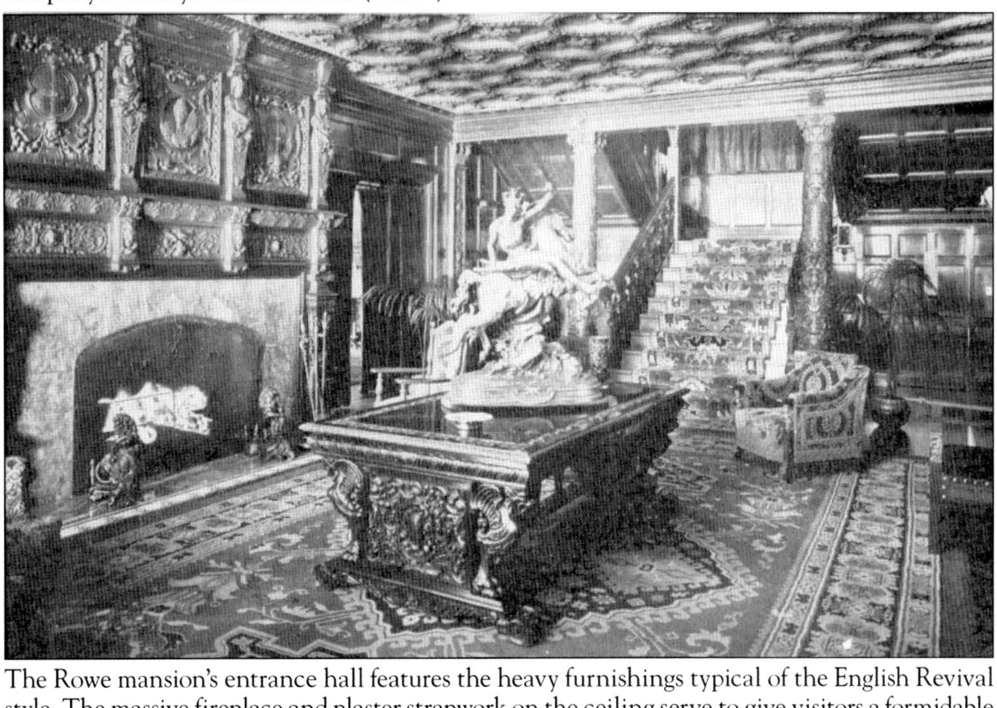

The Rowe mansion's entrance hall features the heavy furnishings typical of the English Revival style. The massive fireplace and plaster strapwork on the ceiling serve to give visitors a formidable first impression of the place. (CMU.)

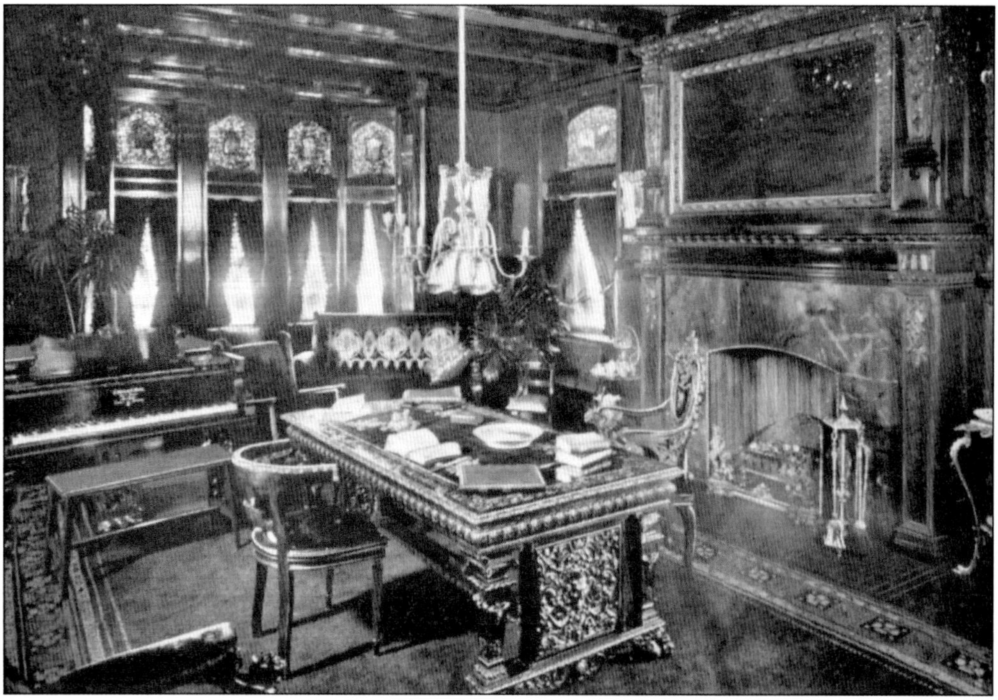
The library in Wallace H. Rowe's home continues the look of massive English-inspired furniture. (HHC.)

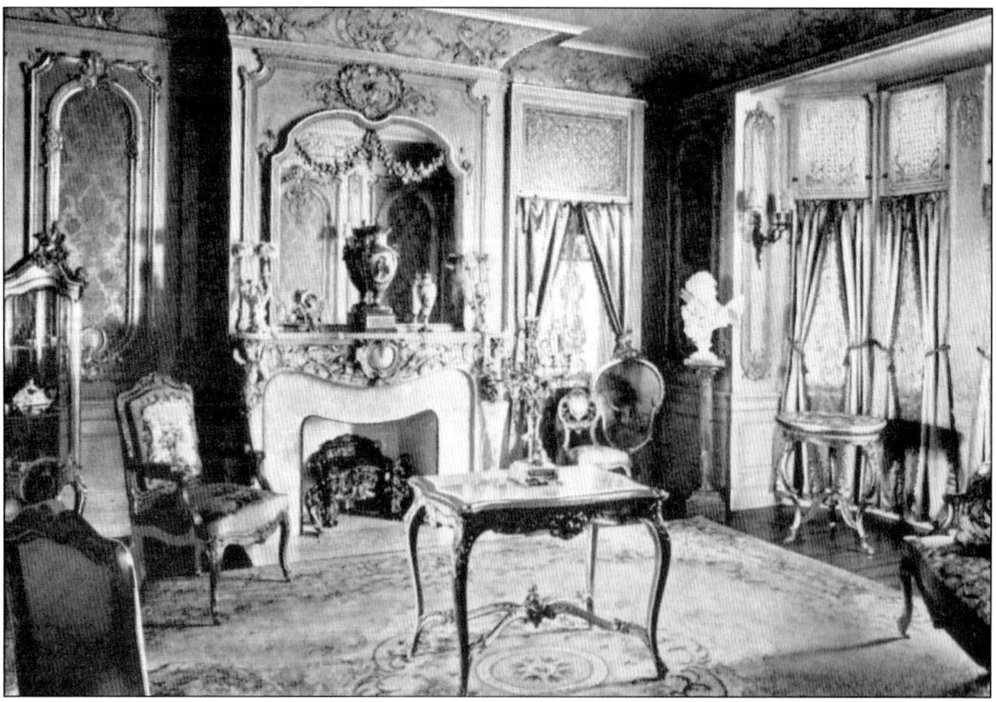
Rowe's drawing room reflects a French Louis XV decor, with much daintier furnishings than the other rooms of the house. Rococo-style drawing rooms were popular at the time, lending a continental flair to many stateside Victorian-era homes. (HHC.)

Emmet Queen lived in this eclectically styled Shadyside home with his wife, Susan, and their children. He was one half of the firm of Guffey & Queen and had made his fortune in the oil industry, being one of the first to concentrate on natural gas production as distinct from oil production.

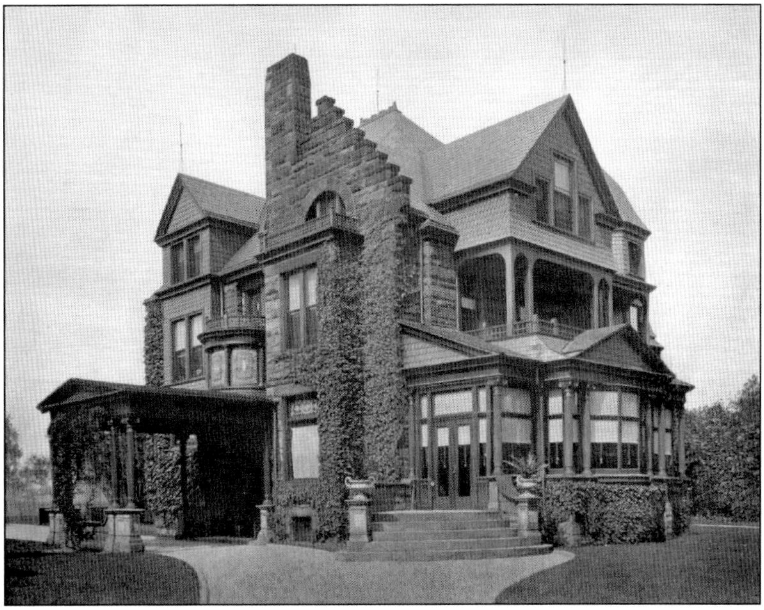

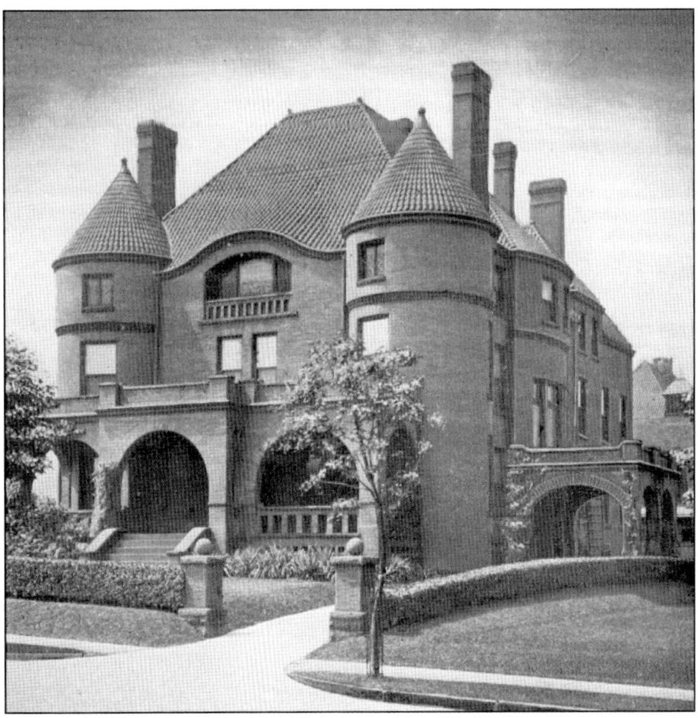

William Latham Abbott lived at 808 Morewood Avenue in this Romanesque fortress of a home with his wife and seven children. He was president of the Iron City Trust Company and also sat on the boards of the National Bank of Western Pennsylvania, the United Engineering & Foundry Company, and the Carnegie Steel Company.

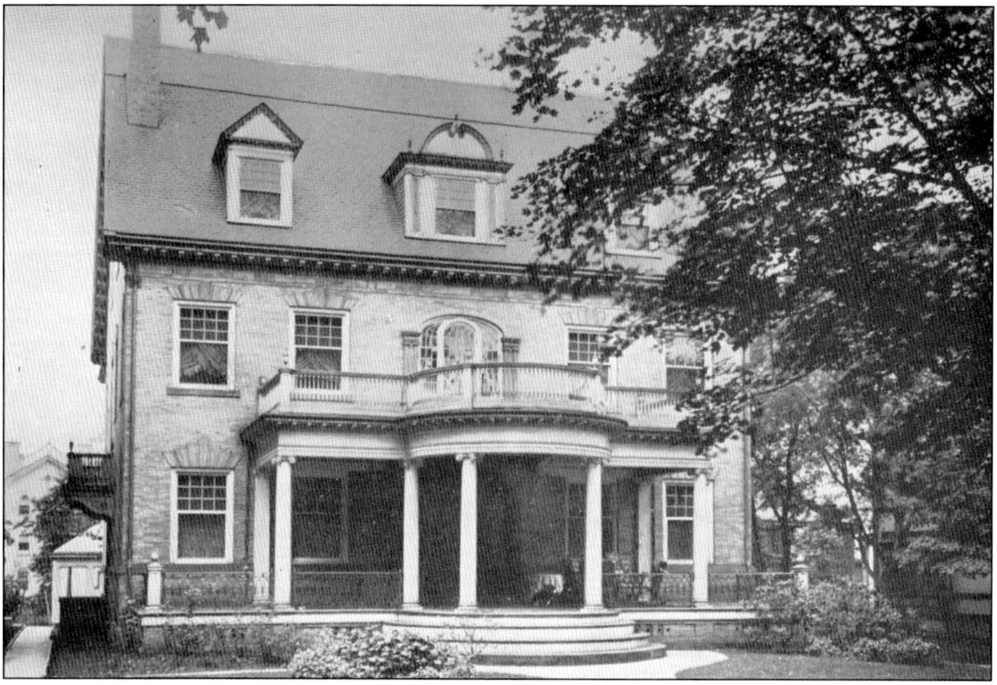

Wenman A. Lewis lived at 826 Amberson Avenue in this Georgian Revival house. Lewis became president of the West Virginia Pittsburgh Coal Company after his previous coal interests were consolidated.

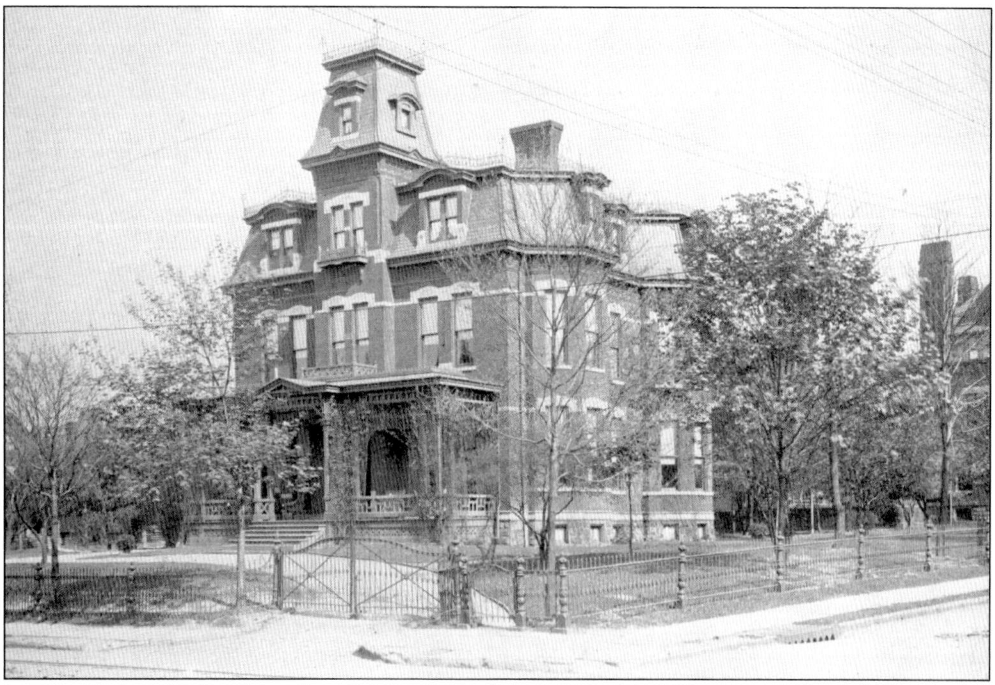

August E. Succop lived at Ellsworth and South Negley Avenues in this Italianate home. He held various banking interests throughout the city, at one time serving as president of Germania Savings Bank.

Three

Allegheny City and the Outskirts of Pittsburgh

The prosperity that grew out of Pittsburgh's industrial wealth spread to the city's surrounding towns and throughout Western Pennsylvania. As the closest and most successful of these areas, Allegheny City, just across the Allegheny River from Pittsburgh, attracted its share of millionaires who built spectacular homes there. Alternately called "Allegheny City" and "Allegheny," the town saw the rise of its own "Millionaire's Row" along Ridge Avenue in the late 1800s.

Unfortunately, following Pittsburgh's annexation of Allegheny in 1907, what subsequently became known as the city's North Side began a downward spiral that saw many of its stately homes demolished. Some of the grand old houses have been preserved as community assets; local preservation activists have brought many other properties back from the brink of destruction. This chapter features a selection of stately homes from outside the city's borders, from Allegheny to Greensburg and beyond.

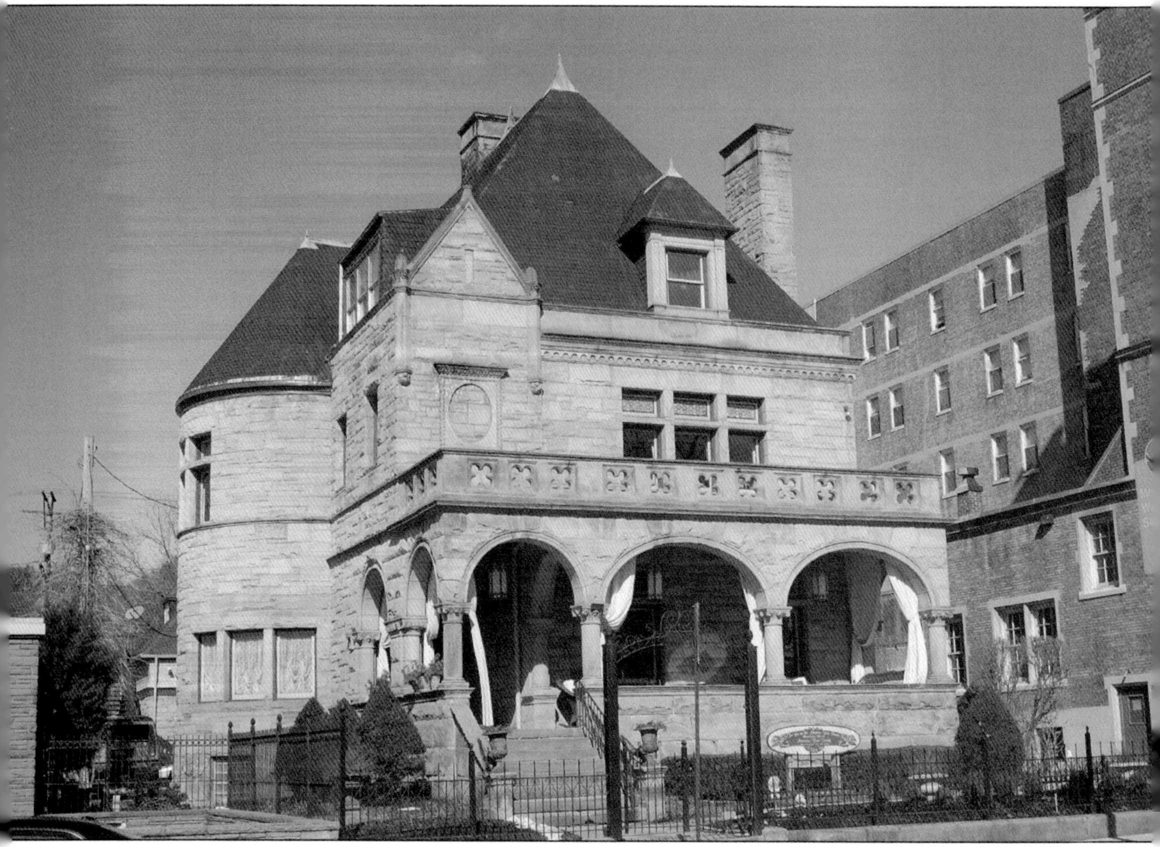

Russell H. Boggs was a partner in the Boggs & Buhl department store. His Romanesque home on West North Avenue was designed by Alden & Harlow around 1888. The home was restored in 1998 and transformed into the Inn on the Mexican War Streets.

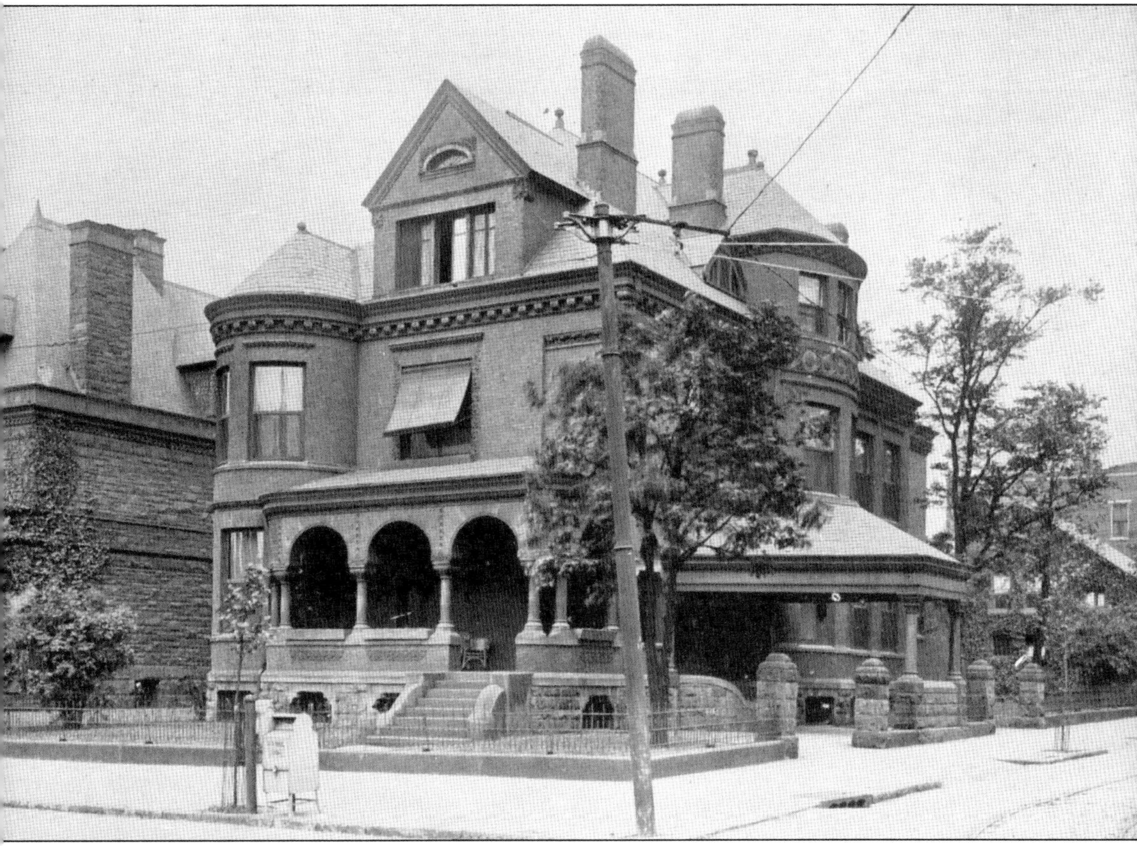

Just next door to the Russell H. Boggs mansion, at the corner of West North Avenue and Monterey Street, was the home of William H. Graham. A Civil War veteran, Graham served in the US House of Representatives for two terms (1898–1903 and 1905–1911). He also held interests in coal, insurance, and railroads.

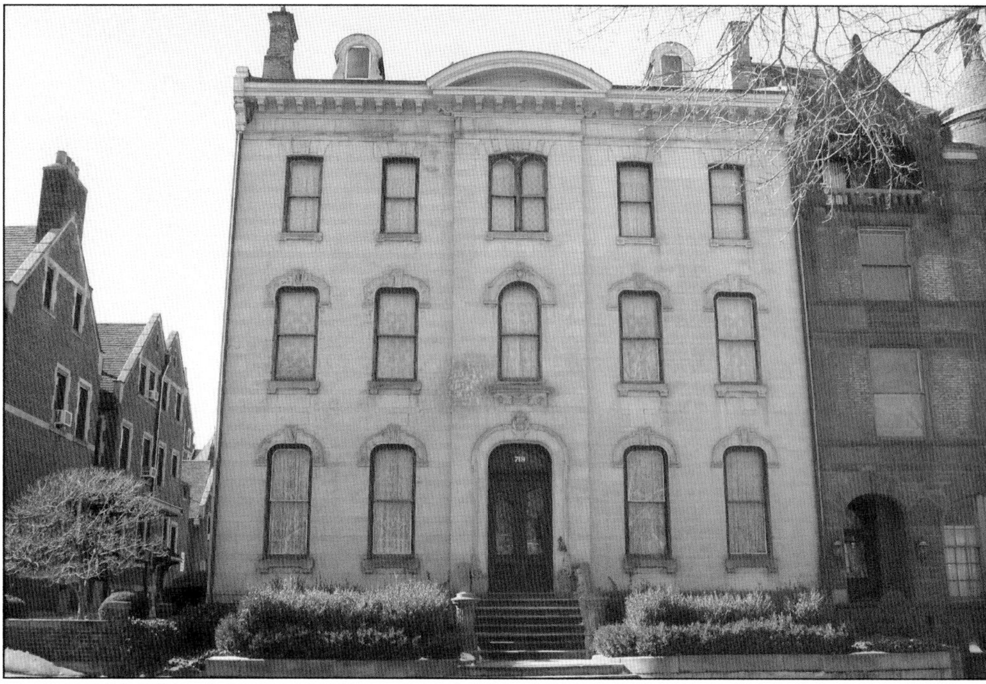

Letitia Caldwell Holmes, a wealthy widow, built Holmes Hall in 1868. The building includes a first-floor ballroom and enough space to house a staff of 14. Today, the house has been handsomely restored and is regularly featured on area house tours.

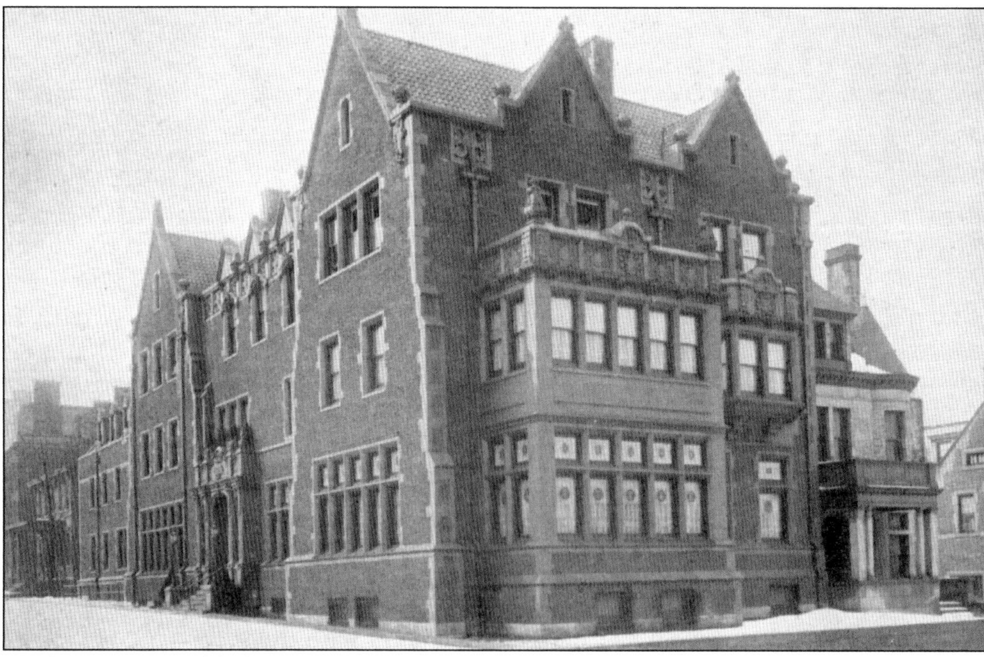

B.F. (Benjamin Franklin) Jones Jr., whose father was a founder of Jones & Laughlin Steel Company, lived on Ridge Avenue, at the time, Allegheny City's own "Millionaire's Row." His 42-room home was designed around 1910 by Rutan & Russell. Today, the house is known as Jones Hall and is part of the Community College of Allegheny County.

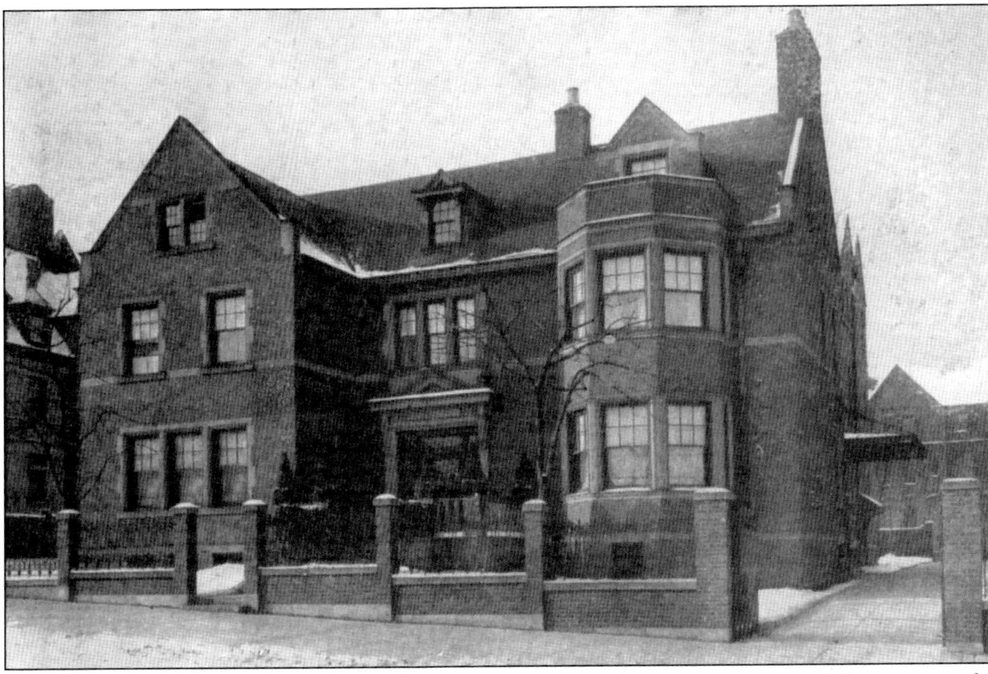

Harry Darlington Sr. commissioned the home at 709 Brighton Road as a wedding present for his son, Harry Darlington Jr. The house was designed by George Orth in 1908. The Darlington family held interests in brewing, steel, coal, gas, and railroads. (CMU.)

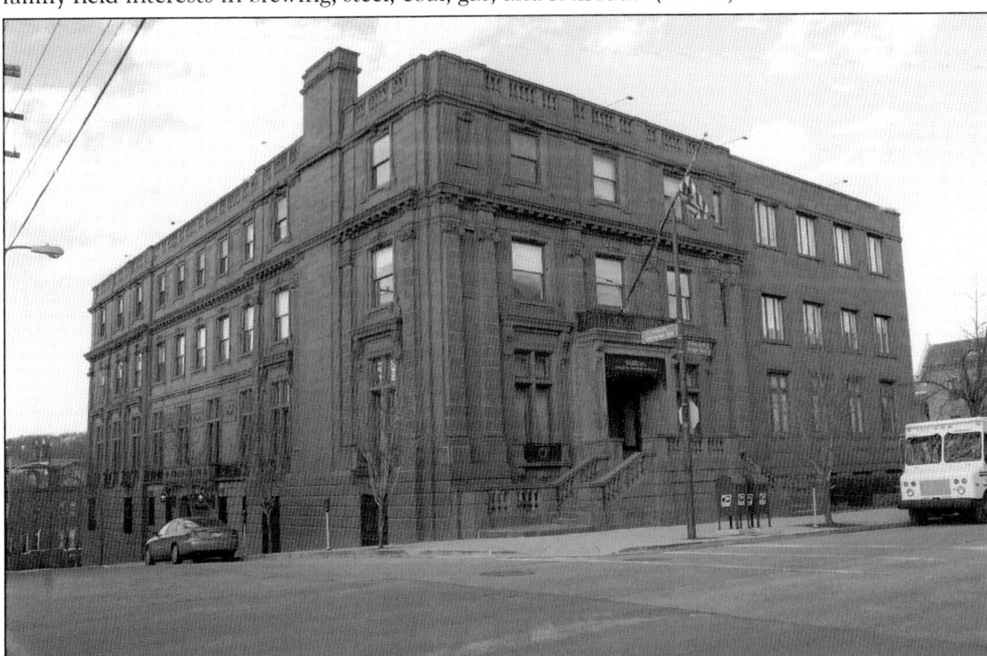

The brownstone mansion at 850 Ridge Avenue was home to William Penn Snyder and his family. Snyder was heavily involved in the coke industry, sitting on the board of directors for McClure Coke Company and H.C. Frick Coke Company. Today, the house serves as offices for an insurance agency.

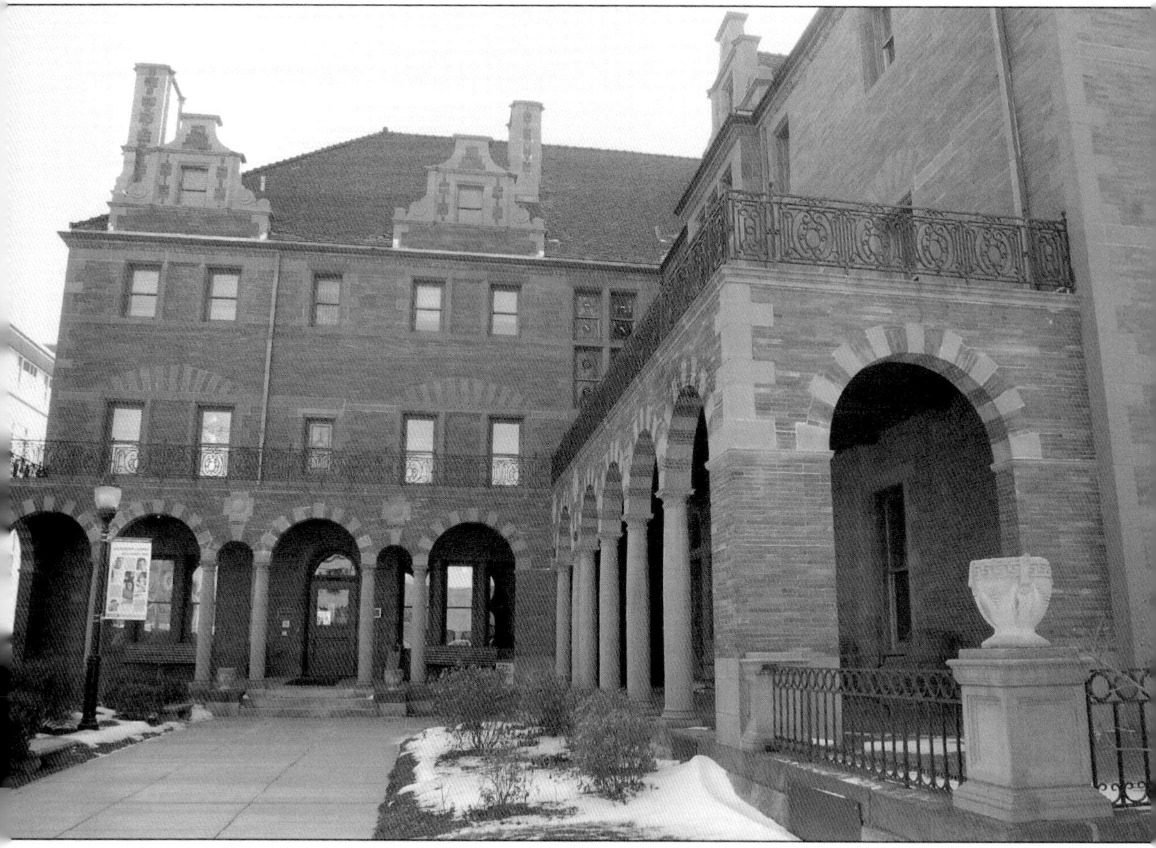

The Spanish Eclectic mansion at 901 Ridge Avenue was a double home to A.M. Byers and his daughter and son-in-law, Mr. and Mrs. John Denniston Lyon. The mansion had a total of 90 rooms and was designed by Alden & Harlow around 1898. A.M. Byers, his wife, and three children occupied one half of the house, while his daughter Maude lived in the other half with her husband.

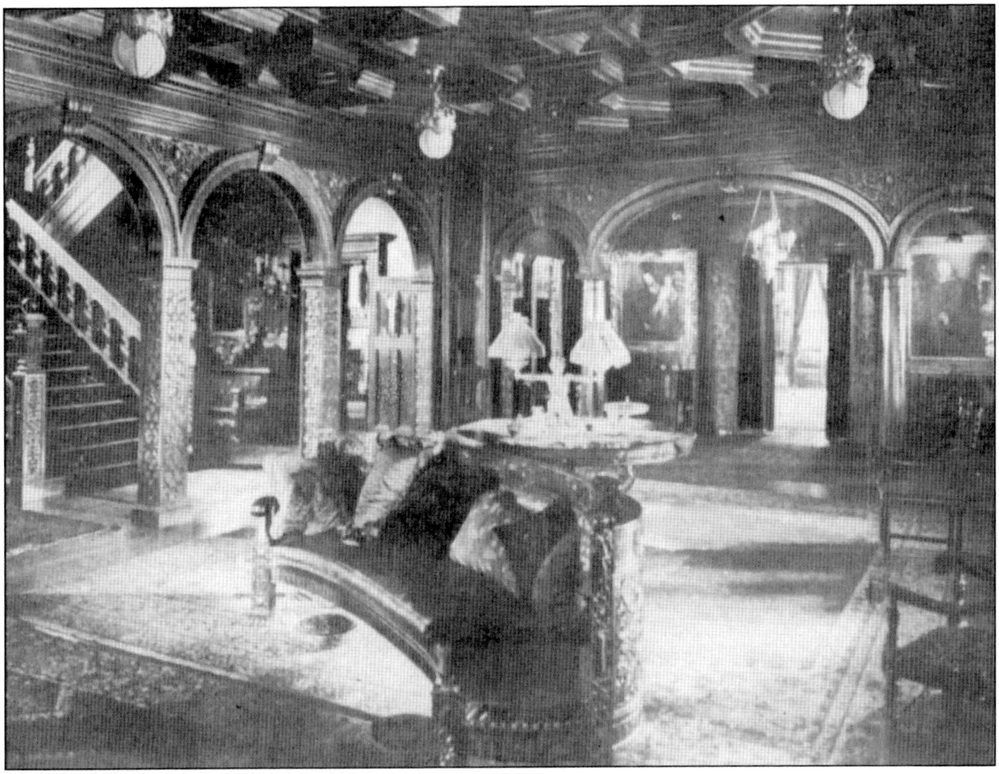

The Spanish style of the Byers home's façade did not extend to its interior. The entrance hall displays a spacious yet typical Victorian aesthetic. Part of Byers's art collection can be seen to the right; it is said that this collection rivaled those that were being amassed in neighboring Pittsburgh. (CMU.)

The dining room of the A.M. Byers home features more of the family's art collection, as well as a marble fireplace and what appears to be heavy mahogany furniture. (CMU.)

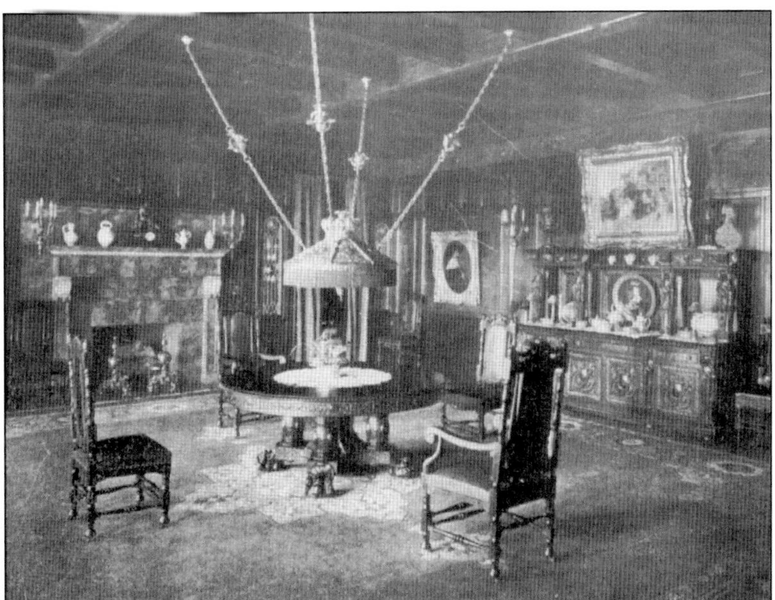

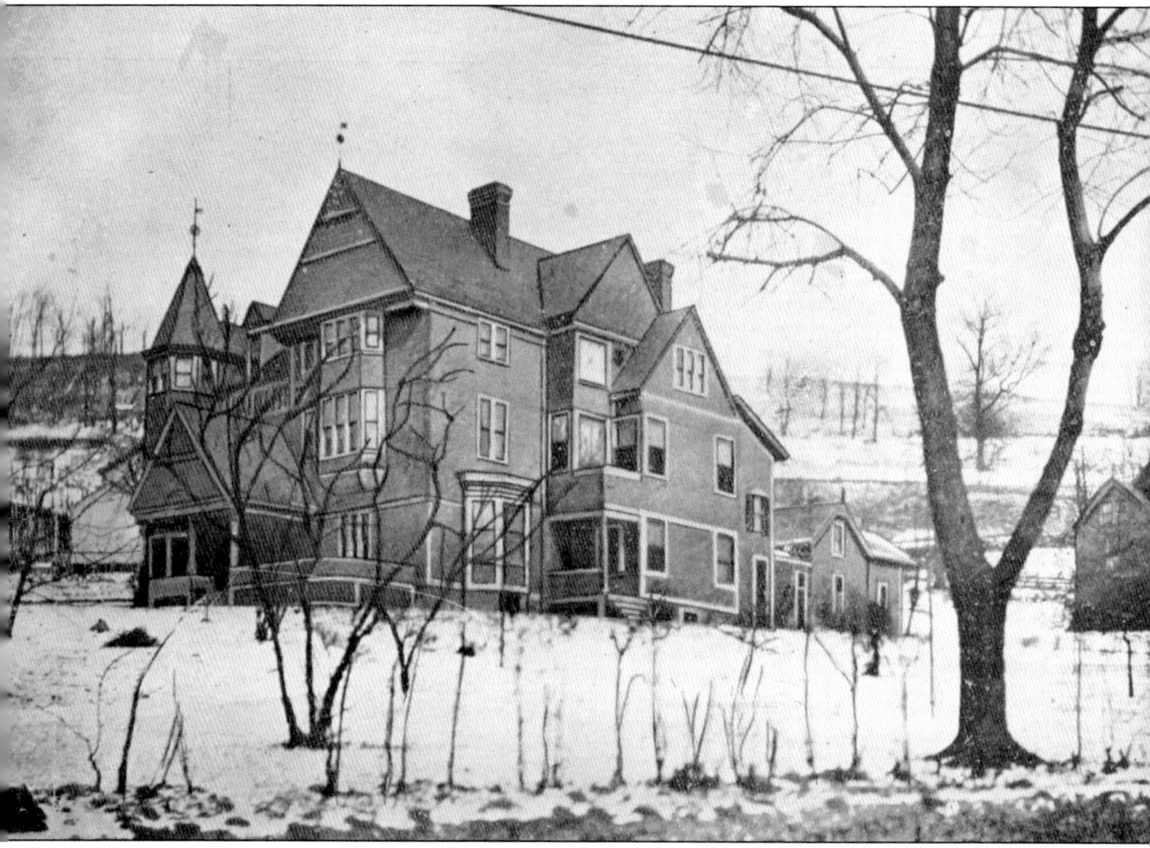

John Dalzell's home, The Wisterias, was located in Swissvale near the Pennsylvania Railroad's Hawkins station. Dalzell served several terms in the US House of Representatives between 1887 and 1913. Dalzell and his wife, Mary Louise, had five children.

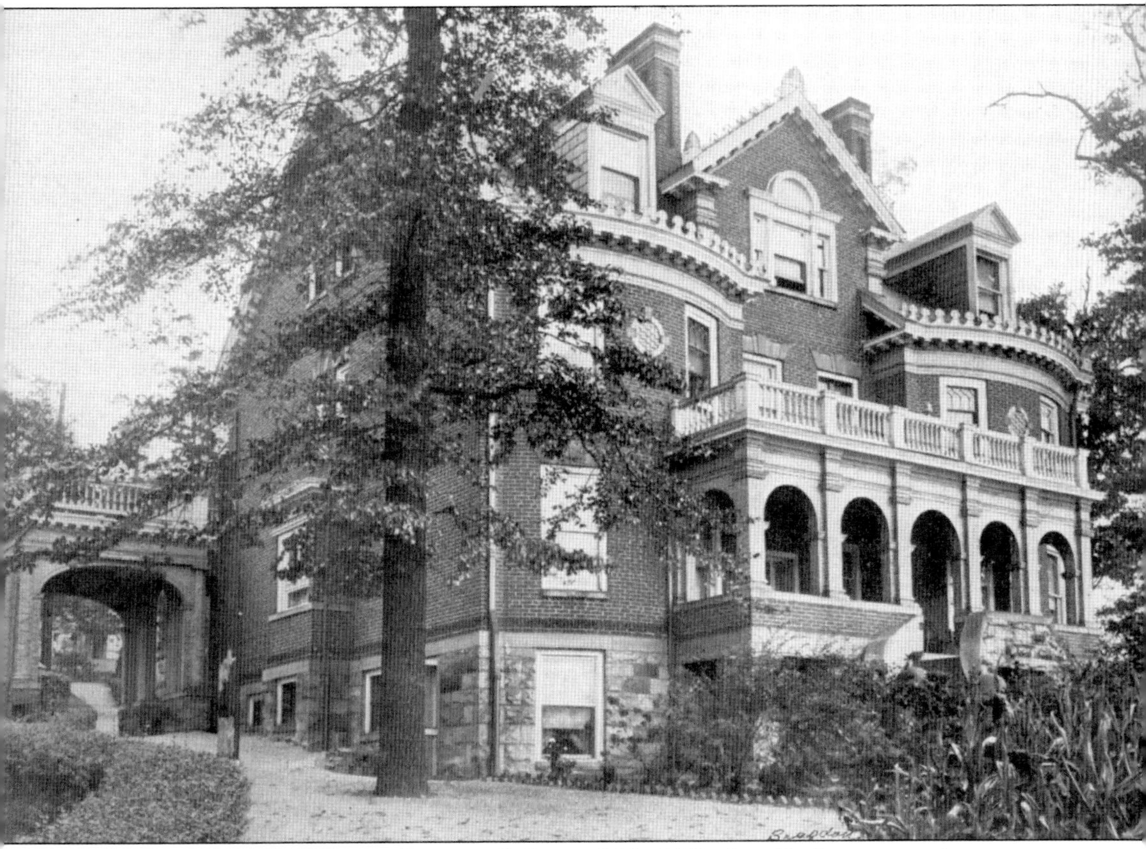

Capt. W.B. Rodgers lived in this home in Bellevue dubbed Windsor. Rodgers was a rivermaster and also held interests in the Tide Coal Company, which eventually became part of the Rochester and Pittsburgh Coal & Iron Company.

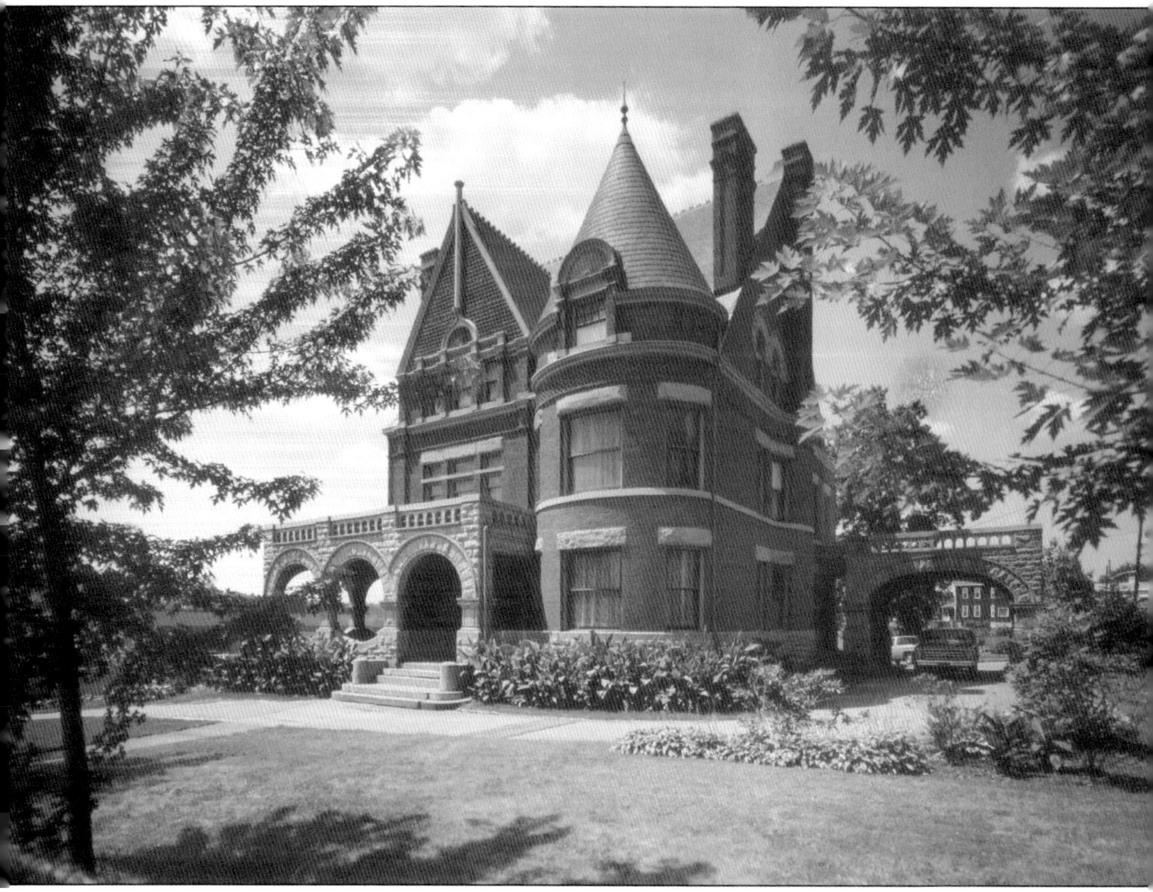

Charles Schwab's home on Jones Avenue in Braddock represented the intersection of two very young yet very successful men of Gilded Age Pittsburgh. Schwab was 27 when he commissioned Frederick J. Osterling, 24, to design his home. The resulting red brick châteauesque home still stands today. Schwab was a former president of U.S. Steel. (Library of Congress.)

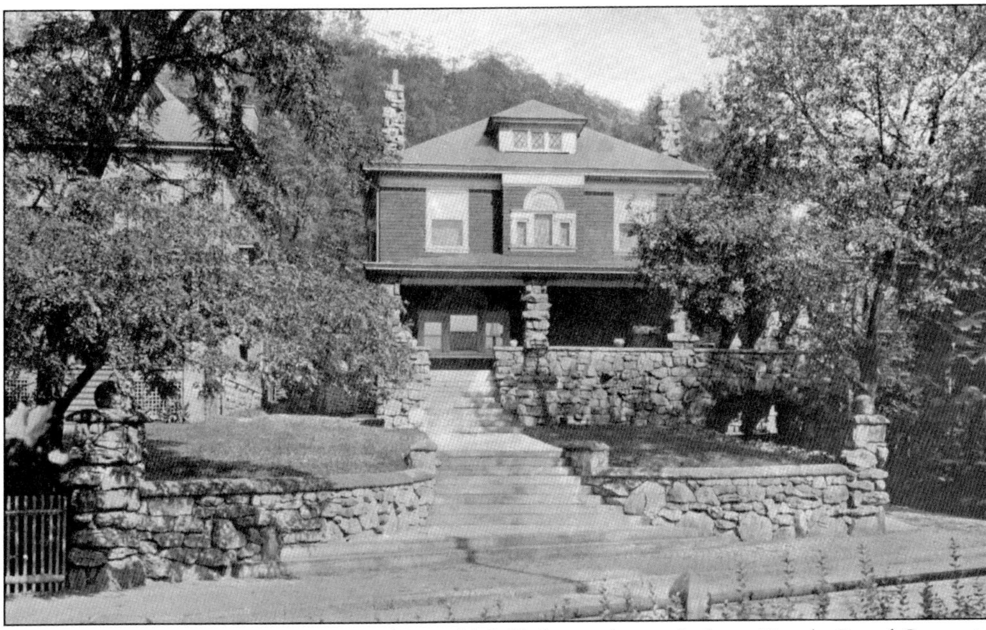

The handsome shingle-style home of David M. Kirk was located along North Canal Street in Sharpsburg. Though the building still stands today, it is now zoned for commercial use and no longer used as a residence. Along with fellow Scotsmen Andrew Carnegie, Thomas Morrison, and Robert Pitcairn, Kirk donated a statue in memory of poet Robert Burns that stands near Phipps Conservatory in Schenley Park. (HHC.)

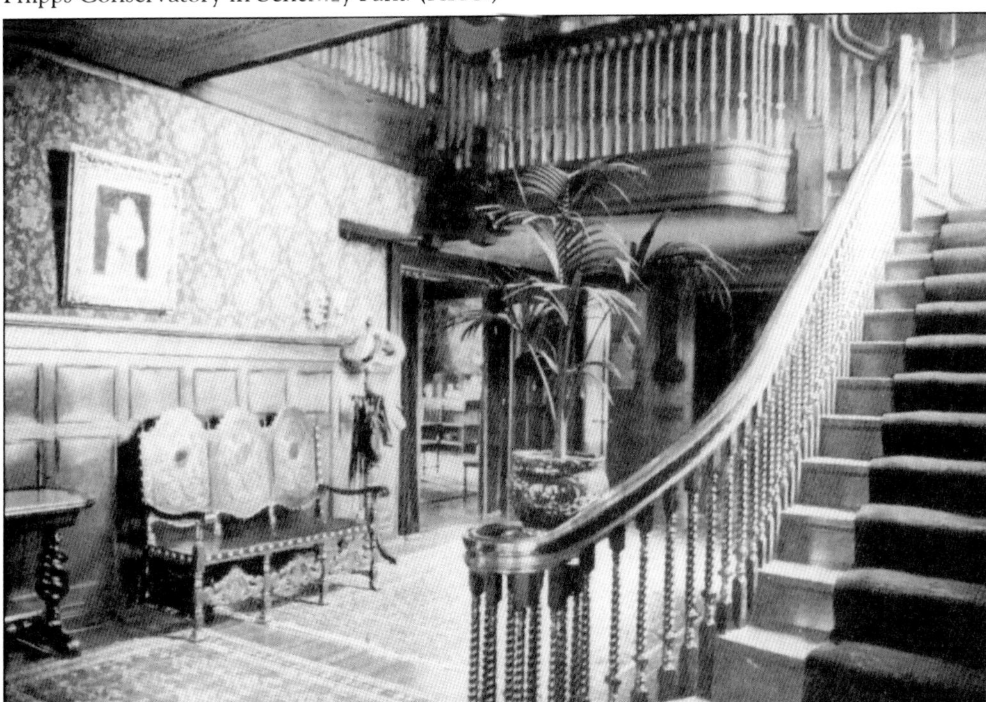

Kirk's home was a showplace, starting with its entrance hall. The wainscoting and staircase appear to be made of oak, and the space is flooded with light thanks to a window on the landing. (HHC.)

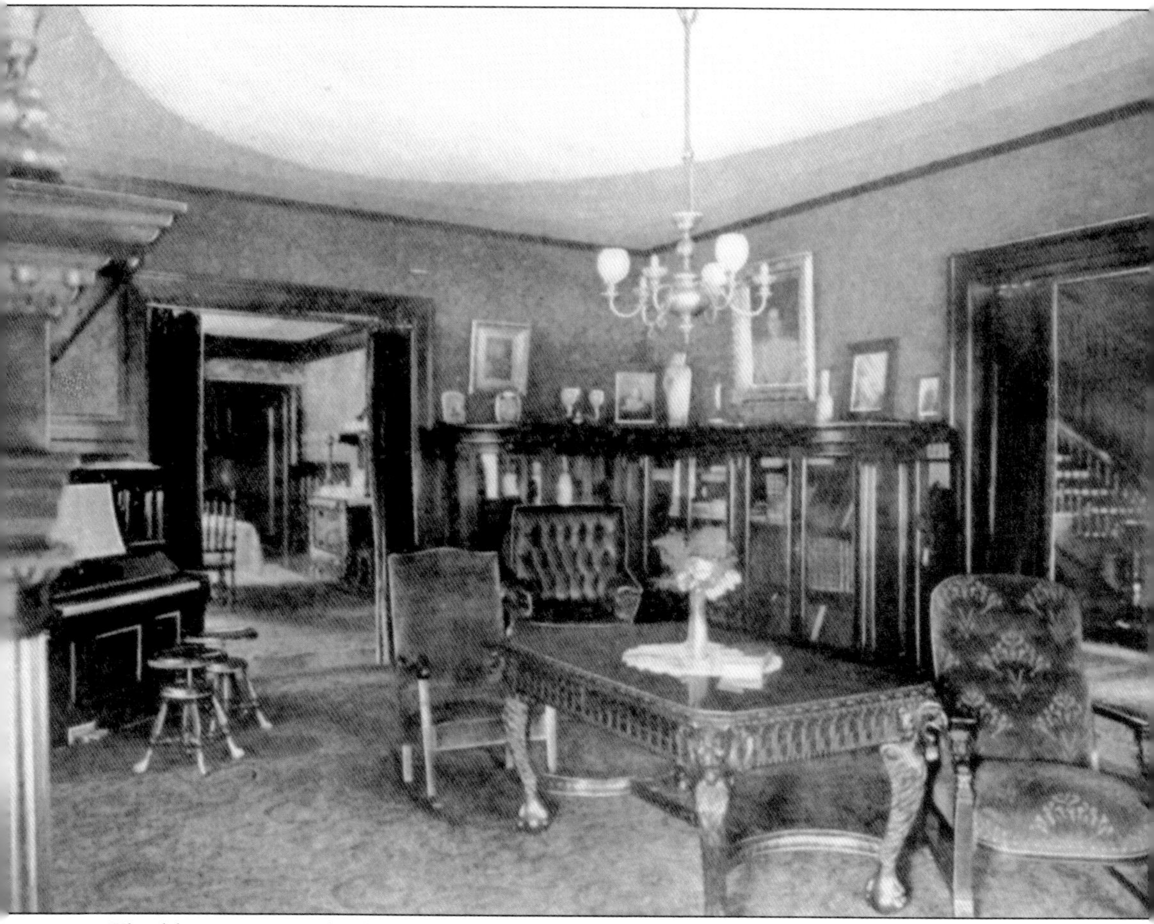

The library, just to the left of the entrance hall's staircase, featured heavily carved furniture displaying a griffon motif. The pair of stools at the piano suggests that one of the Kirk children took music lessons. Velvet portières and dual gas-electric light fixtures further demonstrate the family's wealth. (HHC.)

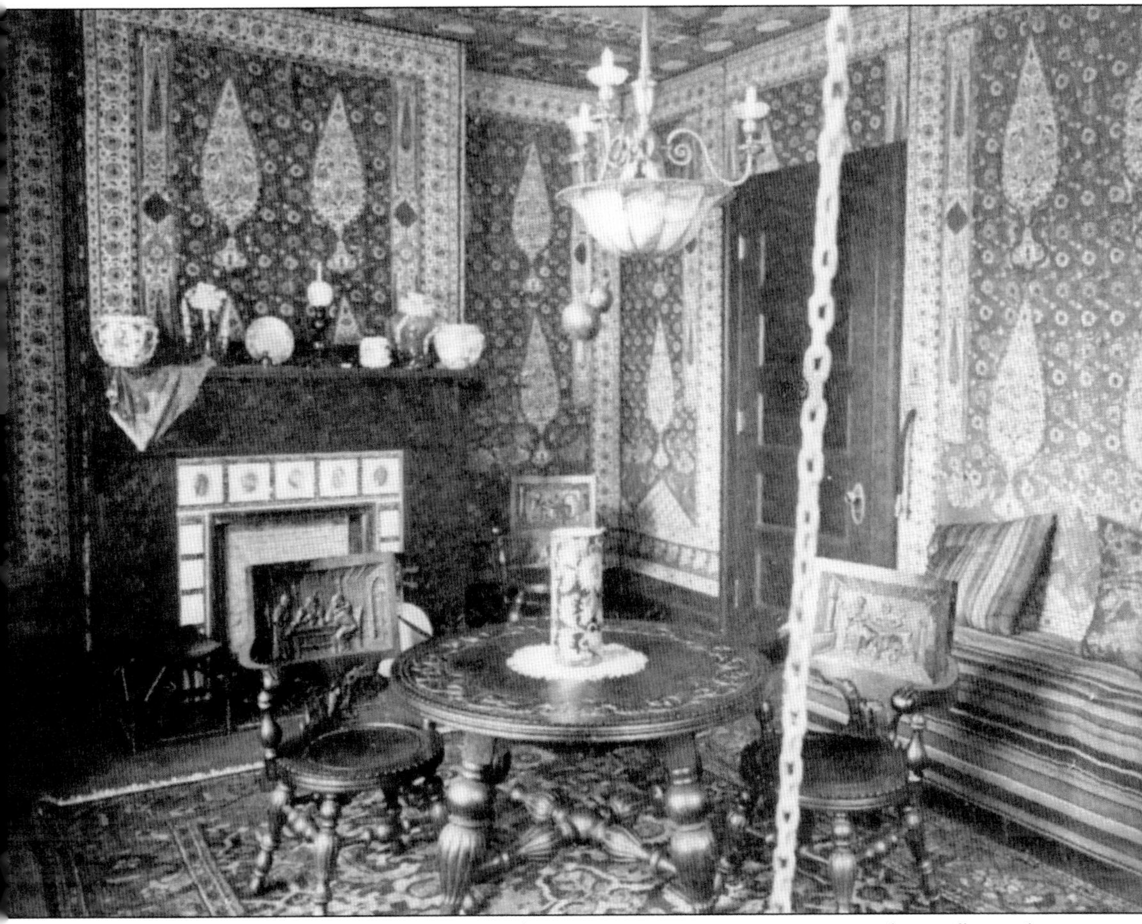

David M. Kirk's home featured an East India Room, an exotic sitting room that reflects the influence of Middle Eastern design that was becoming popular in the late Victorian period. The room may also have been used as a smoking room. (HHC.)

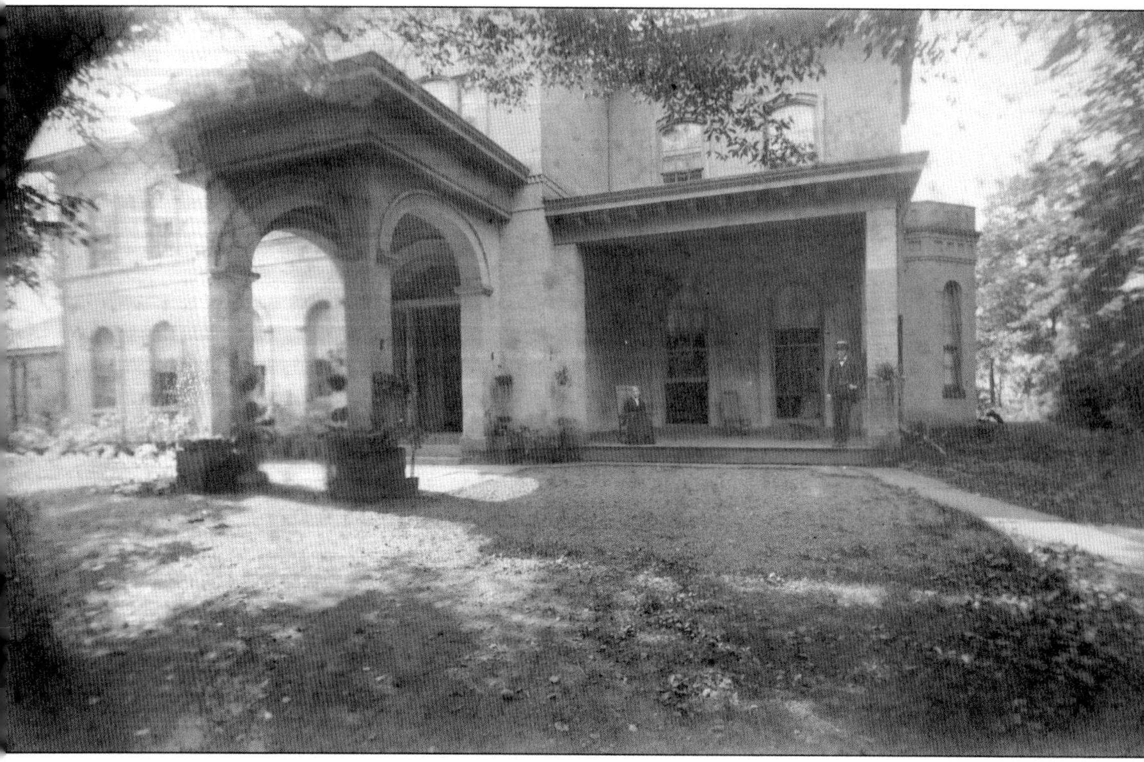

Guyasuta, ancestral home of the O'Hara family, was the residence of William McCullough Darlington and Mary Carson Darlington, who, along with Mary Croghan Schenley, was a granddaughter of James O'Hara. The estate sat on a bluff overlooking present-day Sharpsburg and Aspinwall. Today, the land is part of O'Hara Township, named for the land's original owner. The estate took its name from Seneca Indian chief Guyasuta, who was O'Hara's friend from his days as a military officer. (Darlington Collection, Special Collections Department, University of Pittsburgh.)

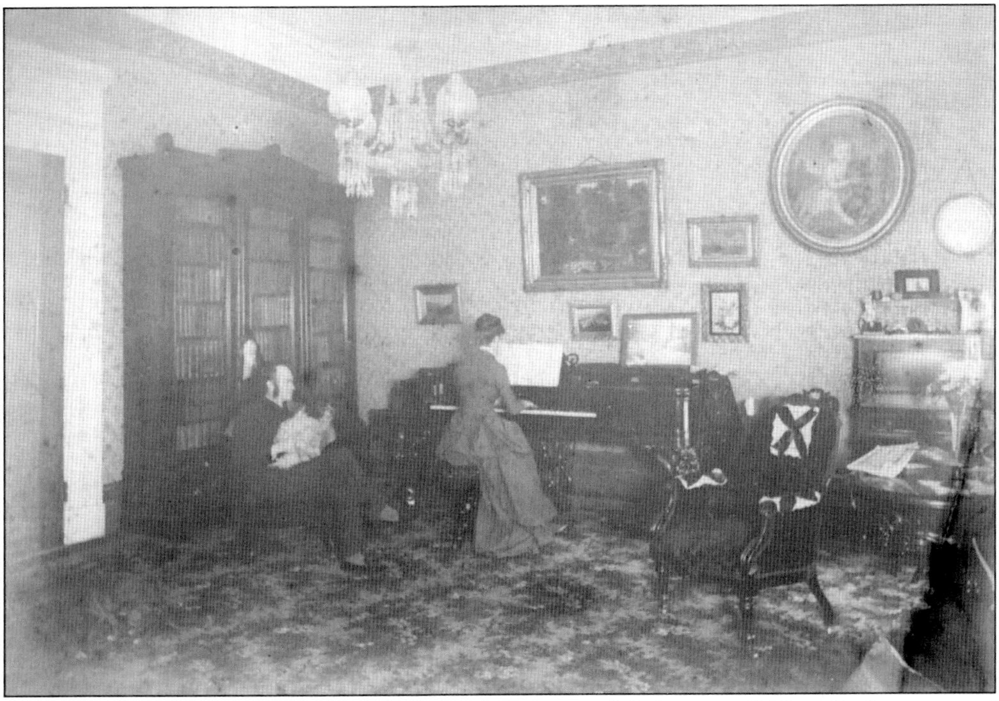

Here in the parlor, Mary Carson Darlington plays piano while her son, O'Hara Darlington, and a family dog serve as an audience. (Darlington Collection, Special Collections Department, University of Pittsburgh.)

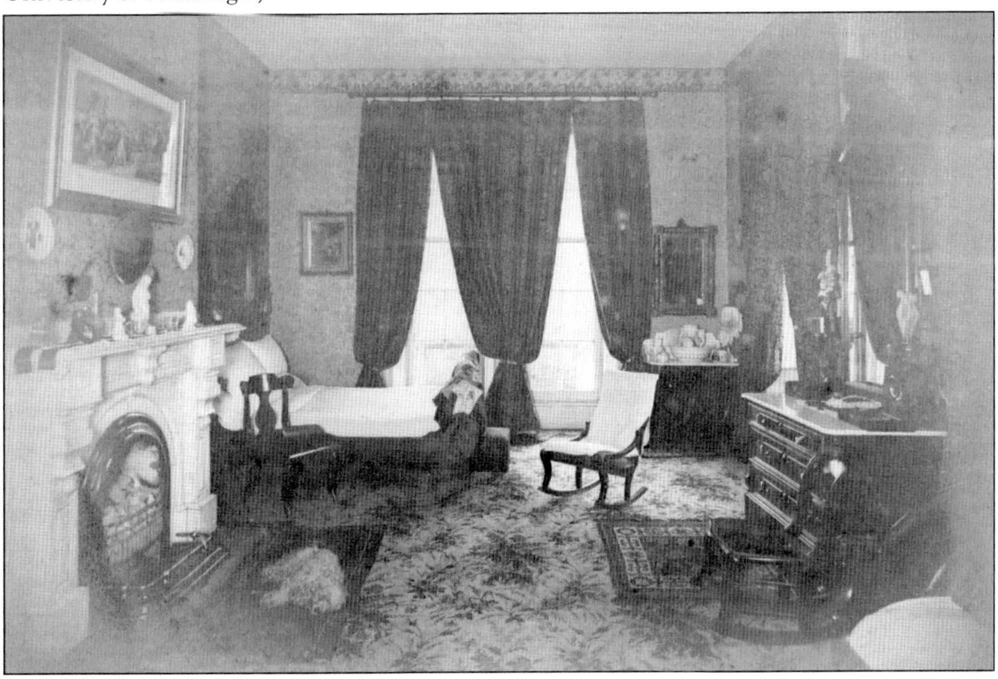

This cozy bedroom scene at Guyasuta features Panza, one of the family's dogs, enjoying the warmth of the hearth. (Darlington Collection, Special Collections Department, University of Pittsburgh.)

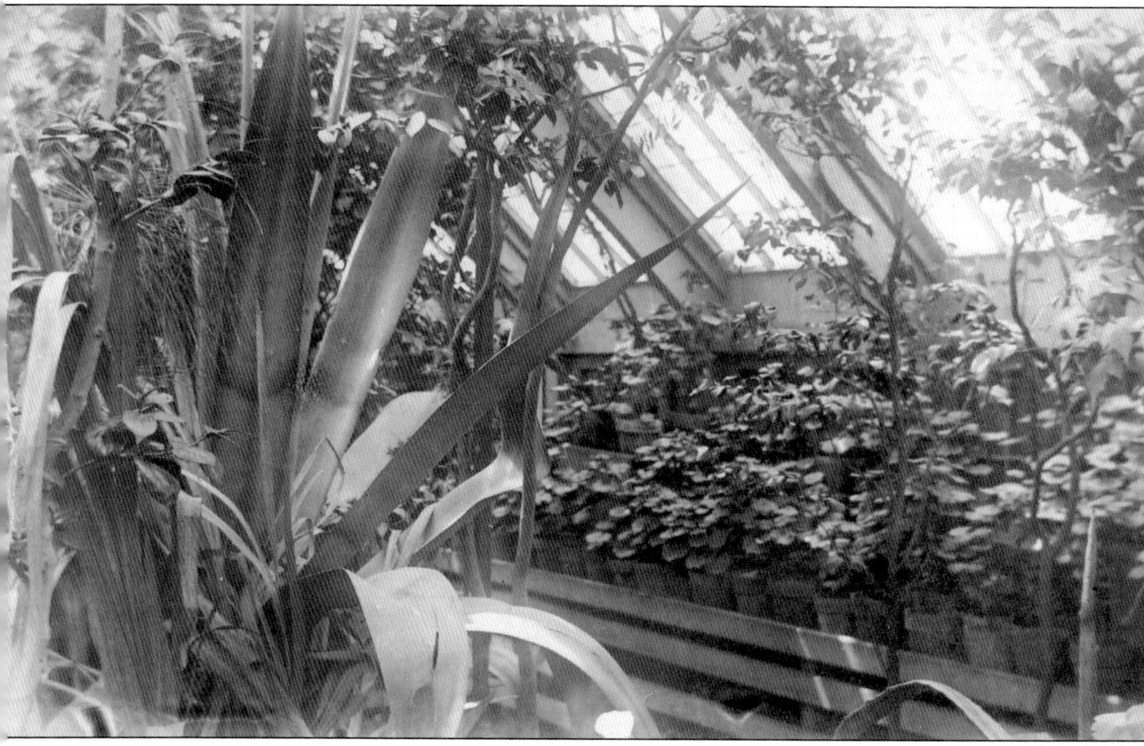

Glasshouses were popular features of many Victorian-era estates. Conservatories were used to house collections of plants, while greenhouses served to produce plants that were used by the owners in cooking or floral arranging. Guyasuta appears to have had a working greenhouse. (Darlington Collection, Special Collections Department, University of Pittsburgh.)

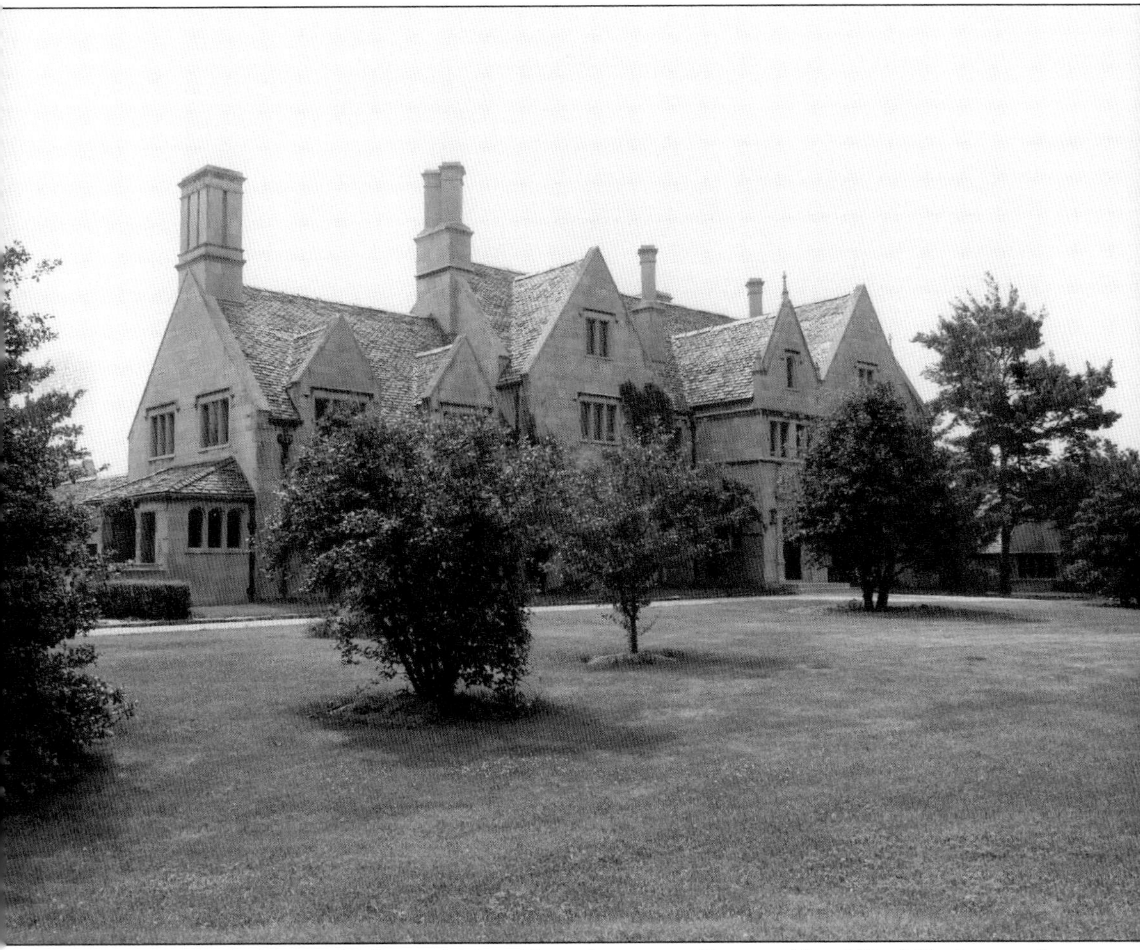

Hartwood was the home of John and Mary Flinn Lawrence. Designed by Alfred Hopkins and built in 1929, the mansion is styled after a manor house the couple had seen while vacationing in Britain. Mary was the daughter of local politician and English immigrant William Flinn. Today, the home, which is open for tours, and its surrounding grounds are known as Hartwood Acres Park, part of the Allegheny County parks system. (HHC.)

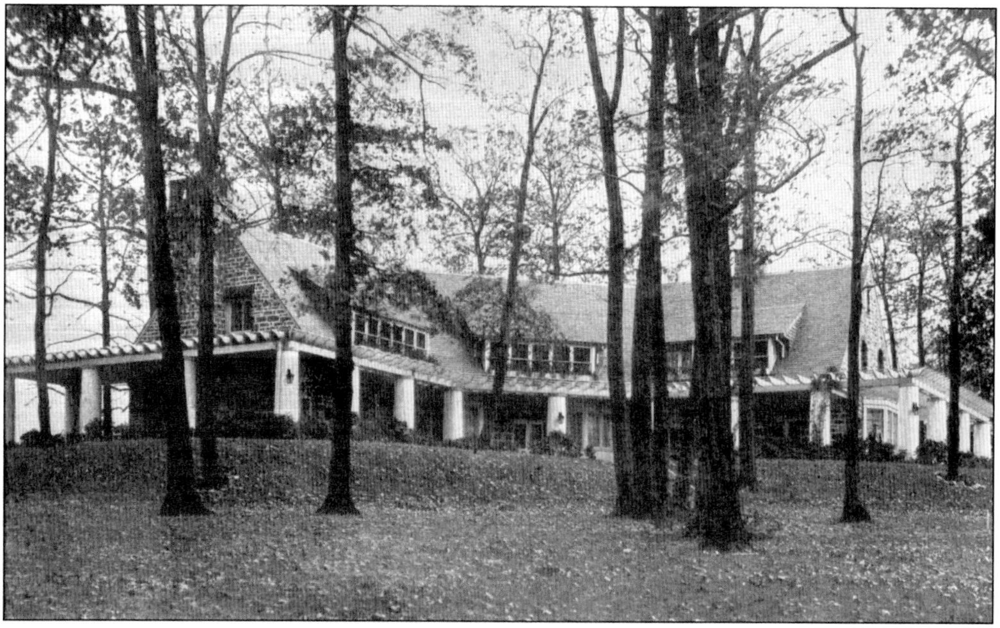

George Calvert was a lawyer and senior partner at Calvert, Thompson & Wilson law firm. Born in Etna, he commissioned Janssen & Abbott to build this home in Hampton Township around 1912. Calvert was known as one of the best-informed authorities on corporation law in the Pittsburgh area. (CMU.)

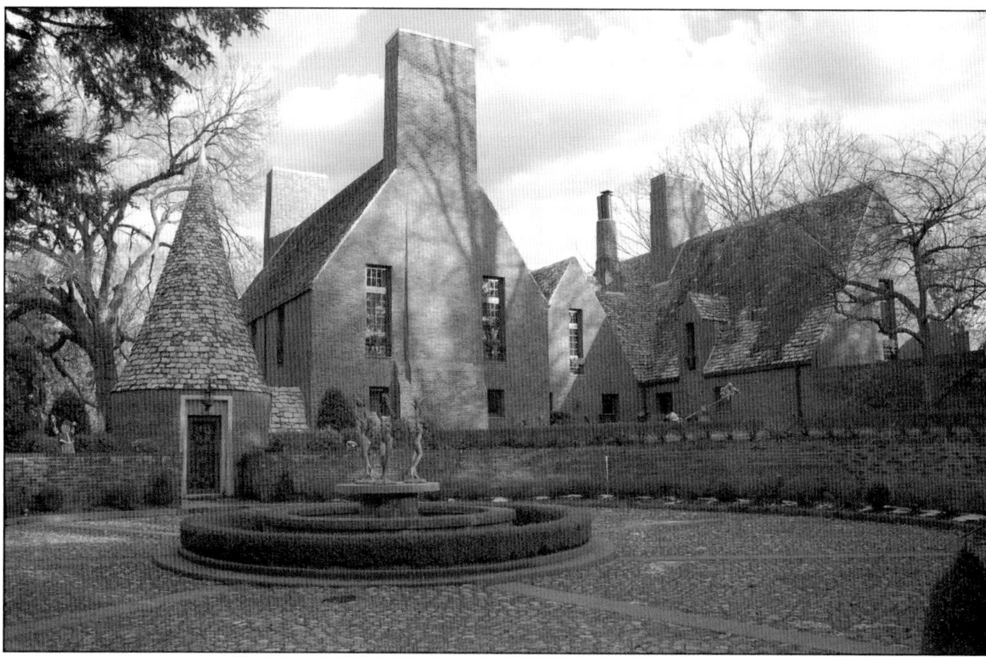

La Tourelle in Fox Chapel was the home of Edgar J. Kaufmann, his wife, Liliane, and their son, Edgar Jr. Designed in 1925 by Janssen & Cocken, the house is said to have been influenced by Benno Janssen's 1904 trip to Carcasonne, France. While La Tourelle is privately owned, the Kaufmann family's summer home, Fallingwater, designed by Frank Lloyd Wright in 1935, is open to the public.

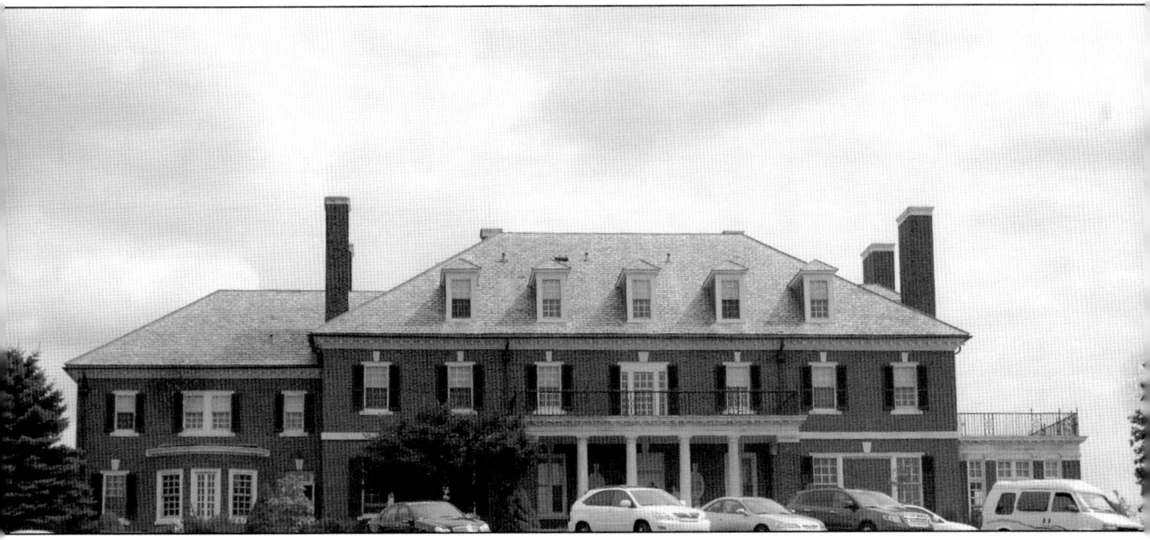

Daniel Burnside Zimmerman commissioned Horace Trumbauer to design this Georgian Revival mansion in Somerset County in 1915. Zimmerman, a cattle baron whose later interests turned to coal, was only able to enjoy the home for about 10 years following its completion before his death in 1928. In the 1990s, the area around the home was developed into a shopping center known as Georgian Place. Today, the house is an inn and restaurant open to the public.

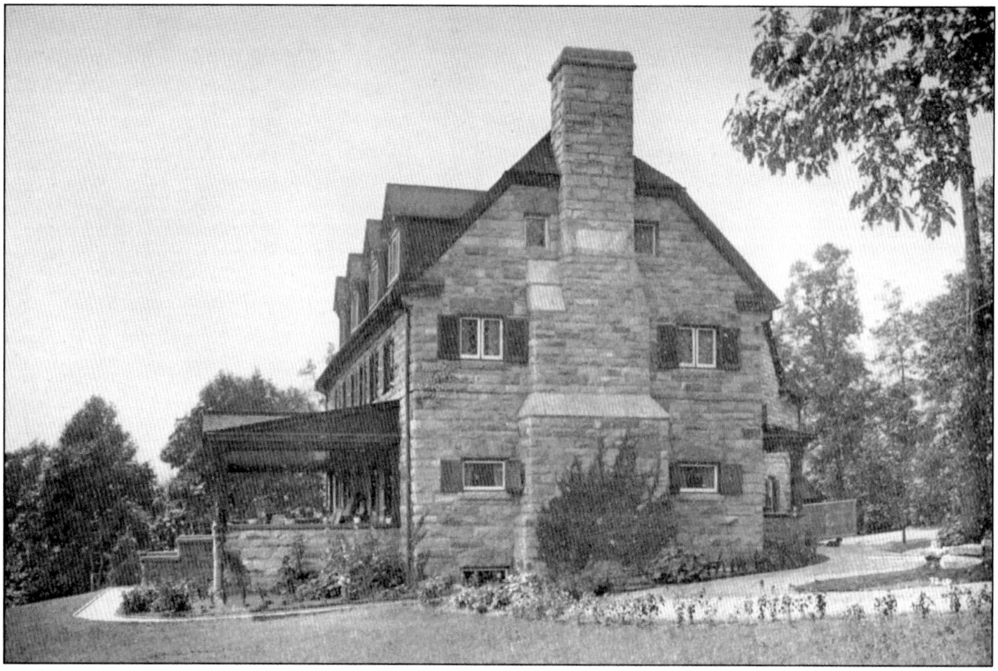

Melrose Farm was the Greensburg home of H.C. (Henry Clay) Bughman. Bughman sat on the board of directors of the Second National Bank and National Union Fire Insurance Company.

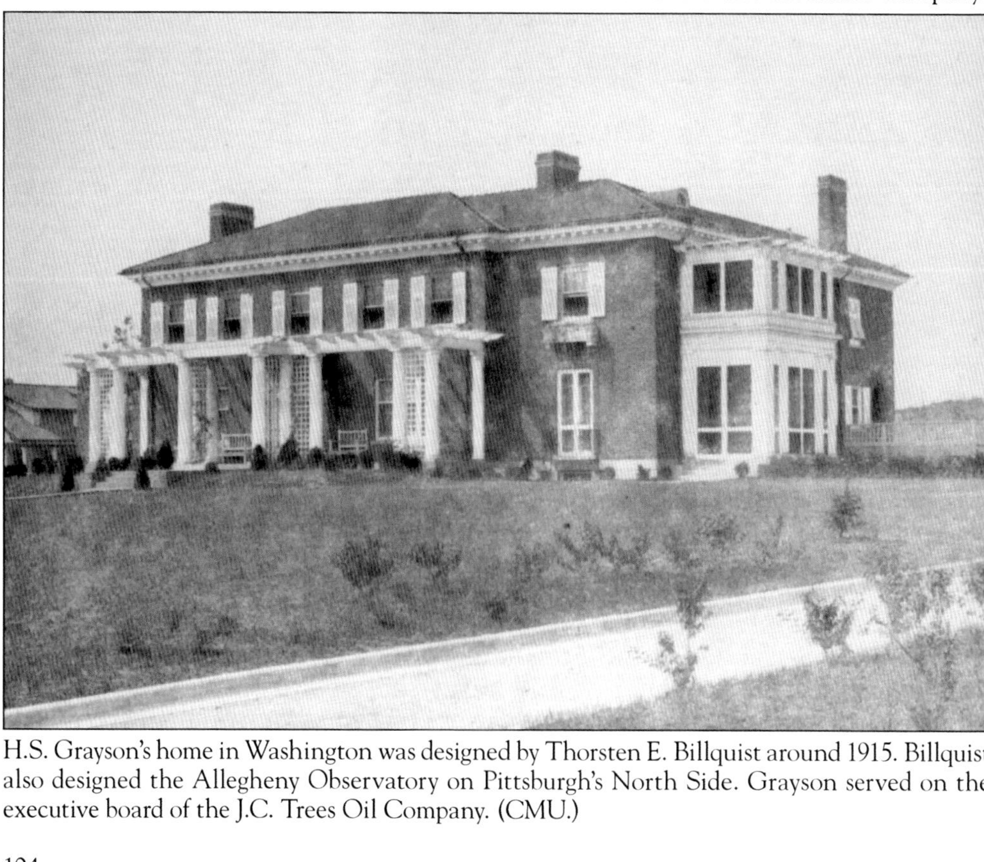

H.S. Grayson's home in Washington was designed by Thorsten E. Billquist around 1915. Billquist also designed the Allegheny Observatory on Pittsburgh's North Side. Grayson served on the executive board of the J.C. Trees Oil Company. (CMU.)

Four

Sewickley

The Sewickley Valley was a popular location for wealthy Pittsburghers to build country retreats. Escaping the bustle and pollution of the city limits of Pittsburgh and Allegheny City had long been pursued, but far-flung Central Pennsylvania areas such as Cresson Springs and South Fork obviously posed travel challenges. Sewickley offered the advantage of being a relatively brief rail trip away from the Golden Triangle.

Many of the area's "country estates" were initially only summer homes, but with improvements in automobile travel at the turn of the 20th century, many of these dwellings were put into use year-round. Sewickley was originally a farming community, but the homes built there from the 1890s to 1930s lent the area an upscale character that it retains to this day, though many of the grand homes are now gone.

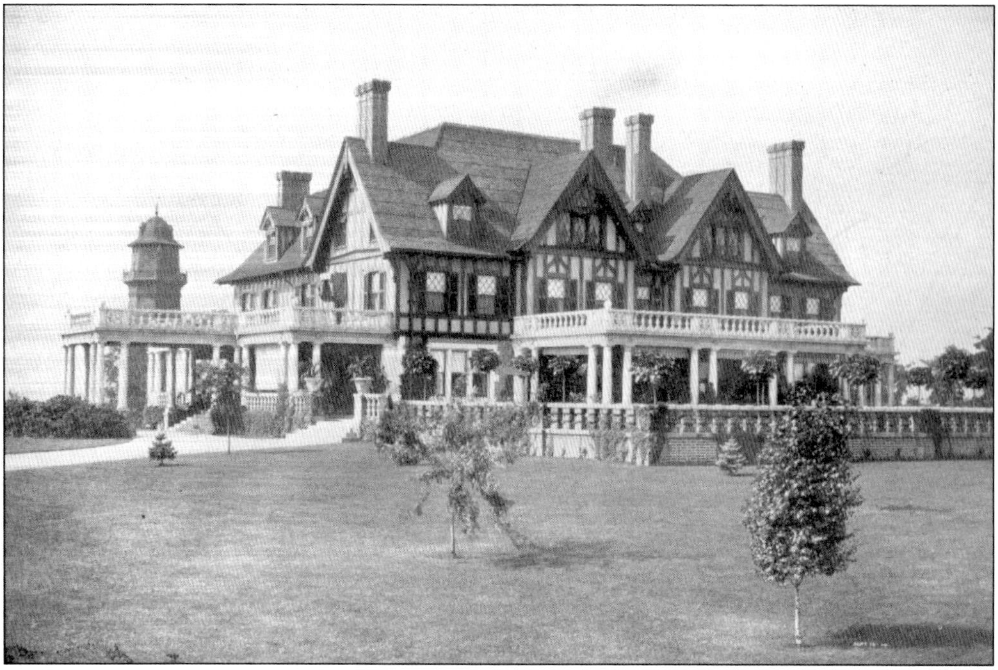

Franklin Farm was the home of B.F. (Benjamin Franklin) Jones Sr. Designed in 1899 by Rutan & Russell, the property featured a greenhouse and water tower. Jones was a founder of the Jones & Laughlin Steel Company. Franklin Farm was demolished in the 1960s. (HHC.)

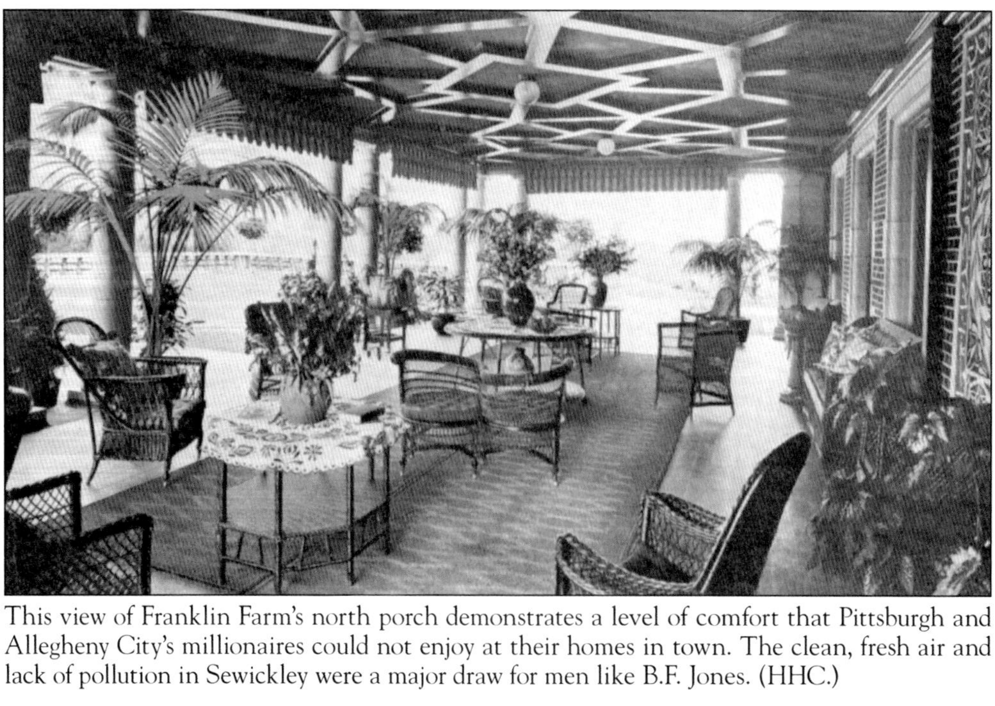

This view of Franklin Farm's north porch demonstrates a level of comfort that Pittsburgh and Allegheny City's millionaires could not enjoy at their homes in town. The clean, fresh air and lack of pollution in Sewickley were a major draw for men like B.F. Jones. (HHC.)

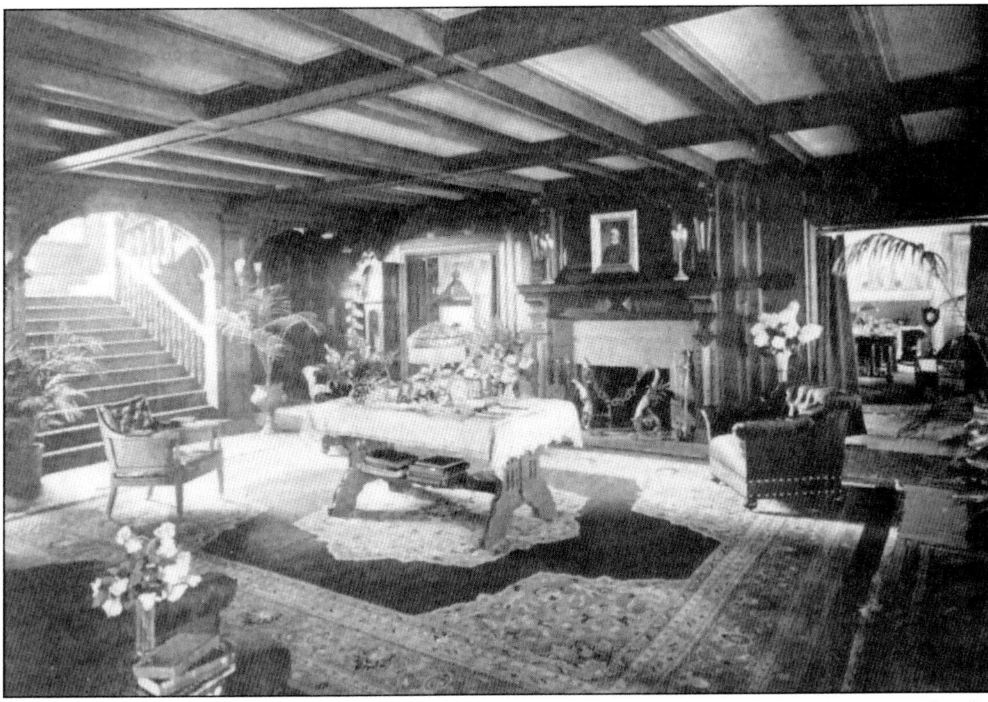

Franklin Farm's Elizabethan Revival exterior was carried into the home's interior, as seen by the half-timbered ceilings in the entrance hall (above) and billiard room (below). Massive stone and wood fireplaces and comfortable furniture demonstrate the more laid-back nature of country living. (HHC.)

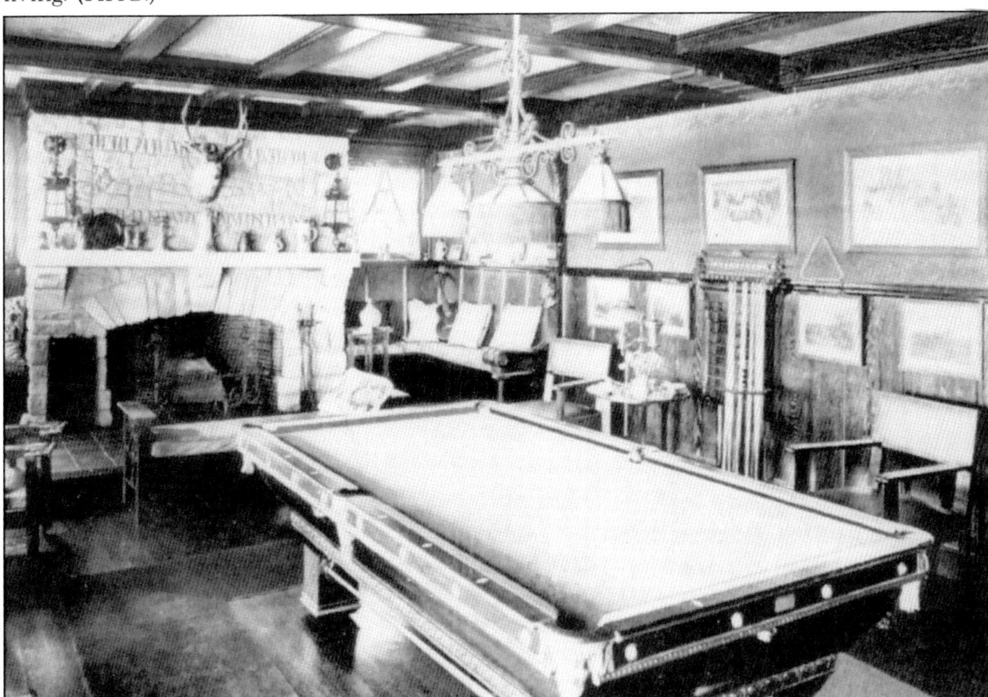

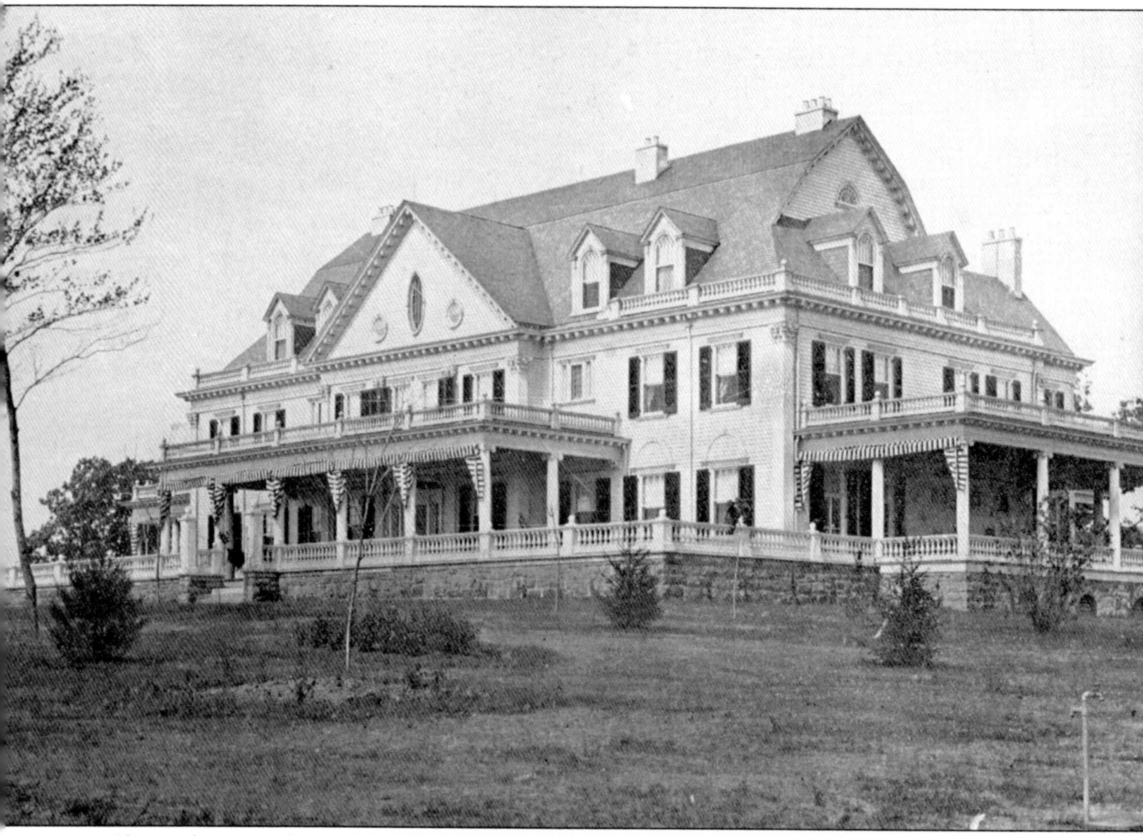

The architectural firm Vrydaugh & Wolfe built Woodmont for Mr. and Mrs. Charles Cook Scaife in 1902. Scaife's fortune was made in the family business, William B. Scaife & Sons Co., manufacturers of tanks and steel buildings.

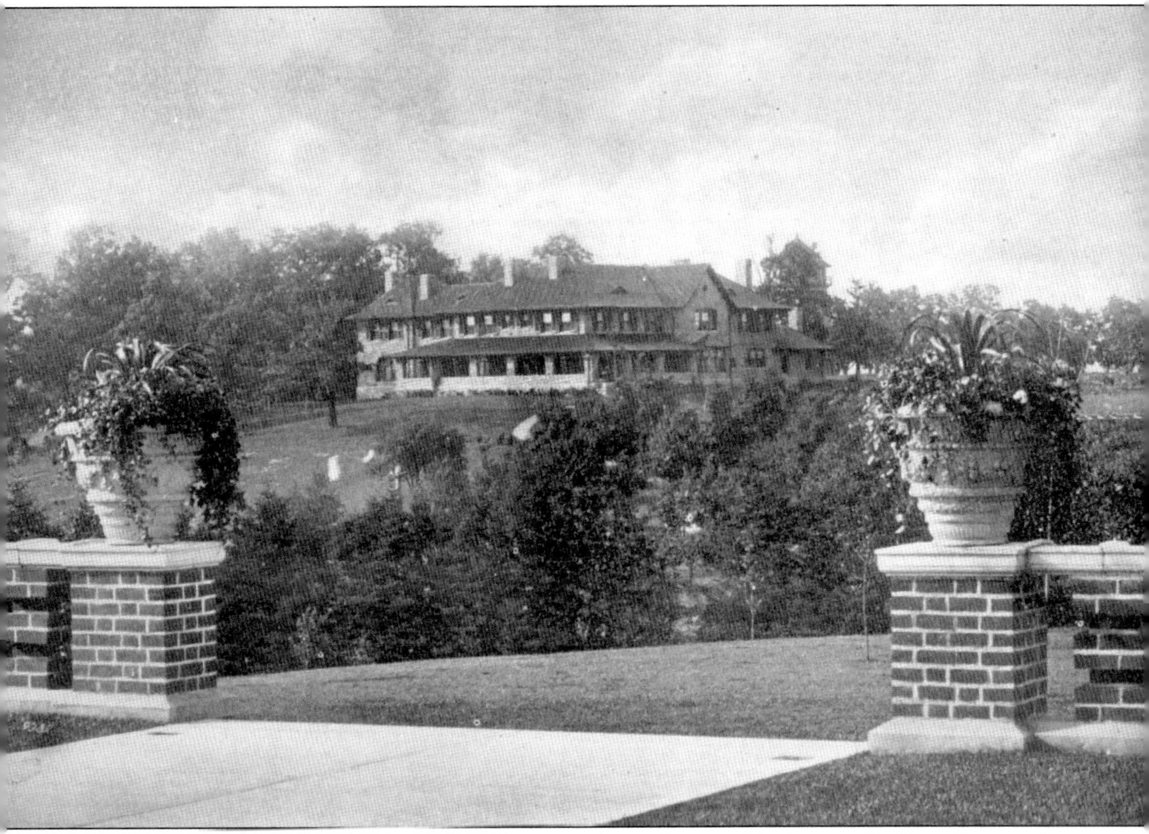

Skipton was the home of Ralph Holden Binns and was designed by Rutan & Russell around 1900. The Harry Darlington Jr. family bought the home in 1919 and renamed it Highlawn. The home was eventually demolished.

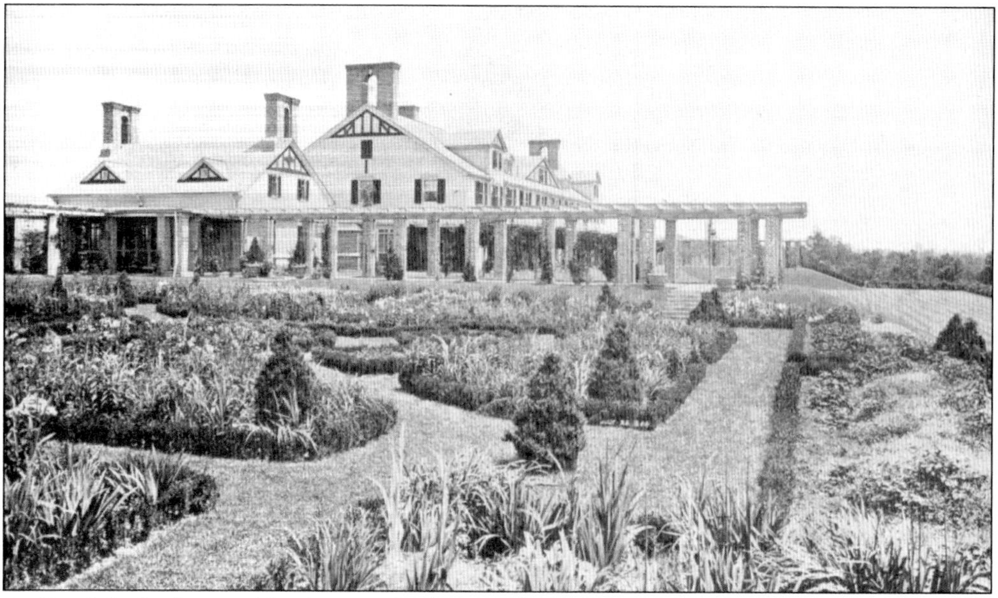

As You Like It, designed by George Orth around 1907, was the home of Elizabeth Dohrman Thaw, wife of William Thaw Jr. Mrs. Thaw was the daughter-in-law of William Thaw Sr. and his first wife, Eliza Burd Blair, and also a step-sister-in-law to the notorious Harry K. Thaw. Elizabeth Dohrman Thaw ordered her home to be demolished in 1937 and had the land turned into a subdivision known as Thawmont. (CMU.)

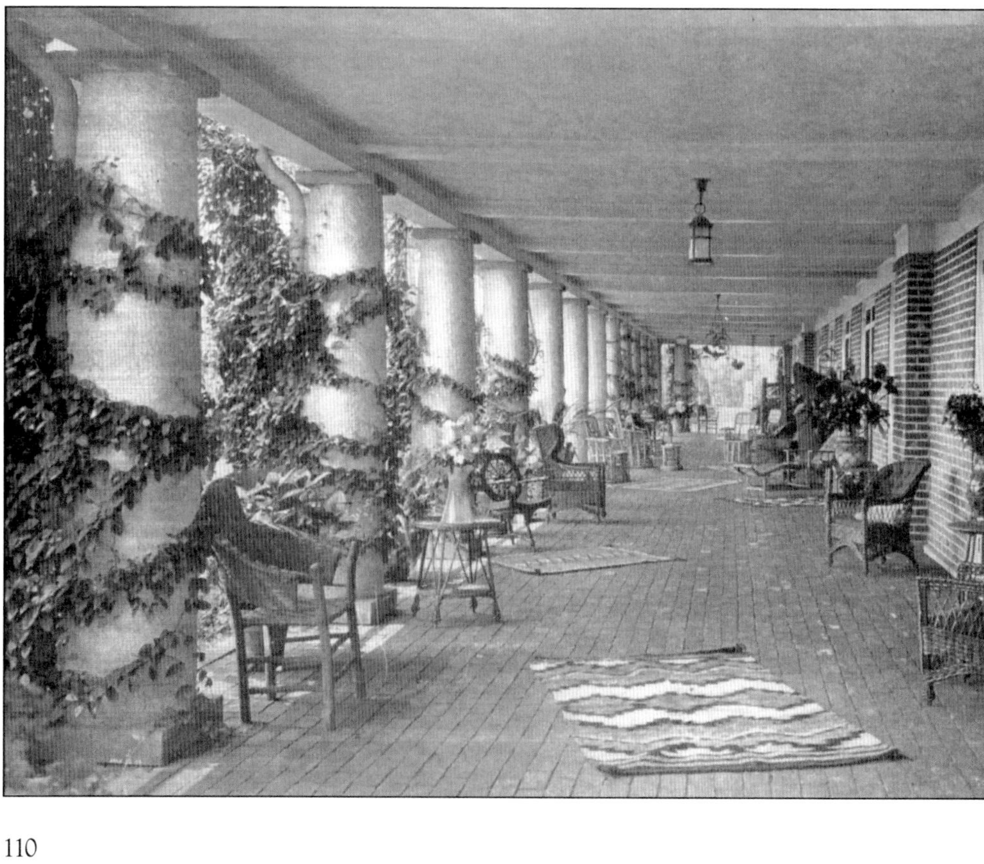

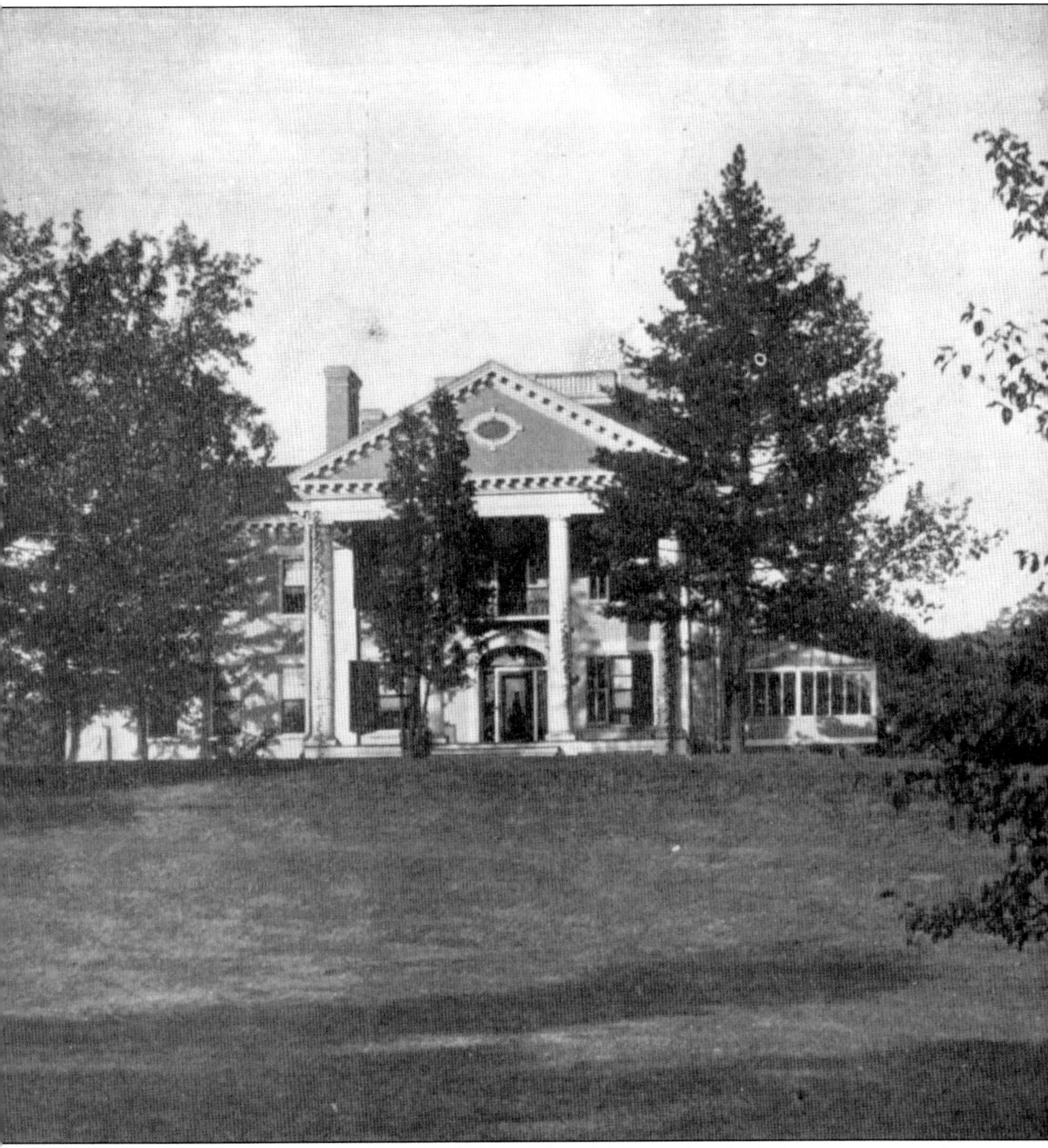

Originally built in 1864 by a Dr. Miller, this Neoclassical home first had the appearance of a Gothic Revival Victorian structure. The man responsible for the dramatic change in the façade was Henry Davis, who bought the home in 1897. Davis hired Rutan & Russell to add a two-story portico, porte cochère, and glass-covered solarium.

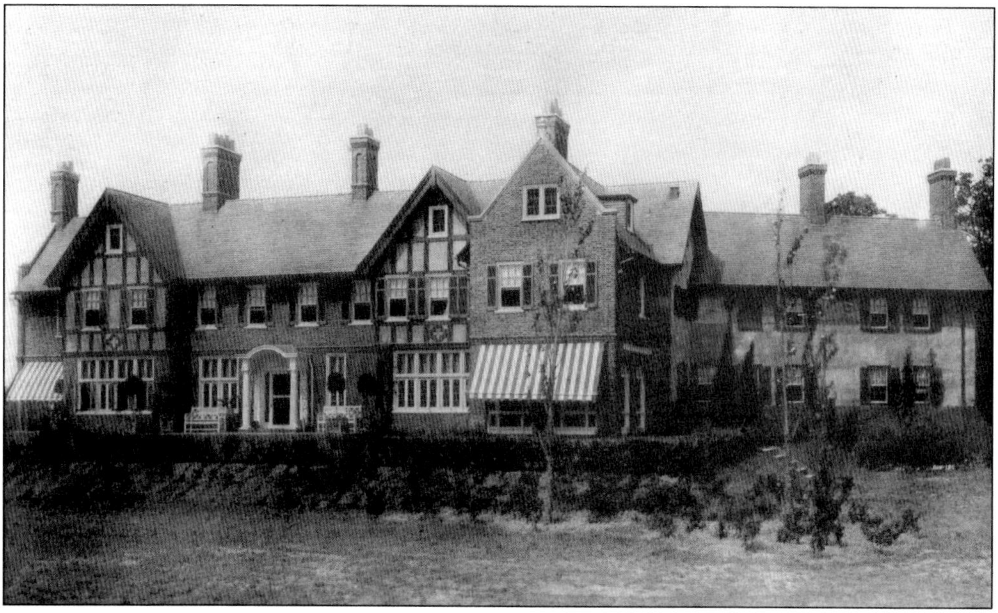

Goodwood was the Elizabethan Revival home of J.F. Byers, eldest son of A.M. Byers of Allegheny City. Though the home, designed by MacClure & Spahr, was built around 1912, Byers did not use it as a permanent residence until 1932, after the death of his brother Evan. Goodwood is seen here from the front (above) and back (below). (CMU.)

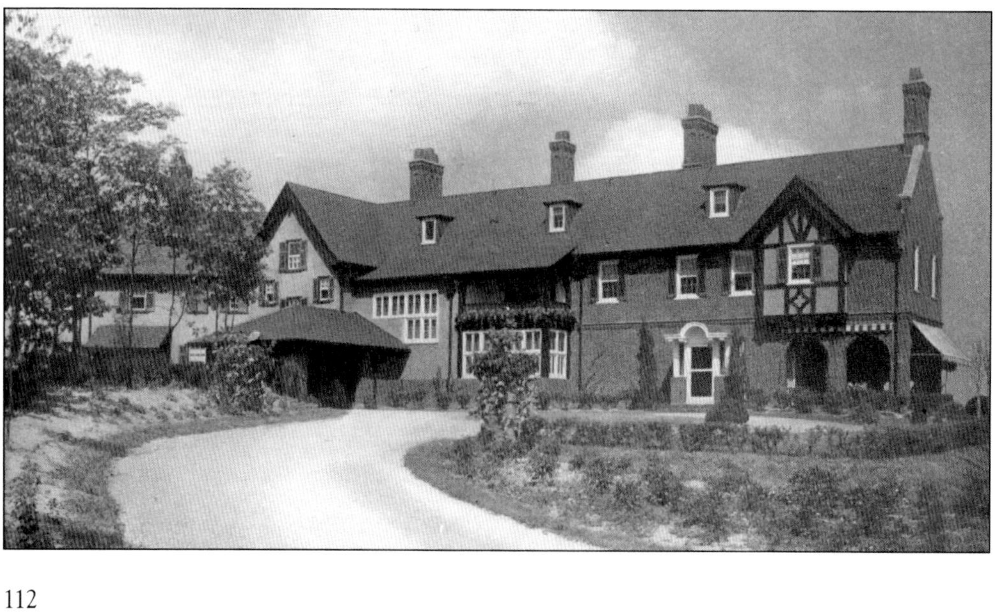

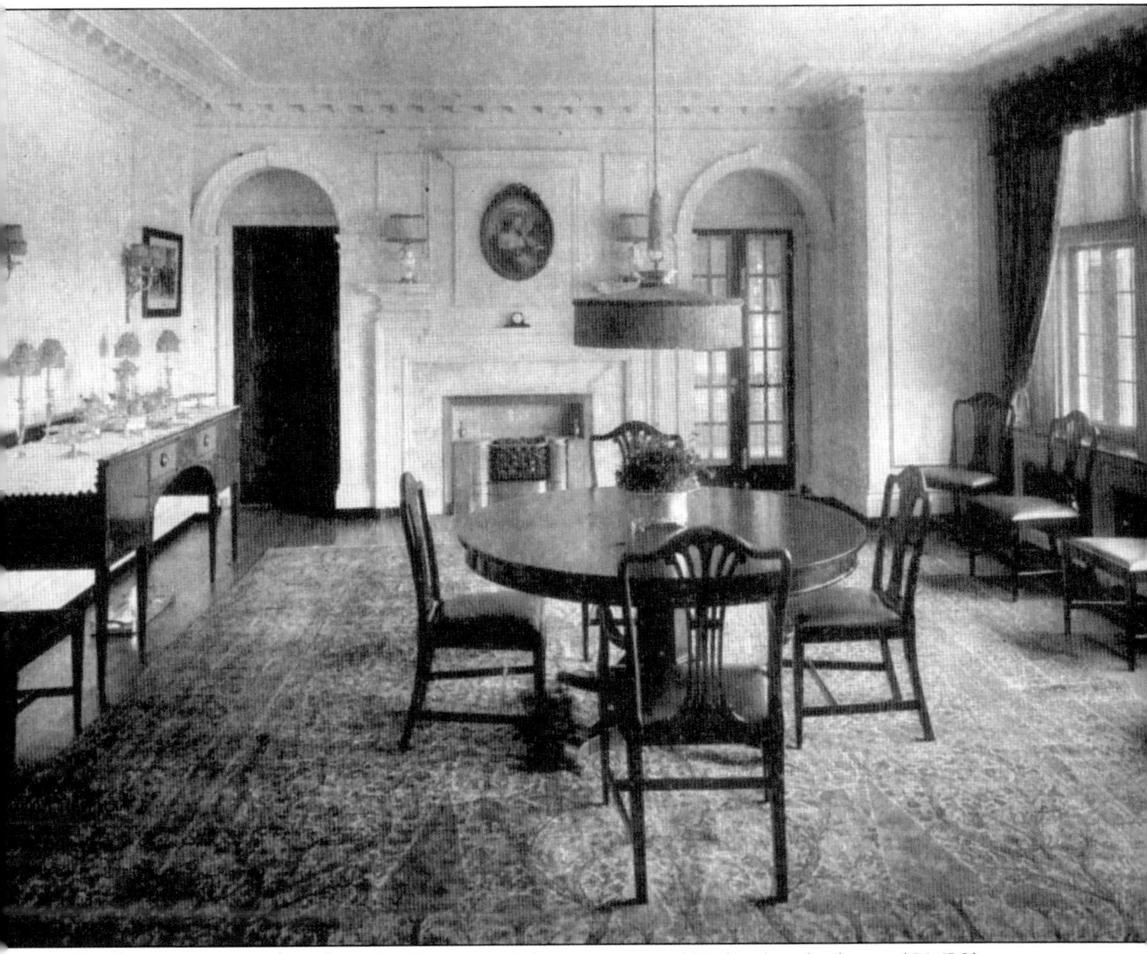

The dining room at Goodwood reflects a bright yet reserved Federal-style decor. (CMU.)

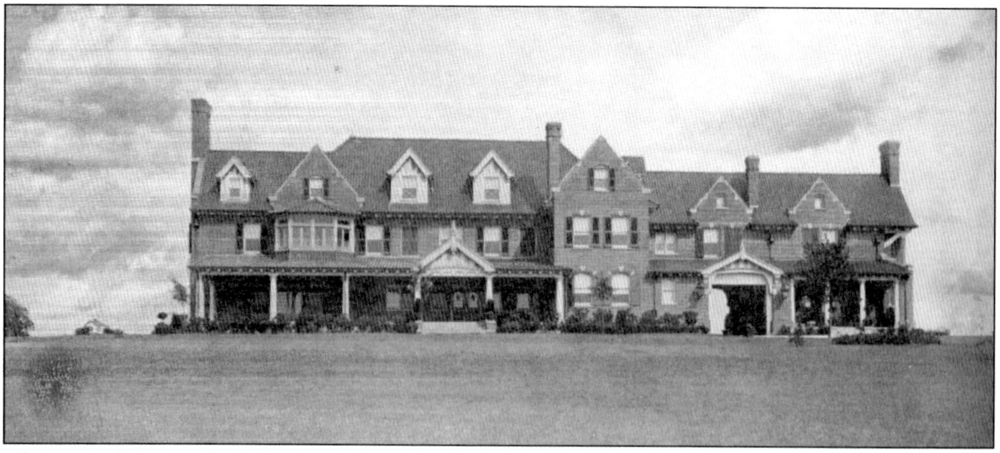

This sprawling Jacobethan Revival mansion by Rutan & Russell, dubbed Bellamona, was the home of Richard Roberts Quay and his mother. The mansion was originally commissioned by Richard's father, Matthew S. Quay, a Civil War veteran and politician, but he died before its completion in 1904. The home was demolished in 1959.

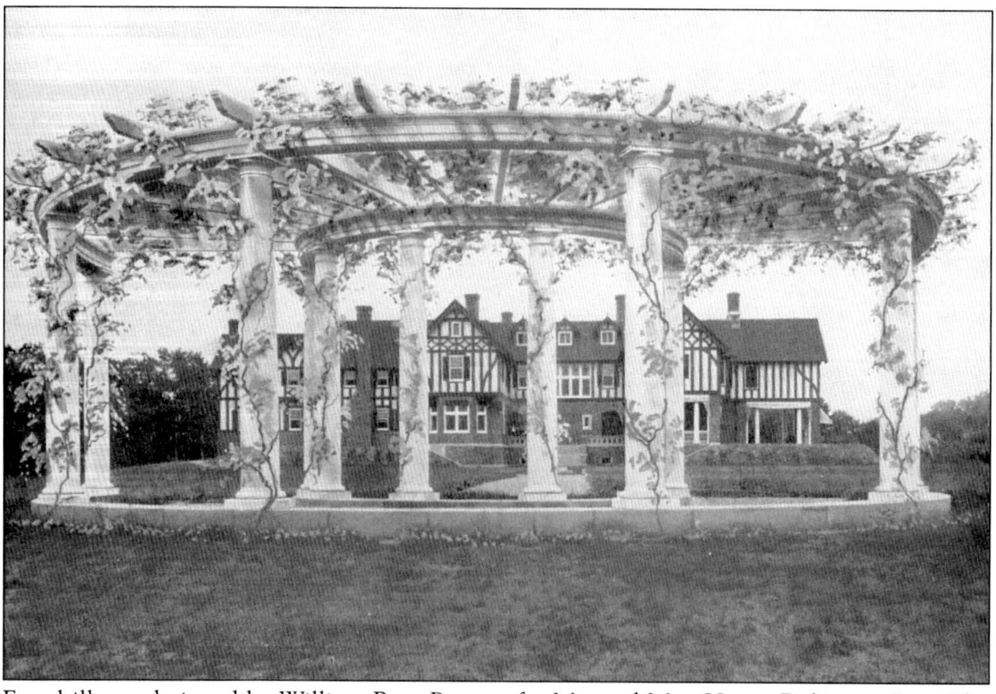

Farmhill was designed by William Ross Proctor for Mr. and Mrs. Henry Robinson Rea. The spectacularly landscaped grounds included a 60-foot waterfall and a lily pond in addition to the Neoclassical pergola seen here.

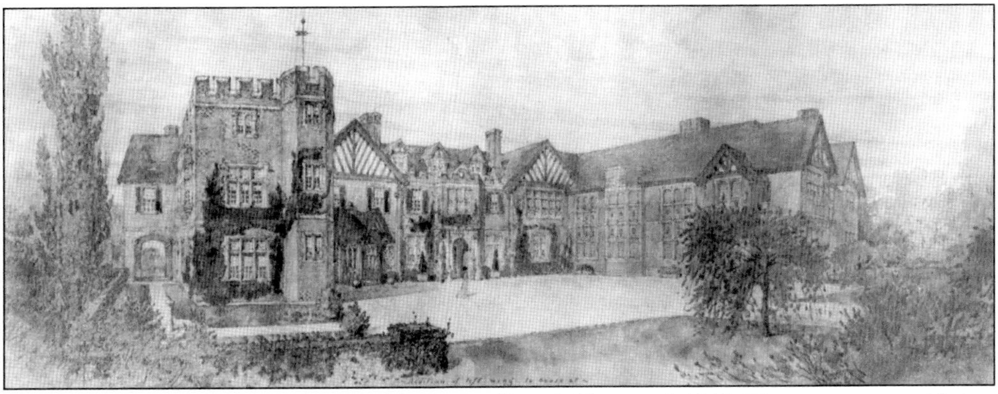

MacClure & Spahr designed new additions to Farmhill around 1913. The west wing addition featured a large stone crenellated tower, turning the Elizabethan Revival home into a sort of composite Jacobethan building. (CMU.)

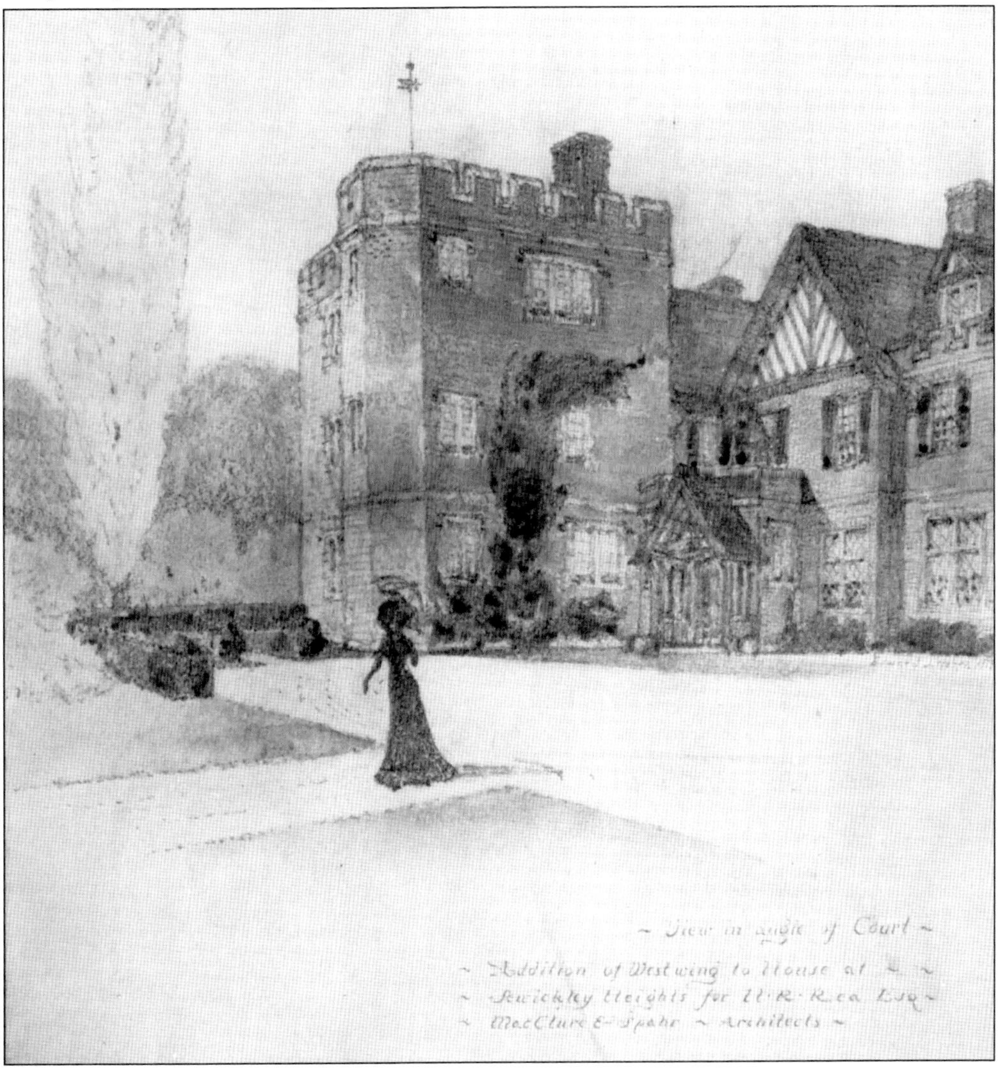

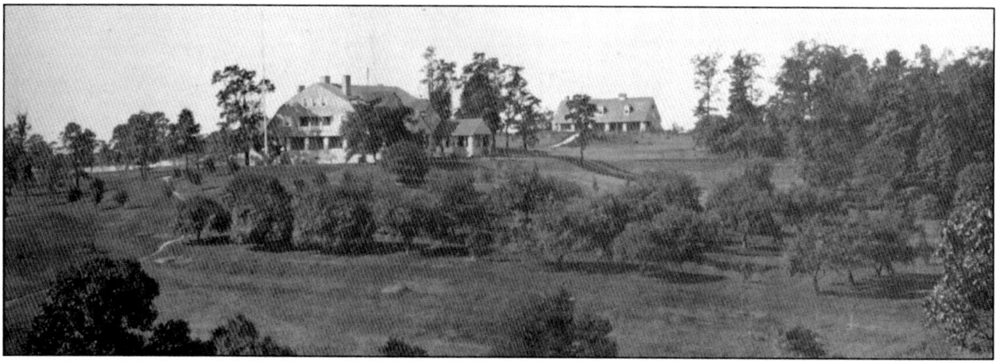

In 1898, William Penn Snyder commissioned George Orth to design a summer home as an escape from bustling Allegheny City. In addition to his interests in the coke industry, Snyder was a partner in Oliver & Snyder Steel Company and was a close friend of Henry W. Oliver. Wilpen Hall serves as home to some of the family's descendants today. (CMU.)

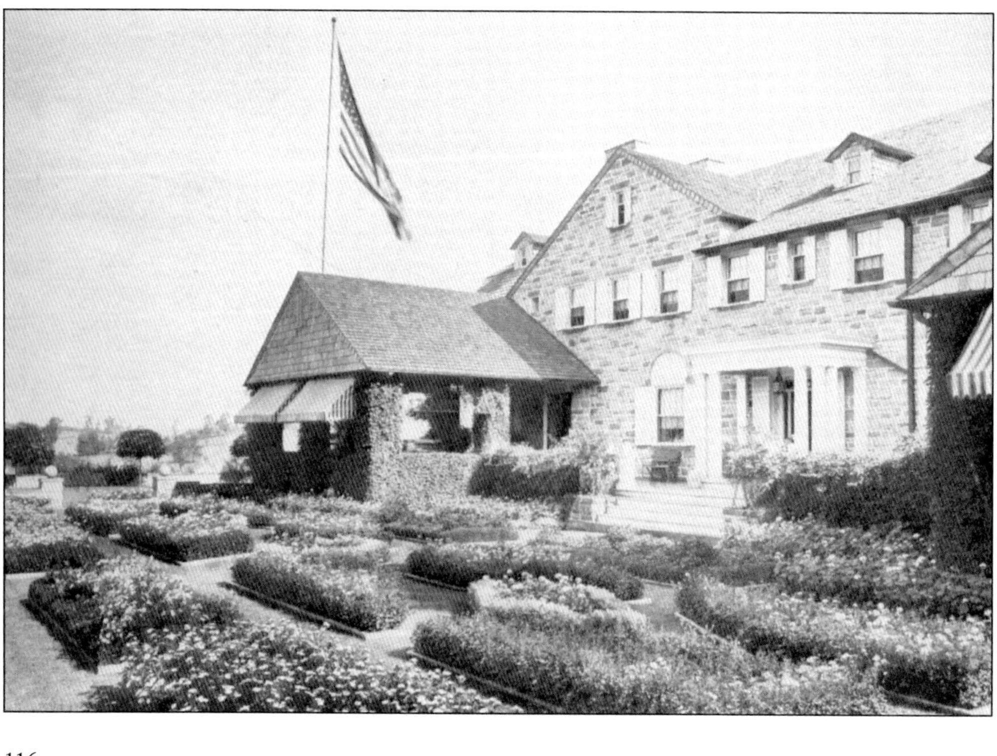

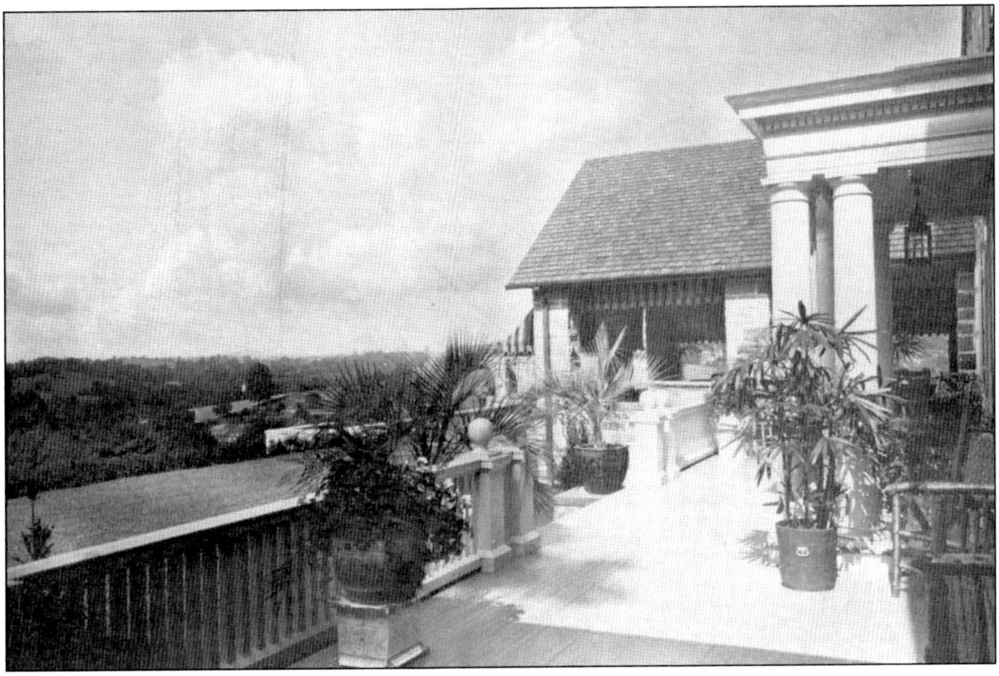

Like all of the Sewickley country estates, Wilpen Hall was comfortably furnished both inside and out. A spacious porch (above) offered beautiful views and fresh air. Around 1912, MacClure & Spahr designed some interior spaces for the family, including the mantel at right. (CMU.)

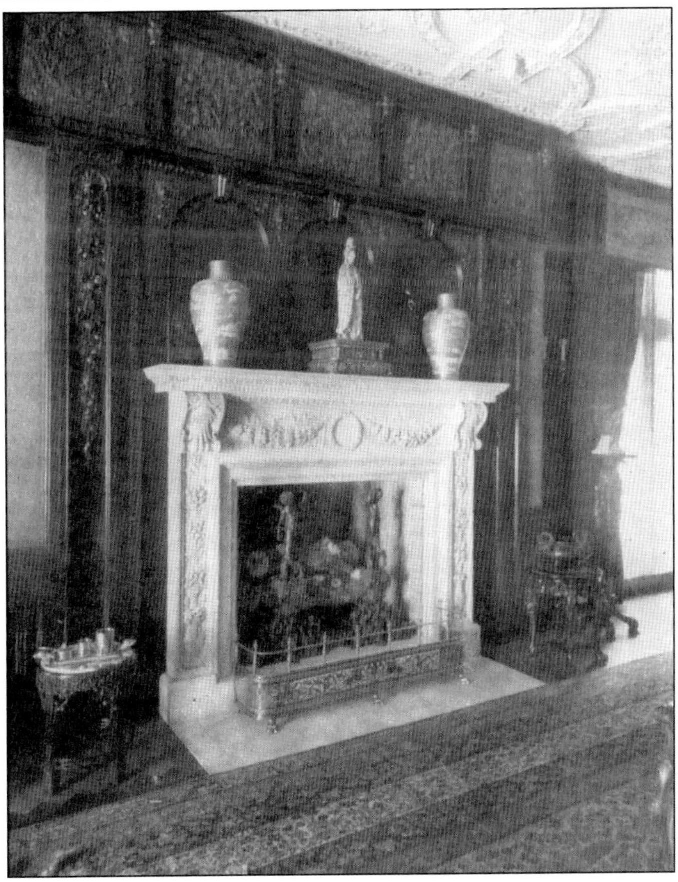

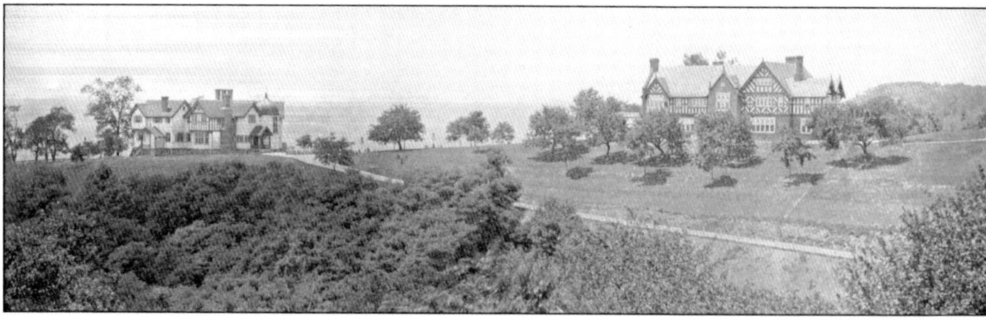

This image shows two of the Singer family's Sewickley mansions. George Harton Singer's home (left) was designed by his brother-in-law, William Ross Proctor, in 1902. The home on the right belonged to George's brother, William H. Singer Jr. Their father, William H. Singer Sr., was an inventor and held interests in Carnegie Steel.

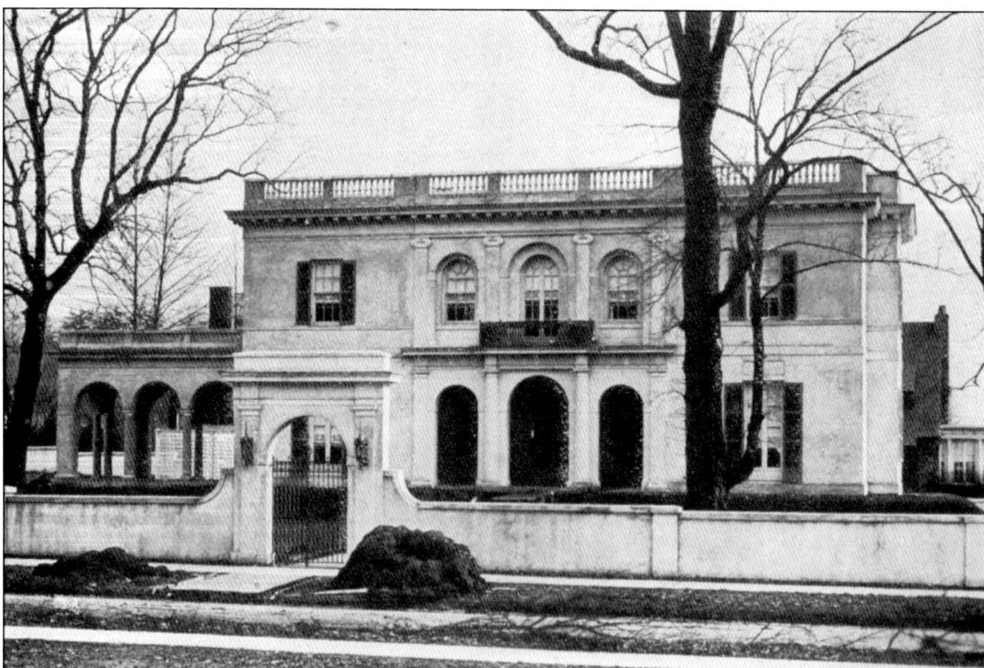

All that remains of this Italian villa in Edgeworth is part of its wall. Originally designed for Florence Walker Wallace, wife of Daniel Henry Wallace, it was occupied by its owner for only a short time. Florence Walker Wallace moved to Italy not long after the home's completion. (CMU.)

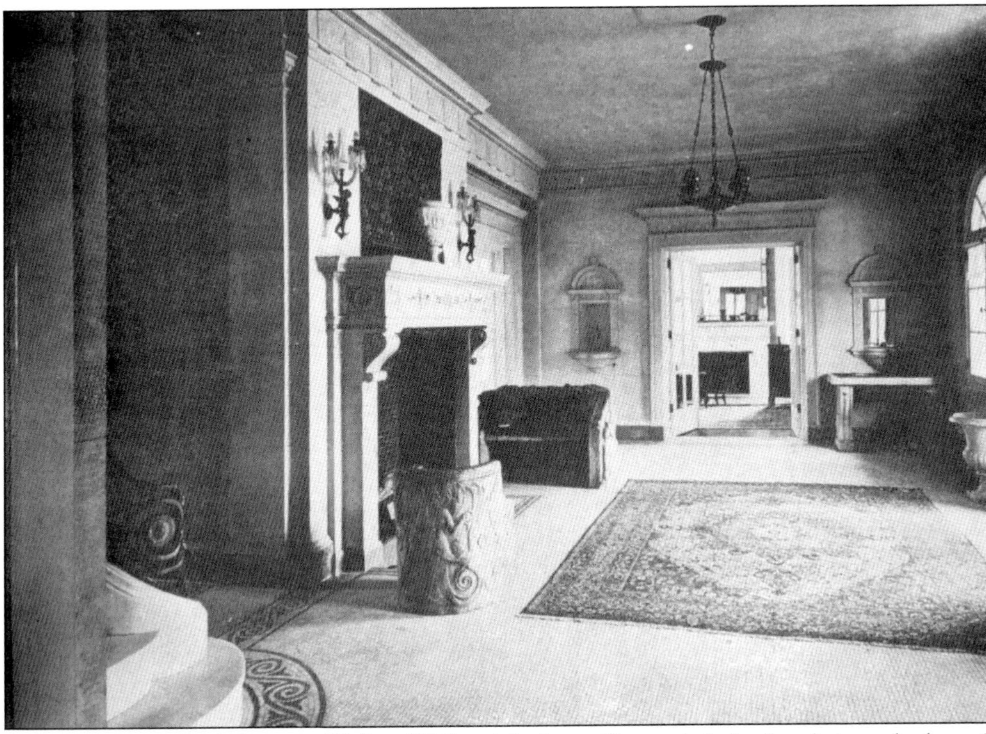

The entrance hall of Florence Walker Wallace's Italian villa carried the façade into the home's interior. With the massive fireplace, dentil molding, and carved stone furniture, the room certainly reflects its owner's passion for the Italian Renaissance style. (CMU.)

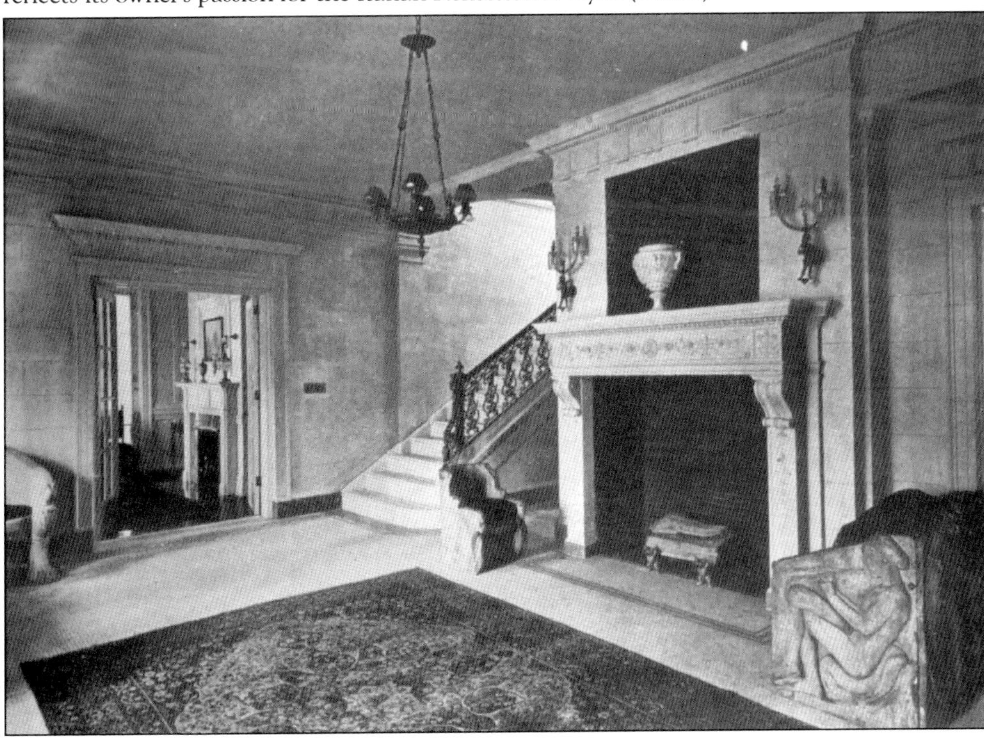

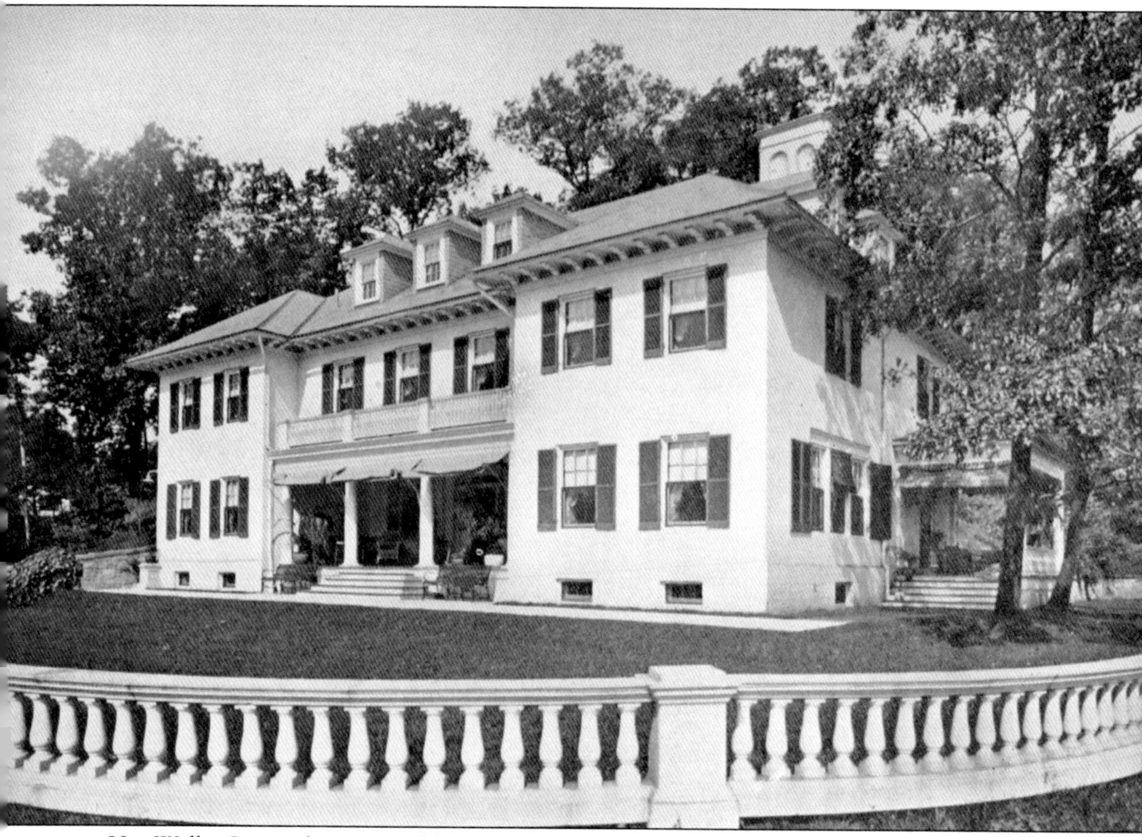

Hay Walker Jr. was the owner of this Neoclassical home. The Walker family spent many generations in Pittsburgh and Sewickley; their fortune came from various industries, including candle- and soap-making, pig iron manufacturing, and the Harbison-Walker Refractories Company.

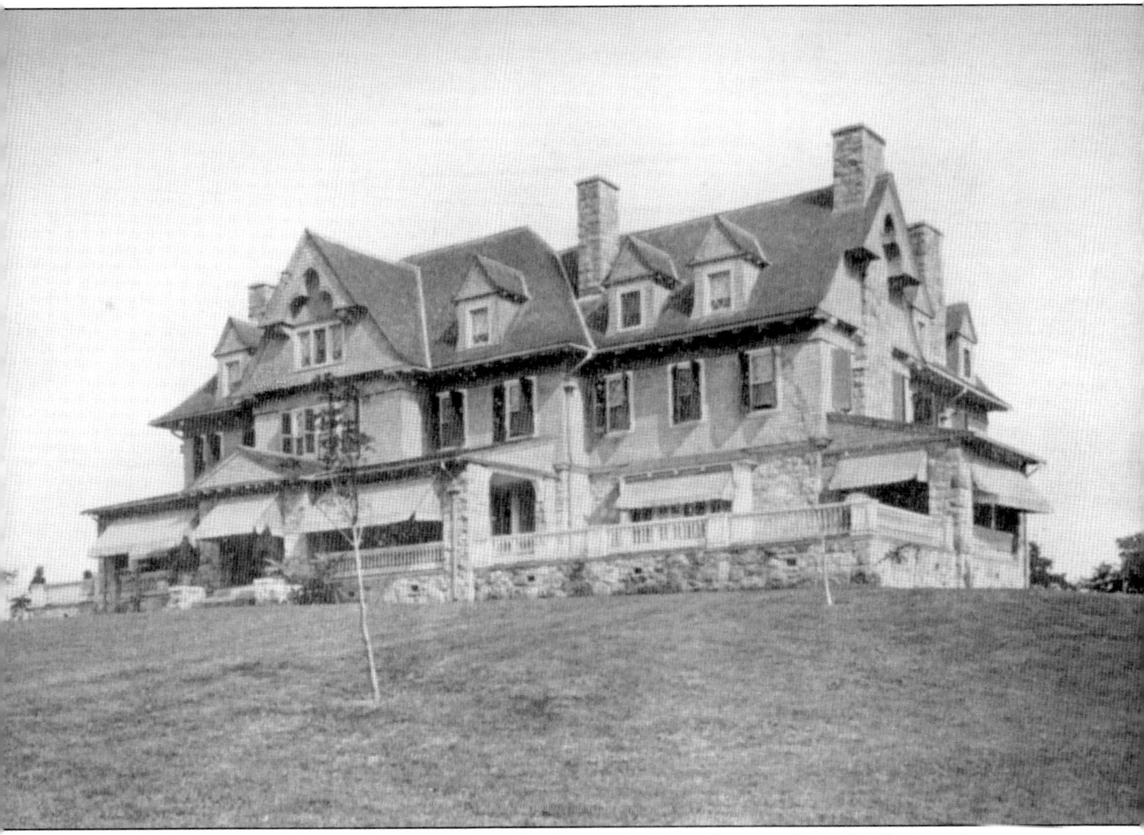

Henry Buhl Jr.'s Leetsdale home was designed by Rutan & Russell around 1904. The façade seems to have a bit of French influence about it, with the slightly flared corners of the roofline and the trefoil gingerbread design. The home's design was meant to allow views of the surrounding countryside from all principal rooms of the house and to impede the free flow of air as little as possible.

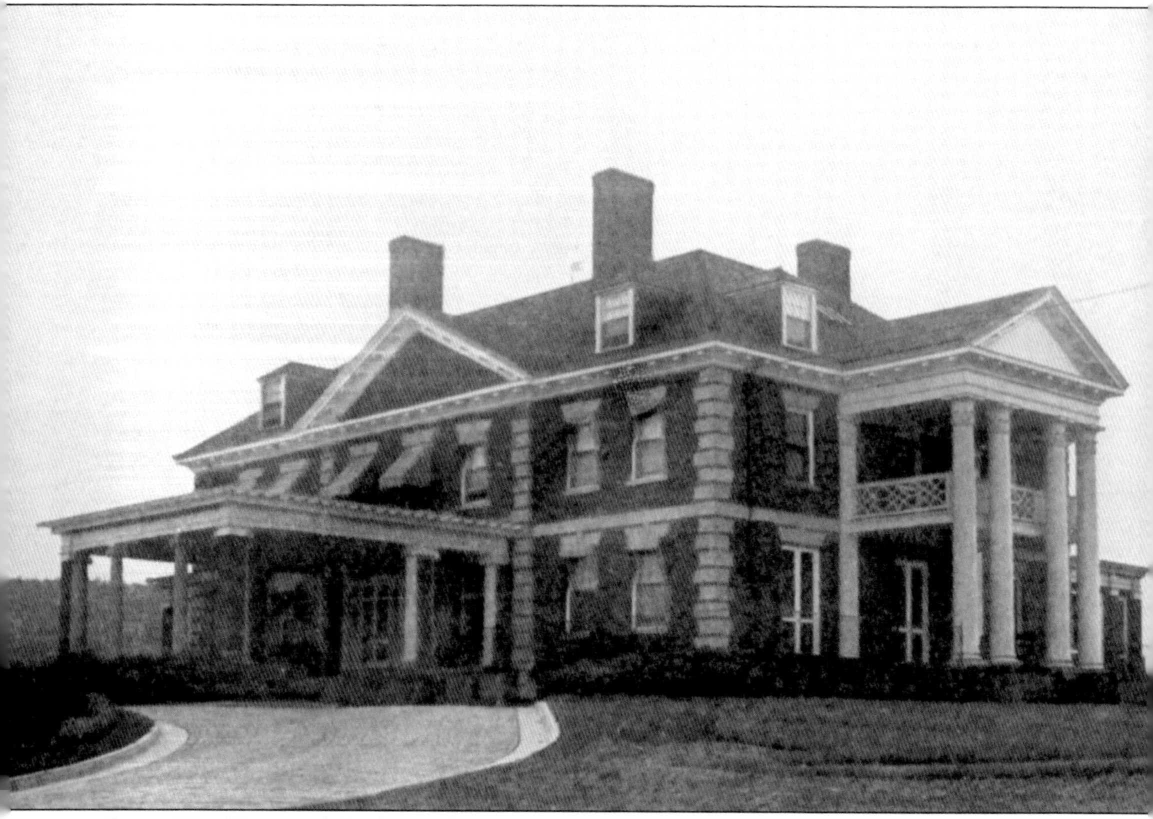

James Ward Jr. owned this home, designed by Louis Stevens in the Georgian Revival style, around 1915. Ward held coal and riverboat interests and was in partnership with the Brown family's coke operations. (CMU.)

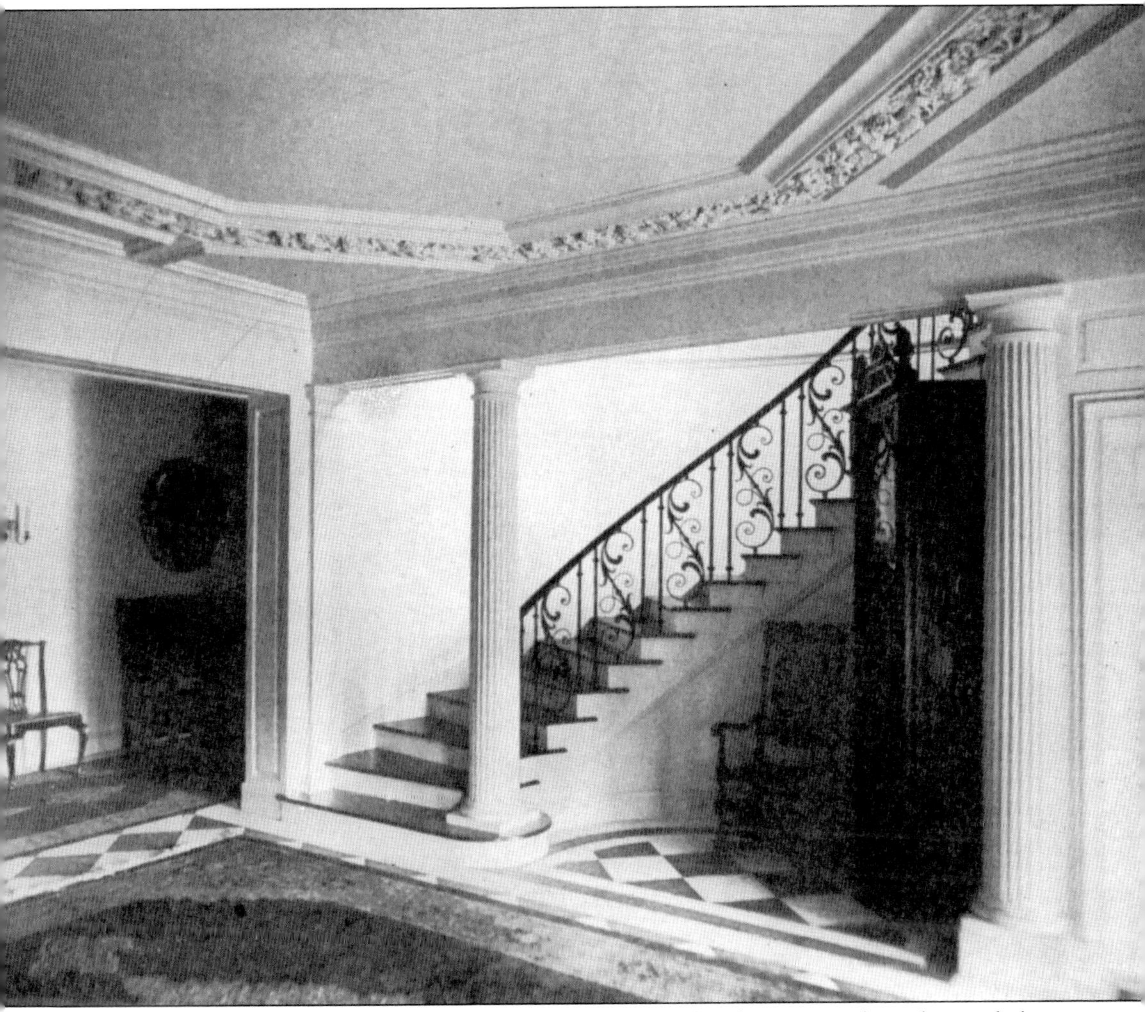

The Doric columns flanking the exterior of the James Ward Jr. home were brought inside by architect Louis Stevens to achieve a harmony between façade and interior.

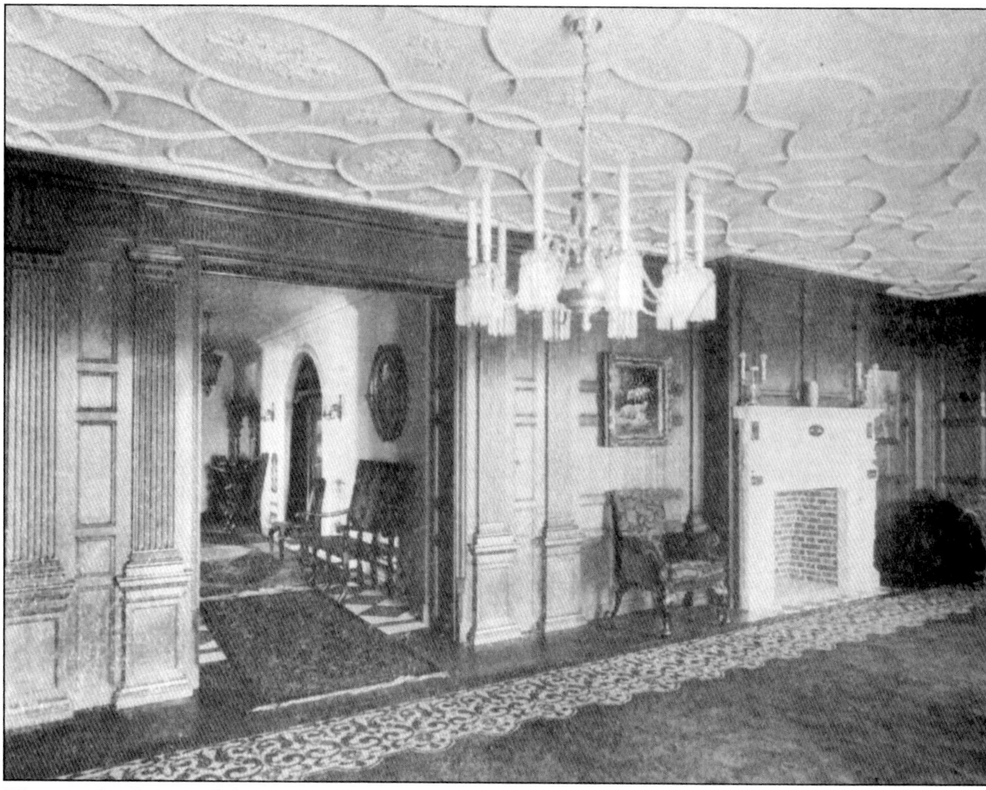

The stately design of the James Ward Jr. home continued in the living and dining rooms, both of which had elaborately decorated ceilings—plasterwork in the living room (above) and carved, painted wood in the dining room (below). The light fixtures, though electric, are meant to look as though they house candles alone.

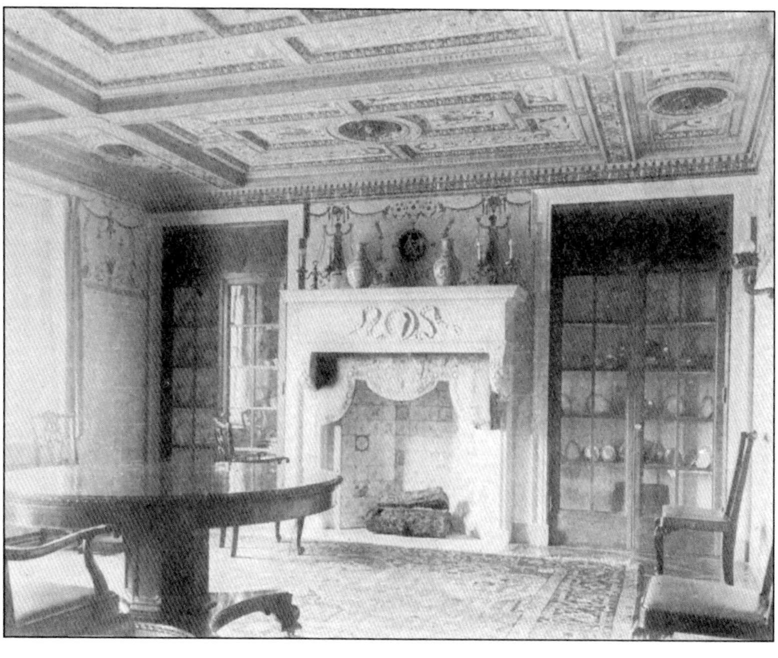

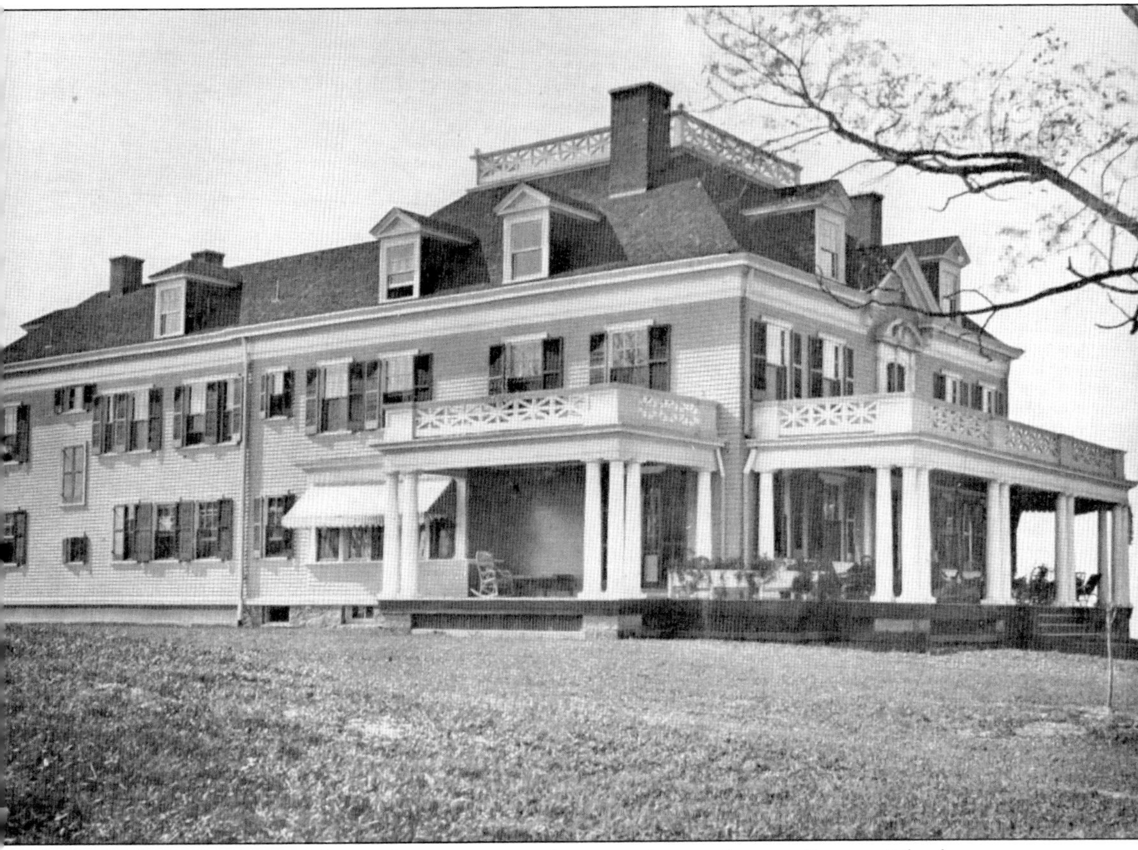

This enormous Colonial Revival mansion was home to James Stewart Brown. The house was known as Uplands. Its widow's walk and elaborate porch afforded an expansive view of the heights above Sewickley.

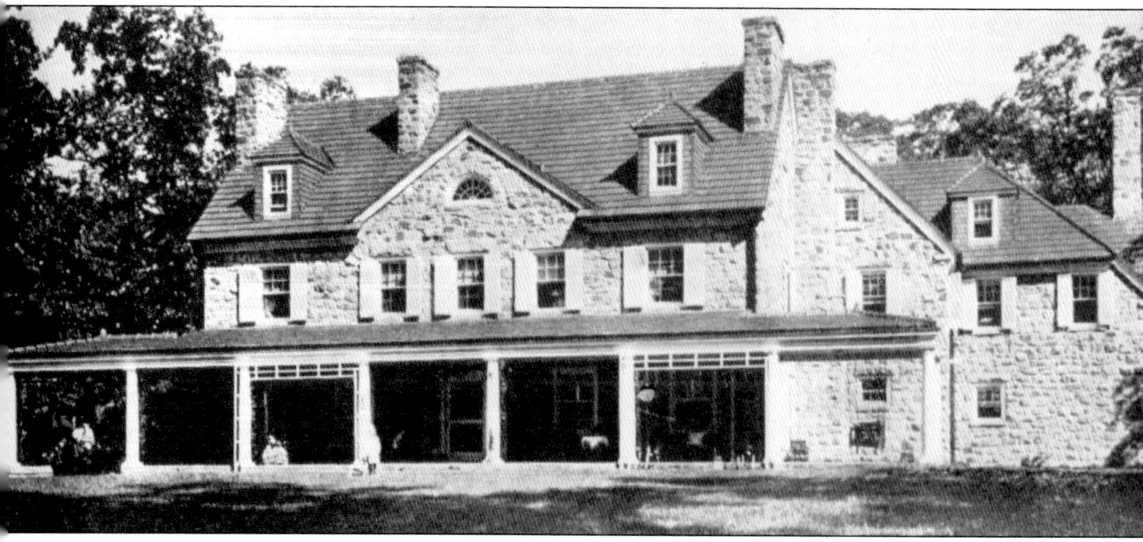

Muottas, a handsome stone mansion with a red tile roof, was home to William Walker and his wife, Jane Dill Wilson. Walker was treasurer of the Harbison-Walker Refractories Company. Designed by Alden & Harlow around 1904, the name of the home means "hilly, U-shaped land" in Old High German. The residence still stands today. (CMU.)

Bibliography

The Book of Prominent Pennsylvanians. Pittsburgh: Leader Publishing Co., 1913.

Donovan, LaVerne D. *Chatham Houses*. Pittsburgh: Chatham University Archives, 1981.

Foster, Gerald. *American Houses: A Field Guide to the Architecture of the Home*. New York: Houghton Mifflin, 2004.

Gall, George. *Homes and Country Estates of Pittsburgh Men*. Pittsburgh, 1905.

McAlester, Virginia and Lee McAlester. *A Field Guide to American Houses*. New York: Alfred A. Knopf, 2006.

Palmer, R.M. *Palmer's Pictorial Pittsburgh and Prominent Pittsburghers Past & Present, 1758–1905*. Pittsburgh: R.M. Palmer, 1905.

Pittsburgh Press Club. *Prominent Men of Pittsburgh and Vicinity*. Pittsburgh: Pittsburgh Press Club, 1912–1913.

Rook, Charles Alexander, ed. *Western Pennsylvanians*. Pittsburgh: Western Pennsylvania Biographical Association, 1923.

Slater, Elizabeth F. *One Family and One Road: Their Legacy to Chatham College*. Pittsburgh: Chatham University Archives, 1981.

Toker, Franklin. *Buildings of Pittsburgh*. Charlottesville: University of Virginia Press, 2007.

———. *Pittsburgh: A New Portrait*. Pittsburgh: University of Pittsburgh Press, 2009.

Writers' Press Association. *Mainly about Pittsburg: Some of Pittsburg's Prominent People, Past and Present*. New York City, 1903.